THE
BIG
HITTERS

THE BIG HITTERS

BRIAN BEARSHAW

Macdonald
Queen Anne Press

PICTURE CREDITS

BBC Hulton Picture Library 42, 93, 122; Patrick Eagar 28, 56, 70, 74, 126, 137, 151, 184; David Frith 110, 141, 164, 170; Kent C.C.C. 89, 147; Leicestershire C.C.C. 129; Mansell Collection 14, 22, 50, 180; The Photo Source 18, 79, 114, 118, 133, 159, 175, 187, 191; Press Association 38, 46, 61, 84, 102; Somerset C.C.C. 97; Sport & General 155; John Topham Picture Library 34, 65.

A *Queen Anne Press* BOOK

First published in 1986 by Queen Anne Press,
a division of Macdonald & Co (Publishers) Ltd,
Greater London House, Hampstead Road, London NW1 7QX
A BPCC plc Company

British Library Cataloguing in Publication Data

Bearshaw, Brian
   The big hitters
   1. Cricket-Batting-History   2. Cricket
   players-Biography
   I. Title
   35'826'0922   GV927.5.B3

   ISBN 0-356-10684-5

Typeset by Leaper & Gard Ltd, Bristol, England
Reproduced, printed and bound in Great Britain by
Purnell Book Production Ltd., Paulton, Bristol

For Zachary, my own big hit.

CONTENTS

INTRODUCTION

One of my fondest memories of school is when I hit a ball from the form knowall clean out of the playground and down the hill towards town. The pleasure was immeasurable, the feeling unmistakably sensual. I tingled for hours after. Perhaps it was through being born into the town where Learie Constantine was the cricket professional and being schooled alongside the ground where "Big Jim" Smith played that I grew up knowing, just knowing, that cricket had one object: to hit the ball as hard, as high, as far and as often as possible.

Some get their pleasure from seeing a fast bowler tear out the middle stump, or a slow bowler tease out a batsman. There is something to be said, too, for the art and grace of batting. But it is the hitters, the fast scorers, the tinglers who stir the senses and bring the day to life. When Ian Botham walks out to bat you can close your eyes and touch the atmosphere. There is a sense of expectation, a chance of history. One of my sons watched Botham get his great century against Australia at Old Trafford in 1981 and will remember it vividly all his life. But ask him what else happened in the match, like who won and how.

The hitter reminds us that cricket is a game. It is still fun. Gilbert Jessop wrote that the best sensation in all games was the full-blooded smack, out of the midst of a good resilient bat, which sent the ball screaming over the pavilion and many a mile. Jessop played nearly all his cricket before 1910 when a batsman had to hit the ball out of the ground — yes, many a mile in most of them — to be given a six. Modern players do not have to hit that far but they do have to put up with slower over rates.

This book does not include just the *big* hitters but the hard hitters and the fast scorers, and the men who went mad for a day. My brief was to select twenty players well known for their hitting or fast scoring, and twenty more who provided memorable innings. Several could have comfortably slid into either category and in one or two instances I cheated, just a little bit: Bernard Bosanquet, for example, had an outstanding match, Kenneth Hutchings a remarkable season.

Picking the first twenty to twenty-five players was fairly easy: Thornton and Bonnor, Alletson and Jessop, Fender and Barratt, Constantine and Gimblett, Smith and Wellard — what a prospect — Brown and Miller, Botham and Lloyd, such came readily to mind. Then came the difficult, though interesting part, especially in choosing players for one particular innings. A year of research brought me over 120 names and thousands of sixes and the weeding was painful. I chased records and reports in different parts of the world, unearthed descendants and eye-witnesses and, of course, from time to time, the players themselves. There were surprises, notably from Farokh Engineer, the former Indian wicketkeeper who claims the record — in terms of balls received — for the fastest Test century, scored against West Indies at Madras in 1967. He reached 94 by lunch on the first day and his hundred immediately after against the bowling of Wes Hall, Charlie Griffith, Gary Sobers and Lance Gibbs. The over-rate was desperately slow and Engineer believes he might have beaten the 67 balls taken by Australian Jack Gregory. I wrote to India but was told the scorer had not recorded the number of balls, that most scorers still use the ordinary method of scoring, with time important, and not the new-fangled way.

However, the number of balls a batsman faces has become the important statistic in recent years. In many instances the time taken is ignored. Yet for me the time involved still conveys the excitement, the speed of the action, the pace of the game, not just the innings. Measuring an innings by balls is a statistician's figure. Of course, it provides a more accurate comparison, but divorces the innings from the game. I have had to record the number of balls for many modern innings but I have stuck to time where possible. There is still more of a feel to Ted Alletson's 189 in 90 minutes and Percy Fender's century in 35 minutes than in the number of balls received.

If I had worked purely to statistics, the forty portraits would simply have been the men with the outstanding records, the fastest fifties or centuries. That would have been pointless. Character, I am happy to say, often overcame the man in the record book and that is why several otherwise worthy hitters have been excluded. The choice is purely personal and all have given immense pleasure and fun through the years. I have seen only about a third of them in action, but the others gave me enormous delight in reading about them and, in particular, writing about them. They are characters all and most would have found the front of any stage.

HARD HITTERS, FAST SCORERS

1 LESLIE AMES

One or two of the players who have scored a hundred centuries reached their target with real style. No ordinary hundred for them, but one worthy of the day. Glenn Turner got his before lunch, Geoff Boycott chose a Test match against Australia on his home ground, Herbert Sutcliffe put eight sixes in his, Patsy Hendren went to Melbourne for his, and our man, Leslie Ethelbert George, scored 131 in two hours in a successful chase for victory by Kent.

A fast hundred was nothing unusual for Ames who won the Lawrence Trophy for the season's fastest century twice in four years, who scored hundreds before lunch, hit balls over the pavilion, and relished taking on any bowler with a good, healthy swing of the bat. "I don't know whether you could call me a big hitter," he said. "I suppose I could go down as a fast scorer." There was more than a touch of modesty there especially when he went on to say he seldom took more than two hours over a hundred. "You'd pinch the bowling," he declared. "It sounds selfish but if you're going well it's the right thing to do." Shortly before I spoke to him, he and his wife had been in touch with Harold Larwood, the England and Nottinghamshire fast bowler who is now in Australia. Larwood wanted to know if Ames remembered hitting him for six at Trent Bridge. "I bowled a short one, a bouncer, and a gale was blowing from the pavilion end," Larwood recalled. Ames hit it "over old George Gunn's head to fine leg for six".

One innings, played in 1934, typifies Ames as well as any and captures the flavour of Kent cricket in those days. Even now, when I go to Maidstone or Canterbury or Tunbridge Wells, I sense the cheerful atmosphere, and I am always happy when Kent win anything. Ames was twenty-eight at the time and playing regularly for England, with 41 of his 102 centuries behind him. The 41st, incidentally, had arrived in the previous match, played at Portsmouth, when he scored 109 and 19 not out against Hampshire.

That was a Saturday. The following Wednesday, having moved on to Brentwood in Essex, Ames got another hundred, a double hundred to be exact, to follow the 332 from Bill Ashdown and the 172 of Frank Woolley as Kent scored 803 for four declared in just over seven hours. It makes you quite breathless just saying it and in all that Les Todd, Bryan Valentine and Percy Chapman did not even get to the wicket. Ian Fleming, however, did and recalled the match in which Essex scored 408 in their first innings and followed on 395 behind to lose, of course, by an innings. Essex had abandoned Leyton as their headquarters that season and in spreading the game around the county they took what *Wisden* described as "modern county cricket" to Brentwood for the first time. A club match had been played there the week before and one gentleman described it as unfit for the first-class game. No doubt Essex agreed with him by the end of the Kent match.

Arthur Fagg and Bill Ashdown opened with 70 runs followed by Woolley who

was missed when two off a towering hit on the boundary edge. In just over three hours he hit a six and 21 fours and scored 172 in a stand of 352 with Ashdown. According to Mr Fleming's memory Woolley was out just after tea, allowing Ames to go in at 422 for two and rattle off a century, his 42nd, before the close, rather like the way Edgar Wallace used to dash off another novel, before lunch maybe. In six hours Kent scored 623 for two with Ashdown having completed his triple hundred and he and Ames ready to get a few more the following day. Ashdown was third out at 667 and, wrote Fleming for *The Cricketer* magazine: "Alan Watt, a violent striker of the ball when he connected, was promoted from number nine to boost the scoring rate, running at about 117 per hour at the time! It was at this stage that Percy Chapman, as a kind thought, had suggested that as this was my first match, I also should jump the queue. So in due course, on Watt's departure, I walked out to the middle, with a deep prayer not to make an ass of myself, with the score at 707 for four which must be a near record of some sort. The time was 18 minutes to 12 and my mission was obviously to give Les Ames the bowling so that he could make 200 and we could declare. We declared at five minutes past 12, he having made 202 not out in two hours 35 minutes, a glorious display of attacking stroke play. The score had advanced from 707 to 803, namely 96 runs in 23 minutes."

Ames, who was missed at 30, hit a six and 29 fours. Fleming, by the way, in his mission to give Ames the bowling, hit 42 not out himself in those final 23 minutes. Heaven knows how many he might have got if he had been just a teeny bit more selfish. There were only six maiden overs out of 146 and leg spinner Peter Smith finished up without a wicket for 208 runs. That was a Thursday. The following Monday, having moved on to Lord's for the Test trial, Ames got another hundred, batting for England against the Rest. Also standing pretty high, is his century before lunch on the third day of the Oval Test against South Africa in 1935. He scored 123 in the session which is the most by any player before lunch in a Test.

Ames was a fine driver of the ball and twice in one innings against Essex in 1930 — he was still a headstrong young man then of twenty-four — he cleared the Leyton pavilion with straight drives. He first won the Lawrence Trophy in 1936 when he hit a century in 68 minutes for An England XI against India at Folkestone and got it a second time three years later by being a minute faster. That was an innings fit to win a match after Surrey had left Kent 145 minutes in which to score 231 for victory. Ames got 136 of them, unbeaten, to see Kent through. It was no surprise when he chose this innings after I asked him to pick an outstanding one. "That was a particularly good one because of the time," he said. "We had 231 to get against the clock, I took a chance and threw my bat."

Ames had been with England in South Africa the previous winter, 1938-39, and had taken part in the Durban Test, the timeless one. South Africa scored 530 and Ames was England's top scorer in the reply of 316. South Africa batted again to leave England to score 696 to win and the team, due to leave for home on the Athlone Castle, had to make plans to travel by train to Cape Town to pick up the liner there. The tenth day had to be the last of the game with England needing 200 more with seven wickets standing. England had reached 654 for five with 42 more needed when rain finished the game with two Kent batsmen, Les Ames and Bryan Valentine, together and more than capable of seeing England through.

Ames and Valentine played many fine partnerships in their years together but the pick was probably their 205 in just over an hour and a half at Dover in 1933. Kent started the match, against Northamptonshire, by slithering to 52 for five but Ames found such a reliable partner in Tich Freeman that 101 runs, of which Freeman made barely a dozen, were scored in the hour before tea. Valentine got a "duck" in the first innings but scored 104 in the second in partnership with Ames who scored his second century of the match, 145 not out in 195 minutes.

Ames was in his last season for Kent in 1950 when he got his hundredth century and happily it brought victory in his home town of Canterbury. He went in after the first wicket had fallen without a run scored towards the 237 needed in about three hours, enjoyed the spin of Jack Young and Jim Sims and went down the pitch repeatedly to hit John Warr back over his head. He scored 131 in two hours, at forty-four years of age. He was caught in the outfield but, more importantly, Kent won by seven wickets.

During the following winter he captained a Commonwealth team in India and although suffering from back trouble and able to play in only two of the five unofficial Tests, he hit two more centuries, one of them coming in the last match of the tour against the Prime Minister's XI, a typically dashing 116 not out. He played one more first-class match after that for Kent, unhappily retiring from the opening game of the 1951 season with more back trouble. "I hurt my back moving furniture," he recalled. "The captain made me play and when I went in to bat I tried to hit on the legside and fell in a heap."

I should have said more about his wicketkeeping which was good enough for forty-seven Tests between 1929 and 1939 and which brought him 127 victims in 1929 and 121 in 1928, still the top two in first-class cricket. He also had 100 in 1932 — and 64 of them were stumped. But brilliant wicketkeeper though he was, surely it is his batting that will be remembered and recalled longer. It was Denzil Batchelor who said of him that he never got his runs less than magnificently. "It was as a hitter into the deep with a bat with lofted face that he will be remembered."

2 FRED BARRATT

As Ted Alletson was approaching the end of his relatively short career, Nottinghamshire were already producing another player whose big hitting would for ever be
remembered by those who saw it. Fred Barratt made his debut for Nottinghamshire
in 1914 at the age of twenty and immediately lost good years to the war, during
which he was gassed at Verdun and injured both feet. Once he got going he hit with
the sort of power and regularity that had hardly ever before been matched. He hit 46
sixes in 1928, a figure that had been surpassed only once, and that by another
Nottinghamshire player, Arthur Carr.

Barratt was first and foremost a fast bowler, straight from the Nottinghamshire
coal seams. He was a genuine, genial man, modest and popular and straightforward.
He belonged to the Nottinghamshire team which won the championship in 1929. In
his debut season of 1914 he took over 100 wickets and when the war was over he was
to prove the backbone of the bowling for a dozen years. His batting was a little
slower to develop. In his debut year he did not top 14 in 26 innings but immediately
after the war he got in a few good swipes with three successive sixes off Wilfred
Rhodes at Sheffield, 20 runs in one over from Arthur Somerset when he hit 82 in 50
minutes against Sussex at Hove, and five sixes and six fours in an innings of 42
minutes that brought him 78 runs against Lancashire at Old Trafford. All those were
in 1919 and the following year he took 22 runs in an over off Jack King of
Leicestershire with three sixes and a four.

In 1921 Barratt hit 33 out of 34 in 15 minutes against Essex at Leyton before playing what was, up to then, his best and most rewarding innings in a dramatic two-
wicket win over Hampshire at Southampton. Nottinghamshire, with 31 from Barratt,
had replied to Hampshire's 190 with a total of 412. But with Phil Mead scoring 280
not out in Hampshire's second innings of 507, Nottinghamshire were left to score 286
for victory in under three hours. Six wickets fell for 65 runs but Bill Whysall found
such staunch partners in Tom Oates and Barratt that a sensational victory was
achieved. Oates scored 56 in a stand of 91 for the seventh wicket but it was Barratt
who brought victory close by hitting 79, with five sixes and seven fours, of an eighth-
wicket partnership of 129 in 50 minutes.

Barratt's hitting was remarkable. James Iremonger said one hit of his went over
the stand at the Radcliffe Road end and through a shop window on the other side of
the road. One of his five sixes against Essex at Trent Bridge in 1923 was described as
a "prodigious hit". When he went in to bat there were only 50 minutes of the first day
left, but in that time he scored 70. He was caught the next morning after adding 16
more and altogether claimed 86 in 62 minutes in a stand of 120 with Willis Walker.
The report of his hitting in Pelham Warner's *The Cricketer* prompted Mr L.P. Kirk to
write from West Bridgford with more detail of Barratt's "prodigious hit".

"Barratt was batting at the Pavilion end and P.E. Morris bowling from the

Nottingham end sent down a short-pitched leg break which Barratt smote to square leg, clean over the top of George Parr's tree — a familiar landmark at Trent Bridge and doubtless well known to you, Mr Editor! I think that this hit is without doubt the biggest hit ever made on the Trent Bridge enclosure, even including 'Ranji's' famous drive from the Nottingham end into the clock face on the Pavilion. Barratt's hit was certainly bigger than the historic drive credited to the 'Giant of the North' for two reasons: (1) In George Parr's day the wickets at Trent Bridge were pitched much nearer the western boundary of the enclosure than is the case nowadays; (2) The tree has undoubtedly grown considerably since George Parr's hit 'carried' it."

Barratt came close to his first century in 1923 when he returned to the team after having flu and in the last home game of the season gave a wonderful display of hitting against Leicestershire before he was run out for 92. Mr Warner was moved to write: "Everyone who knows him would have been glad if he had succeeded in reaching three figures. It would never surprise us to hear that he had got his eye in and had run up anything from 150 to 200 in about an hour and a half." But it was five more years before that first century did arrive, and then two came together in the 1928 season when he did the double of 100 wickets and 1,000 runs. The first was at Coventry where he scored 139 not out in 84 minutes, being promoted to number five in the order as Nottinghamshire's batting slaughtered the Warwickshire attack. He took such advantage of a strong position that he hit seven sixes and 18 fours before Nottinghamshire declared at 656 for three! His second century was not far behind, 110 not out in an hour and a half against Glamorgan at Trent Bridge with five sixes and 12 fours.

Barratt was a big, strong man, over six feet tall and weighing 14 stone with a neck like an ox and massive, slightly knock-kneed legs. Not surprisingly, he was also a professional footballer, a full back with Aston Villa and Sheffield Wednesday. He was the tallest man in the cricket team and his trousers often came above his ankles as if he had perhaps picked up Ben Lilley's or Eddie Paynter's by mistake. A study for the camera was likely to see him with slightly bent head, studying, considering. If he had been wearing glasses he would have been peering over them. A picture of the 1929 championship-winning team shows Barratt, then thirty-five and at the peak of his career, an England player at last and with a M.C.C. tour of Australia and New Zealand coming up. Bill Voce was only nineteen at the time and Barratt was opening the attack with Harold Larwood, taking over 100 wickets again and producing some wonderful displays of lusty hitting.

In that season of 1929 he hit 39 sixes, seven of them against Middlesex at Trent Bridge in what was described as the best display of hitting that summer, seven more in an innings of 74 in 33 minutes at Bristol, and another six — three of them in four balls off Len Hopwood — against Lancashire at Trent Bridge. Lilley was lbw to the first ball of Hopwood's 14th over and Barratt went in to play the remaining five with some care. They must have been good sighters for he went through Hopwood's next over with 66.6.., before taking a four and six off Frank Watson. The attack resumed on Hopwood two overs later with two more sixes which gave Barratt five sixes in 15 balls against him. Barratt, in at 278 for five, was out 20 minutes later for 50 at 347 for six and Hopwood, once the proud bearer of the analysis 14-4-28-3, finished up 17.5-4-67-4. "Frank Watson thanked Fred later for letting him off so lightly," Len

Hopwood told me. "And Fred, then thirty-five, put his arm round Frank's shoulder and said: 'We old 'uns must stick together, Frank, and put these young whippersnappers in their place.' I was twenty-five at the time and Frank thirty."

Many of Barratt's finest innings were played at home — 94 in 80 minutes against Surrey with three sixes, one of them on to the top balcony of the members' pavilion, 90 not out in 75 minutes against Middlesex, 75 in an hour against Warwickshire with two sixes and 12 fours, and 38 in 25 minutes against Northamptonshire, including three sixes in an over off Vallance Jupp. He kept on hitting right up to the end of the season and in the last match of 1929, in the middle of September while playing for Nottinghamshire against the Rest of England at the Oval, he hit 54 in 40 minutes with three sixes.

That winter he toured Australasia with four Tests against New Zealand and thoroughly enjoyed his first experience of ship life. He could not be bothered with deck sports. He took to a deck chair instead and when invited to play would reply: "Mine's a Bass". The big man had probably added to his 14 stone by the time he got to Australia and as he ran up to deliver his first ball at Sydney, there came a shout from the Hill: "What do you do with your milk, Fatty?" And the genial Fred just laughed and laughed.

Barratt has the unusual distinction of having fielded in an overcoat. The end of the second day's play at Southampton in 1930 saw Hampshire one run from victory with five wickets standing. The batsmen were dressed properly the following morning but Nottinghamshire were in lounge suits and trilbies with Barratt and Voce wearing overcoats for what turned out to be two balls.

He was to get 1,000 runs in a season only once, in 1928, and at the end of a career that included 77 "ducks" he averaged 15 an innings. His greater strength and real purpose lay in his bowling where he topped 100 wickets in a season four times and finished with over 1,000, including 12 in a match twice. He became the licensee of a pub in Eastwood, the birthplace of D.H. Lawrence, after retiring from cricket at thirty-eight and died early, in hospital, when he was fifty-two. The big man had sadly wasted away to seven stones.

3 GEORGE BONNOR

George Bonnor was a giant of a man — "one of the grandest specimens of manhood that ever stepped upon a cricket ground," W.G. Grace said of him. "Six feet six he stood, erect, broad-shouldered, straight-limbed, splendidly proportioned, a giant of strength and an Apollo of grace." In his obituary *Wisden* declared: "Australia has sent to England many finer batsmen, but no other hitter of such extraordinary power." That statement is still true, more than seventy years later. Yet Bonnor achieved little in Test matches in England, although evidence of his hitting powers was produced in many of the less significant matches.

He played seventeen times for Australia and toured England five times, all in the 1880s, a natural hitter who stood firm-footed, swung the bat with the strength of a blacksmith and could hit the ball out of even the enormous Australian cricket grounds. He was an attractive figure, a striking personality, and his achievements were constantly recalled and re-lived.

Bonnor was born at Bathurst in New South Wales, 100 miles from Sydney beyond the Blue Mountains, in 1855, of English parents. His father came from Herefordshire, his mother from Lancashire, an alliance that produced "one of the most perfect specimens of humanity on a large scale that ever existed ..." He was muscular without any superfluous flesh. When Gilbert Jessop went to Australia in 1901-02 he met Bonnor at a sheep station in Orange where he had settled in partnership with a brother in the timber trade. "A fine figure of a man then in his forty-sixth year though his appearance suggested a man of the mid-thirties," said Jessop who added that Bonnor had two chief regrets — at not having cleared Lord's pavilion and that a single-wicket match with Charles Thornton, England's champion big hitter, had never been arranged.

Bonnor first came to England in 1880, but was a complete failure as a batsman with a total of 145 runs in 17 innings. Yet one of those innings, played in the first Test match in England, provided an incident that was to be remembered for years. All three Grace brothers, W.G., E.M. and G.F., played in the game and trust W.G. to mark the first Test match in England with an innings of 152. The Australians followed on 271 behind and it was during their second innings that Bonnor hit a ball from Alfred Shaw to a tremendous height. The batsmen ran — and so did Fred Grace, galloping around the edge of the huge Oval field, his eyes on the ball which reached for the sky, then hung there as if undecided which way to go before setting off for earth again. The batsmen were well into their second run, Grace had passed the second gasometer and still the ball was in the air. It was only when the batsmen had completed two runs and were setting off for their third that Grace, after running a colossal distance, took the brilliant catch. He said later that it was the only catch about which he ever felt "funky". He thought his heart stopped while waiting for the ball. Two weeks later he died in a hotel in Basingstoke aged twenty-nine. He had had

a cold before and during the great match and died, it was believed at the time, "from his having slept in a damp bed". In his reminiscences nearly twenty years later, W.G. wrote: "My brother, G.F., who was playing in this match — it was the last big match in which he did play — atoned for a pair of spectacles by dismissing Bonnor with a catch which is remembered to this day. Bonnor got hold of a ball from Shaw and sent a tremendous skier into the long field, which G.F. judged in a wonderful way. Mr Frederick Gale, who chained the distance himself with two of the Oval Ground men, stated that the hit measured 115 yards as a minimum. When at its greatest height the ball seemed to hang in the air, and two runs were finished before it dropped into G.F.'s hands."

By 1882 Bonnor was known in Australia as the biggest hitter in the world. Despite his failures two years earlier, he was again chosen for England, part of a great all-round team which embarked in the Assam in March, 1882. And it was on the ship that Bonnor struck up a bet that was to win him £100 on his first day in England. George Giffen, another of the Australian players, was at the same table when Bonnor remarked that he could throw a cricket ball a distance of 120 yards. Someone doubted whether he could pitch it 115 yards. Bonnor offered to do so in one throw after landing and a wager of 100 sovereigns was made. "Most of our fellows, splendidly though they knew Bonnor could throw, considered that he had embarked upon a risky undertaking," said Giffen. "After his long spell of idleness on board he would be out of form and, moreover, might slip without having a second throw to recover his sovereigns." In a letter to W.G. Grace a man called William Hearder referred to the landing of the Australian team at Plymouth on 3rd May, 1882. "They drove up to my business house and explained that a bet had been made on board that Mr G.J. Bonnor would not throw a cricket ball 110 yards. The conditions were to be, first throw on landing, and no other attempt to be made previous. I took them to our cricket ground, as both parties concerned asked me to act as judge. On arriving at the cricket ground, Mr Bonnor objected to the grass and said he would prefer a hard road or parade ground. We then drove to the Raglan Barracks where there is plenty of space. He said that would suit very well. The distance was marked off by news-papers and he took his stand, toeing a line. The ball, which he had previously purchased from me, was an ordinary match ball. This I handed to him, and I had placed in my hand the two cheques for £100 apiece. He threw the ball from where he stood to the line and did not run. It was a grand throw; it seemed as if the ball would never stop rising; and it pitched on a spot which was measured after to be 119 yards 5 inches from where he stood. As there was no objection made, I handed over the two cheques to Mr Bonnor."

It was during this summer that Bonnor made himself famous as a hitter in England. He started against Yorkshire at Bradford, a bright little innings of 35 in which he drove a ball from Billy Bates into the pavilion, then hit one from Edmund Peate over the stand. Two more from Peate went out of the ground and in the following match, against Nottinghamshire, he hit a ball from Shaw out of the Trent Bridge ground. Against the Gentlemen of England at the Oval he played his first innings of consequence, making 74 in 80 minutes including an on drive off Charlie Studd which cleared the stand beside the pavilion and landed on the old racquet court. It was during this match that the Surrey secretary, Mr C.W. Alcock, was about to unlock a cupboard in the office when a ball hit by Bonnor knocked the keys out of his hand and smashed an engraving of the Kent v. Sussex match.

Bonnor was dismissed for three "ducks" in two consecutive matches against Yorkshire at Dewsbury and Bradford, got a fourth against Northumberland, and managed only a single against the Gentlemen of Scotland. There was still some fine hitting left in him, however, particularly at Scarborough and Portsmouth. The Australians played I Zingari at Scarborough where Bonnor scored 122 not out in 105 minutes, a spectacular innings that included four sixes — out of the ground, of course — 11 fours and only nine singles. The Australians were already 256 for six when Bonnor joined Alick Bannerman who had taken the sting out of the bowling and had been batting five hours for 84 not out. He hit with astounding power and freedom and between being dropped twice in the deep he drove Lancashire's A.G. Steel clean out of the ground. "A ball from Mr Lucas was served in the same way" and off four balls in Alfred Lucas's third over he scored 20 runs — 6-4-4-6. Bonnor scored 122 to Bannerman's 36, giving his partner five hours start and overtaking him in 105 minutes before getting out.

Steel was also a member of the Cambridge University Past and Present team which played the Australians at Portsmouth, a game which included Charles Thornton, the chief rival to Bonnor in the world as a big hitter. The Australians were set 208 to win and sent Bonnor in early, a move that produced 66 runs in half an hour with the ball hit out of the ground four times and the sightscreen splintered as he drove hard and often. Three of the sixes came off Studd, prompting Steel to observe: "His hitting of C.T. Studd's bowling was appalling."

There was only one Test match again in 1882, also at the Oval. When Billy Murdoch won the toss he batted first. The wicket was not easy and perhaps in the hope of succeeding before it got worse he sent in his hitters, George Bonnor and Hugh Massie. The move failed. Both were quickly dismissed on an opening day that saw 20 wickets fall for 164 runs with England taking a first-innings lead of 38. Bonnor, who was temperamental and given to bouts of melancholia, was concerned about the slow left-arm spin of Edmund Peate and before the game had dealt with some imaginary deliveries in the privacy of his bedroom in the Tavistock Hotel. Well, part privacy, for his unnamed teammate let his secret out. Bonnor tried going forward, going backward, ending with a tremendous swing that connected with a china jug and basin and shattered them. "How do you like that, Peate?" he commented. However, he was bowled by Dicky Barlow in the first innings before he could face Peate and that night, with the second innings in prospect, he practised privately again. All to no avail. This time Ulyett got him out quickly. He might well have murdered Peate if he could have stayed around long enough to face him. But the Australians were not worried. They won by seven runs in the match that led to the creation of the Ashes.

Bonnor was a boaster and by all accounts, while a handsome figure of a man, was not all that engaging a person. On a train journey to Brighton, Bonnor, a great betting man, laid a wager that he would hit Walter Humphreys, the lob bowler, out of the ground. He was very contemptuous of lobs. Humphreys was told that the big man had backed himself to hit him into the sea and baffled Bonnor by keeping the ball low. Bonnor did not even hit a boundary, let alone clear the ground, and did not get into double figures in either innings. On another occasion Bonnor and Charles Thornton were dining after a match in which Thornton had hit a century and hit a ball 135 yards. Said Bonnor; "You think you can hit hard? I have a sister in Australia who can hit as hard as you."

In the obituary in *Wisden*, only two of Bonnor's innings were mentioned, those in 1882 against the Gentlemen of England and I Zingari. Strangely enough, much more space was devoted to two of his dismissals. One was the catch by Fred Grace, the other was a catch, just as remarkable, but quite a different kind, by George Ulyett on Bonnor's third tour in 1884. Barlow, the Lancashire all-rounder, described it as "the finest and most marvellous of all the catches," he had ever seen. And he was talking with the experience of forty first-class seasons as player and umpire. This, too, was a Test match, the first ever held at Lord's. When the Australians batted for a second time they were 150 runs behind and faced a wearing wicket. Peate had the batsmen in difficulties but Lord Harris surprisingly called on Ulyett who worked up to full speed and destroyed the Australians with a return of seven for 36. One of his wickets was that of Bonnor, whose instructions were to knock Ulyett off his length. He did his best. He drove mightily at a half volley, Ulyett sprang and somehow caught it. "The ball came from the batsman with the speed of a shot from a gun, straight into the hands of the bowler, which were forced backward over his shoulder with the impetus of the ball," wrote Barlow. "Had the ball struck a vital part, it must have meant certain death and it would have shattered any bone which had happened to get in its way. Ulyett afterwards remarked to me that this catch was as much due to good luck as to skill; he had just time to see the ball coming, and threw up his hands." George Giffen, Bonnor's partner at the time, described the catch as one of the most brilliant he had ever seen. "Bonnor got one fourer, then made a mighty drive. Every one looked down the ground to see where the ball landed, and the spectators began to open a space in the ring, but the ball did not reach the crowd. Ulyett put up his hand, and meeting it with the right spot of his hand held it." Said W.G.: "The way he caught Bonnor has never been surpassed."

The catch was important enough to also play a prominent part in Ulyett's obituary in *Wisden* in 1899. "Bonnor's mission was to knock the fast bowler off, and he did his best. He drove a half volley with all his force, but the ball — travelling faster than an express train — went into Ulyett's right hand instead of to the boundary. Bonnor wandered disconsolately back to the pavilion and the England players gathered round Ulyett curious, perhaps, to know what manner of man he was, and anxious to congratulate him on his escape from imminent danger. One can remember, even now, the look of wonder on the faces of A.G. Steel and Alfred Lyttelton. Ulyett himself was very modest about the matter. Complimented on the catch when the day's play was over, he said simply that if the ball had hit his fingers instead of going into his hand he should have played no more cricket that season."

One of Bonnor's most interesting innings came that year at Lord's when he played in a charity match between Smokers and Non-Smokers, a collection of English and Australian cricketers playing together. W.G. Grace said Bonnor smoked occasionally but not regularly and was allowed to play for the Non-Smokers as he wanted to be on the opposite side to the famous bowler, Mr Spofforth. "Once set, he treated the 'Demon' as severely as he did the rest of the bowlers," said Dr Grace.

Bonnor had once told Spofforth he would punish him if they ever met and took advantage of the unusual situation to score 124 out of 156. And he reached his century with a six off Spofforth which went over the wall behind the pavilion. Another enormous hit off the Australian fast bowler landed on the roof of the pavilion. And they gave him four for that. Spofforth himself suggested he helped Bonnor. "Part of the match we were feeding Bonnor just to enjoy his glorious hitting," he said. "I was more pleased to be punished by him in that friendly game than at getting lots of wickets."

Bonnor's finest innings — at least, his most important — came on his home ground of Sydney during the fourth Test against England in 1885. England had scored 269 and Australia were sinking rapidly at 119 for six when Bonnor went out to bat at 3.30 p.m. on the second afternoon. Fifteen minutes later, with Australia 134 for seven, he was joined by Sam Jones with the follow-on in prospect. Jones blocked, Bonnor slogged in cold weather and poor light and between them they put on 154 runs for the eighth wicket. After a slow, uncertain start Bonnor reached 50 in 65 minutes, 100 in 100 minutes and in just under two hours hit 128 out of 169 with a joyous display of pure hitting which enabled Australia to take a first innings lead of 40 and win the match by eight wickets. Bonnor narrowly escaped being bowled several times but did not give a chance in the field until he was 81 when Peel missed him. He was missed in the slips off Ulyett, enabling him to run two and reach his only Test hundred, and was also missed in the deep when he was 105. He was finally caught in the slips at 5.40 p.m., having batted 115 minutes.

Unfortunately, the comedian wanted to play Hamlet, the hitter aspired to playing it straight. The result was disastrous and Bonnor would exasperate his teammates with his futile efforts to play scientifically. Said Giffen: "We often used to wish that Bonnor would not get the idea into his head that he could, if he chose, bat as scientifically as anyone. This was generally after he had heard someone say: 'Oh, Bonnor is nothing but a slogger.' Then he would go in and play his 'sweetly pretty game', and sometimes last a while, too; but it was almost painful to watch a giant of six feet and a half playing that barndoor game when we knew that if he chose, and got going, he could pulverise the bowling and disorganise the field. Bonnor had some very quaint sayings. He used, for instance, to remark: 'If I could only remember that balls hit on the ground can't be caught, and make it my pet proverb, I'd have these English bowlers looking both ways for Sunday in every match I played.'"

Bonnor died on 27th June, 1912, aged fifty-seven, and "in poor circumstances". W.G. Grace was among those to pay tribute to him. "His own strength he scarcely knew but when he got a ball well in the centre of his bat people made guesses as to the horse-power behind it. When he threw in from the long field the ball whistled as it clove the air." In 30 innings in 17 Tests against England he averaged only just over 17. Yet he was one of the most attractive figures in the Test matches of his day. "He was born to be a hitter," said Giffen. "He had a distinct mission as a demoraliser of bowlers and fieldsmen."

4 IAN BOTHAM

If God had made me a world-class sportsman I would have asked nothing else than to play the Botham way, always, always to win but able to lose with dignity as well as disappointment. At the Oval in 1979 India, trying to score 438 to beat England, finished desperately near at 429 for eight after a double century from Sunil Gavaskar who was out in the final hour. At the end of the game Botham picked up the stumps and kept them as souvenirs — for Gavaskar, who described the action as "the gesture of a person who has always treated the game as a sport". I remember, too, a day at Sydney only a few months later when Australia beat England by six wickets to take a winning 2-0 lead in the three-match series. Greg Chappell had to get the winning runs with a six if he were to get his 16th Test century. Botham tried to oblige by bowling a slow, long hop but Chappell's shot fell a few feet short of the fence and he had to be satisfied with a four and 98 not out.

Botham has played his cricket as much with his heart as with his head. It is still a game at Test level. It is still to be enjoyed. Perhaps being brought up in the game in Somerset has helped. There is a much more relaxed, sportive approach there than in the dour seriousness of the game further north. Somerset has a rich history of big-hitting batsmen, from W.H. Fowler and Guy Earle, through Arthur Wellard — perhaps the mightiest of all — and Harold Gimblett to Botham himself. Dashing batsmen are as much a part of the county as its scrumpy and so many of them have delighted spectators over the years, although Somerset members might have been quick to point out that of Botham's 24 first-class centuries up to the start of the 1985 season, only three had been scored in the county of his cricket adoption.

The 1985 season made up for a lot with four of his five centuries coming at home, all thundering, joyful hundreds after a winter away from the game. Dozens of sixes climbed for the heavens like disturbed starlings and he waltzed past Arthur Wellard's record of 66 in a season with five weeks of the season in hand. Somerset finished bottom of the championship but with Viv Richards also rattling off nine centuries, they at least died with a smile on their face.

Botham's first came at Taunton at the beginning of May when he took 76 balls to reach 100 and finished with eight sixes in his 112 against Glamorgan. The next hundred was on the same ground three weeks later and again took 76 balls. This time, however, he went on to score 149 against Hampshire to lift Somerset from 58 for four to 298 all out with six sixes and 20 fours. Trevor Gard contributed nine to a stand of 58, Mark Davis managed two in a partnership of 85! Perhaps he was too busy marvelling, open-mouthed at the master.

The quickest century of the season came at Edgbaston in May, an innings of great power in which his hundred took 50 balls and which closed at 138 not out with 12 sixes and 13 fours — all but 14 of his runs came in boundaries. The 67-minute barrage — now that means more to me than 65 balls — included eight sixes off one

man, left-arm spinner Norman Gifford, the Warwickshire captain, who first played county cricket when Botham was four years old. One of them entered the top tier of the East Wing stand through an open door before running down stairs to re-emerge at ground level. Gifford described the innings as a magnificent performance that brought great pleasure to the crowd. He had been hit for 128 runs in 42 overs, 20 of which were maidens! Botham was back at Taunton the following day to face Essex and inflict on them his fourth century of the season, this time in 68 balls with four sixes. He went on to 152 with a mixture of awesome aggression and delicate deflections. His next championship match was two weeks away but he made it three centuries in three games by going to Weston-super-Mare to hit ten sixes in an innings of 134 and at the same time overtake Wellard's record of 66 sixes set in 1935.

He finished the season with 75 first-class sixes for Somerset, 74 of them coming from eleven championship matches, less than half the number Wellard played in 1935. In all, Botham hit 80 first-class sixes in the season, 105 in all cricket including the one-day competitions.

Two of Botham's best centuries before 1985 had come at Taunton, with his top score of 228, which included ten sixes, and 131 in 65 minutes against Warwickshire. His 228 against Gloucestershire in 1980 was an astonishing innings, lasting only three hours and including 27 fours and ten sixes, three of them in one over from left-arm spinner David Graveney. Between lunch and tea, in two and a quarter hours, he scored 182 runs, all part of a record fourth-wicket stand of 310 with Peter Denning. His innings against Warwickshire two years later, though shorter, was even faster with a century in 52 minutes and a final scoring rate still of two runs a minute. Somerset had been set to score 309 in 270 minutes and were struggling at 57 for three until Viv Richards, with two sixes and 12 fours in his innings of 85, had opened the way for the Botham blitz. When Botham went out to bat 160 runs were needed in 145 minutes. Sixty-five minutes later Somerset had won with Botham hitting ten sixes and 12 fours and scoring the fastest century of the season along the way. He scored his second 50 in 14 minutes; he scored 30 in one over from Paul Smith; he shared in a stand of 158 in an hour with Phil Slocombe; he twice hit three successive sixes. Let us not forget, too, that it was the quickest century ever by a Somerset player. In the first 25 minutes he scored only 17 runs. The other 114 took him just 40 minutes after tea, an assault that would have delighted even Wellard or Gimblett.

That was Botham's second century of the year inside an hour, following the even quicker one, scored in 50 minutes, against the Central Zone at Indore during England's winter tour of India. It was the fastest century ever in India. His 122 took 55 minutes, and that included the drinks break and was made out of 137 for the fourth wicket with Mike Gatting. He received 55 balls, seven of which were hit for six and 16 for four.

Botham the buccaneer has enjoyed himself a time or two against India and Gavaskar particularly recalls a Test century at Leeds in August, 1979. The game was ruined by rain and England were still in the first innings of the match when play started on the Monday, the fourth day. Botham started with nine runs, gathered the previous Thursday morning, and in the session to lunch hit 99. One enormous hook off Kapil Dev cleared the dressing rooms behind square leg and landed among the cars. In all he hit five sixes and 16 fours in his 137. "It was hitting which was controlled and at the same time savage," said Gavaskar. "Every time Kapil or Ghavri bowled a little short of length it was hooked into the car park of the Leeds cricket ground. It looked at one stage as if he was more keen on smashing Geoff Boycott's car parked there." Botham was driving south after the game when he was stopped by the police and told he was going a bit quick. "Still," said the policeman, "you played a bloody good innings."

Nothing, however, will ever match his Test centuries against Australia at Leeds and Manchester in 1981, marvellous, memorable pieces of mayhem that kept the Ashes for England. He scored 149 not out with 27 fours and a six at Leeds, and hit 118 with six sixes and 13 fours at Manchester. David Gower said the Manchester innings was more controlled throughout despite the power of his hitting. Mike Brearley, back in the side as captain, agreed. "He played even better than at Headingley," he wrote. "An innings of classical power and splendour; of off-drives, hooks and cuts. To the player, the Manchester innings was the best; to the spectator the performance at Leeds will never be matched. That was the stuff of which heroes are made, when victory is snatched out of thin air."

England had lost the first Test at Nottingham and drawn the second at Lord's under Botham's leadership. Brearley was recalled as captain for the third Test at Headingley and was outplayed for three and a half days as Australia amassed 401 and then forced England to follow on by dismissing them for 174. By the end of the third day England had lost their first second innings wicket — that of Graham Gooch who was dismissed twice in four balls that day — and still needed 222 to make Australia bat again. Botham booked out of the hotel on the Monday morning, and he was not the only one. Brearley would have done the same except that since his county, Middlesex, were playing Lancashire at Old Trafford on the Wednesday, he would be staying in the north. Everybody was ready for home and when England slipped to 135 for seven quite a few bags were packed. Botham, however, was still at the crease. He had started quietly, scoring 39 in an hour and a half to tea. When Graham Dilley joined him at the fall of the seventh wicket he asked him: "You don't fancy hanging around on this wicket for a day and a half, do you?" Dilley did not. "Right," said Botham. "Come on, let's give it some humpty." There was nothing to lose. England were quoted at 500-1 by Ladbroke, the bookmakers, and the entire country was left wishing it had invested just a tenner when Botham started his assault. In 80 minutes he and Dilley put on 117 runs, Dilley claiming 56 of them. In 55 minutes Chris Old, with a mixture of pleas and threats no doubt still ringing in his ears from the dressing room, helped put on 67 with Botham who had now forced seven fieldsmen to the boundary. In one particularly fierce spell of hitting, Botham went from 39 to 103 with a six, 14 fours and two singles. In two hours after tea he scored 106 out of 175 in 27 overs. The over-rate was abysmally slow. If Botham had been batting in Gilbert Jessop's or Percy Fender's time he would probably have had at least 12 more overs — maybe another 50 runs. Quite a few runs came through or over the slips but Botham's 149 not out carried England to a total of 358 and left Australia with a victory target of 130. It was only natural, I suppose, that Botham should open the bowling. Not so acceptable that his first two balls should be hit to the boundary. Still, there was Bob Willis to apply the finishing touches, securing a famous victory for England by taking eight for 43 in the amazing 18-run win.

Botham, however, had not finished. Far from it. When Australia needed only 151 in their second innings to win the fourth Test at Edgbaston, he took five for 11 in 14 overs to give England another astonishing win, this time by 29 runs, and take a 2-1 lead in the series. And then, four weeks after the miracle at Leeds, Botham played the innings still regarded as his best, his 118 in 123 minutes at Old Trafford, his century taking 104 minutes and being the second fastest English Test hundred to Jessop's in 1902. His six sixes were the most ever hit in a Test innings. It was a marvellous display of hitting which brought the ground to life after Chris Tavaré had taken 306 minutes to reach 50, the slowest recorded half-century in English cricket. Botham, who had been dismissed first ball in the first innings, strode out at 104 for five in the second, with England 205 runs ahead. The start was sober enough with five singles in his first 33 balls and the real blitz was reserved for the new ball, taken when Botham was 28. Dennis Lillee, of course, took it and his first over was smashed for 22 runs including two memorable, hooked sixes. Fifty-two runs came in 4.2 overs, 47 of them to Botham who went from 28 to 100 in 37 minutes and who scored his last 90 out of 103 in 55 minutes. Botham gave one chance, a difficult one, when he was 34. Mike Whitney, making his debut for Australia, was left with the swirling skier, an awkward catch with the ball dropping over his right shoulder. He got a touch but could not hold on to the ball.

The following weekend, in a John Player League match for Somerset, Botham hit another sensational hundred with nine fours and seven sixes in 61 minutes against Hampshire at Taunton. His second 50 took nine minutes and Botham remembers looking at the scoreboard and seeing his own score at about 40 and Viv Richards in the eighties. Richards was still in the eighties when Botham reached his hundred.

Through the years Swansea has been the scene of a good deal of big hitting and fast scoring. Botham has twice scored fast centuries there, taking an hour and a half in 1979 and following it two years later with 123 in 137 minutes. The 1979 innings — played on the day Bjorn Borg was winning the men's singles at Wimbledon for the fourth time — was the most spectacular with 12 fours and seven sixes in his innings of 120. And it could all have been nipped in the bud if Robin Hobbs, the former Essex leg-break bowler then captaining Glamorgan, had held a skier when Botham was 16. His 123 not out in 1981 was rather more subdued, including only three sixes — and 18 fours — as he hit his first century for thirteen months, the prelude to the assault that was to hit the Australians at Leeds and Manchester in the following seven weeks.

Botham's first century, his 167 not out against Nottinghamshire at Trent Bridge in 1976, two years after his debut, was a match-winner after Somerset had needed 301 for victory in 225 minutes. His hundred took 134 minutes and he hit 20 fours and six sixes and finished off the game by hitting Bob White for six, four and six.

He scored two centuries in succession at Christchurch, New Zealand, in February 1978 during his first tour, with 126 not out against Canterbury in two and a half hours, and 103 in the Test match. There never seem any nervous nineties for Botham. In the game against Canterbury he moved from 88 to 104 by hitting Dayle Hadlee, in five balls, for a two, two fours and a six.

One of the great pleasures for Somerset followers in recent years has been the sight of Botham and Richards batting together. Cricket can have few more splendid prospects. One of their most delightful partnerships came at Leicester in July, 1983, when Botham batted at number nine because of a stomach upset. Richards scored 216, Botham, who reached his century off 101 balls, hit 152 and between them they added a record 172 for the eighth wicket. It was as well that Botham did not have migraine, too.

5 FREDDIE BROWN

Freddie Brown earned the captaincy of England for the tour of Australia by hitting 122 in 110 minutes for the Gentlemen against the Players at Lord's. So the story goes. And they do say he sealed it with a six, hit into the pavilion to reach his hundred. I hope the story is right. It certainly deserves to be and although England lost 4-1 in Australia Brown proved himself a worthy captain. One or two England captains, it might be said, have been chosen on rather flimsier evidence.

Brown's innings for the Gentlemen was typical of the man and if it did seal the captaincy it marked a triumphant comeback for a popular and talented player who might well have believed during the Second World War that he would never play cricket again. Brown lost five stone in weight as a prisoner-of-war and played only the occasional first-class match in the three years after the war. He had played for Surrey in the 1930s but reappeared in county cricket in 1949 for Northamptonshire where he quickly forced himself back into Test cricket and in line for the captaincy in Australia in 1950-51 and where he spent his fortieth birthday.

Brown, who was born in Peru and went to England when he was eleven, had first made his mark in English cricket in 1931 when he was playing for Cambridge University and for the Gentlemen while still only twenty. He was a regular member of the Surrey team in 1932, taking 95 wickets at 16 runs each — "if at times his bowling did not meet with the success most people anticipated ..." whinged *Wisden* — and played some stirring innings full of fire and brimstone. The twenty-one-year-old Brown was one of the Cricketers of the Year of 1932 and his photograph in the following year's *Wisden* shows a cherub, round cheeked, clean-cut, glossy haired, parted left. Bill Voce, the Nottinghamshire professional whose formative years were spent with a colliery team, stands alongside. He was only a year older than Brown but looked twice his age.

The cherub, who had played four games for Surrey and two for England in 1931, saved his really outstanding pieces of batting in 1932 for the second half of the season. He scored 168 in 130 minutes at Blackheath, 212 in 200 minutes at the Oval, and 135 in just over two hours at Lord's, the last two being against Middlesex, perfect models of timing and earning him a place with the M.C.C. in Australia for the 1932-33 tour. Brown's innings at Blackheath brought him up against the great Kent leg-spinner Tich Freeman for the first time and when he went in to bat Surrey were 139 for four, two of the wickets to Freeman. This soon became 171 for seven but the last three wickets, with Brown in full control, added 174 in 95 minutes. Of those 174, the last three batsmen, Edward Brooks, Maurice Allom and Jack Parker, totalled 19 between them! The last-wicket stand with Parker put on 104 runs of which Brown hit 91. He took an hour to get his first half-century, 35 minutes more to reach his hundred, and then advanced from 100 to 150 in quarter of an hour. He drove and pulled powerfully and hit four sixes and 21 fours. And Tich Freeman? — Four for 163

in the total of 345. A memorable shot for Brown, and one which gave him great joy, was a six over square leg off Freeman." I didn't know it at the time but I think it was his googly and I don't think he bowled me many more in that innings," Brown told me in a letter from his home in Suffolk.

Four weeks later Brown played a significant part in one of the most memorable games between Surrey and Middlesex which Surrey won off the last ball. Middlesex had been bowled out for 141 with Brown taking three for 38 with his leg breaks and then joining his captain, Douglas Jardine, at 195 for five. The pair added 143 in 85 minutes before Jardine was out but the best partnership — perhaps the best of the season — was still to come with Allom helping to add 155 in 65 minutes. It was breathtaking stuff with Brown reaching his hundred in 100 minutes and hitting seven sixes in his 212 in 200 minutes. It was an amazing innings, a great display of hitting in which he hit two balls out of the ground. Brown followed with five wickets in the Middlesex second innings, but Surrey had only just enough time to squeeze out a six-wicket win as they scored 57 in 20 minutes with Jardine having to score ten off the last three balls to secure victory. The two teams met again at Lord's three weeks later and blow me if Brown did not again hammer their bowling and take eight wickets in the 229-run win. This time Surrey were 113 for five when he went in, 311 for seven when he left after hitting 135 in just over two hours.

Brown, who was twenty-two while in Australia, did not play in any of the Tests in what became the Bodyline tour. But he was a regular and efficient drinks waiter and Pelham Warner, a joint manager, spoke in raptures about his dancing on the Orient liner Orontes. "A really beautiful dancer, he was the admiration of all and was much sought after as a partner," he wrote. You cannot say fairer than that ...

He did not play all that much the following year but his two centuries were both worth watching — 108 not out at Old Trafford in an innings that produced three centuries and yet another hundred against Middlesex at Lord's, as Surrey beat them for the second time in a week. The number of appearances continued to drop but he still found time in 1934 to hit three sixes and 18 fours in an innings of 119 at Edgbaston. In a rather splendid win over Derbyshire, in which Surrey hit off 137 runs in under an hour, Brown and Errol Holmes got the last 38 in eight minutes. But his appearances were spasmodic, although he still managed to fit in the occasional flash like his 88 in an hour for the Gentlemen against the 1938 Australians at Lord's when batting at number nine.

Lieutenant Brown of the R.A.S.C. won the M.B.E. for welfare work in the Middle East during the Second World War. He was taken prisoner at Tobruk during Rommel's advance and for three years he and Bill Bowes, the Yorkshire and England fast bowler, were together in various Italian and German prisoner-of-war camps. The usually burly Brown was reduced from 14½ to 9½ stone by his experience as a prisoner-of-war, yet he made such a good recovery that before the end of 1945 he had played at Lord's for a Services side. It was some time before he was able to return to county cricket but there was an impressive 11-wicket return when he captained the M.C.C. against Cambridge University at Lord's in 1947 and a quite special century at Scarborough when he was one of three century-makers in the South innings against the North. His 104 not out, which included two sixes and 16 fours, took 68 minutes, and he moved from 79 to 104 by hitting 25 runs off Johnny

Wardle's last over (4-6-4-6-4-1) before Bob Wyatt declared. Godfrey Evans helped Brown add 67 in 15 minutes and Wardle was left with the rather unpleasant return of three wickets for 236 runs. One six was a straight hit over the stand, a reminder of two huge Brown sixes at Scarborough fourteen years earlier. He was then playing for the M.C.C. against Yorkshire and hit left-arm spinner Hedley Verity over the crowd for one six and into the bushes for another. Brown also played for the Gentlemen against the Players at Lord's in 1947 and after getting a "duck" in the first innings he started the second with two sixes off Jack Walsh, one over the scoreboard by the Tavern, the second on to the roof of the Mound Stand and into St. John's Wood Road.

Brown became a welfare official at a Doncaster colliery and played Saturday cricket with a colliery side. He played for Surrey once in 1948 and was a welfare officer with a Birmingham plastics firm in November, 1948, when Northamptonshire approached him. A job was guaranteed, he moved to Daventry five months later and, at the age of thirty-eight, captained Northamptonshire in 1949. Success was immediate and so impressive that he captained England that same summer against New Zealand and achieved the double of 1,000 runs and 100 wickets after a lapse of seventeen years. But it was the following year, 1950, that he reached the pinnacle, beating off his challengers for the English captaincy in Australia with his 122 in 100 minutes for the Gentlemen, the innings he regards as his favourite. The runs were scored out of 131 and before the match with the Players was over, Brown had been named. "It would be correct to say that Norman Yardley and George Mann had declared themselves unavailable for the tour, which really made me third choice," wrote Brown.

He played five seasons for Northamptonshire; five good seasons in which he followed the double of 1949 by missing it in 1952 by one wicket. Vivian Jenkins paid tribute to Brown's leadership qualities in *Wisden* that year, enthusing about the way he won over the Australian crowds with his fighting spirit, his personality and his skill. It was his courage that stood out and Jenkins enjoyed recalling the cry of a stallholder in Sydney who cried: "Lovely lettuces, only a shilling, and hearts as big as Freddie Brown's." What a tribute. The photograph that stood with the article reminded me of the one nearly twenty years earlier when Brown had been one of the Cricketers of the Year. Now he was turned forty, a pipe rested easily on his fingers, the parting had moved towards middle and leg, but there was still a look of the cherub.

Colin Cowdrey, too, said nice things about him: "Freddie Brown I think was a magnificent personality. He would bowl as long as you wanted him in the nets in 1954, a lovely lumbering action full of slow rhythm, a classical shoulder action to create the dangerous loop in the flight of his leg breaks. I admired his approach to cricket and it is one of my regrets that I did not play more with him. As manager he was, behind the bluff mask, the kindest, gentlest man, unselfish to a degree and always wishing the best for you."

Brown kept on hitting right to the end. In his last season, 1953, he scored 97 in an hour against Somerset with four sixes and 12 fours, his last 47 runs coming in ten minutes. He went in to bat against Kent when Northamptonshire were 85 for five and in two hours hit three sixes and 13 fours in his 101. He hit Raymond Dovey for 20 in an over and was caught on the boundary attempting a six off Doug Wright.

6 ARTHUR CARR

There are players who made less auspicious debuts in the game than Arthur Carr. But not many. He was only seventeen and a bit and still a schoolboy at Sherborne when Nottinghamshire took him to Bristol to open the innings in 1910. He faced George Dennett, who took 120 wickets for Gloucestershire that season, and Charlie Parker, who finished that game with 12 of the 15 Nottinghamshire wickets that fell. Carr might not even have had the pleasure of facing Dennett for he twice fell to Parker rather quickly — for one in the first innings and a "duck" in the second. Still, the seventeen-year-old started with a win and there are not many better places to visit than Bristol for your first match.

Carr got his first hundred in 1913. He was still just a boy, barely twenty, but he laid into the Leicestershire attack of George Geary, himself only twenty, and Alec Skelding to score 169 of his team's 507 for three declared. He and Garnett Lee added 333 runs for the second wicket at over 100 runs an hour. A dazzling innings, drooled *Wisden* ten years on when picking him as one of the Cricketers of the Year. That century, as well as being Carr's first, turned out to be his last for several years. The First World War broke out in 1914 and the young Carr served in the 5th Lancers. By the time he returned to cricket he was twenty-five and captain of a Nottinghamshire team that was to break the Yorkshire-Lancashire domination of the championship by winning it in 1929.

He won a game for Nottinghamshire in 1920 with a great hundred against Surrey at the Oval, he hit 204 in four and a quarter hours against Essex at Leyton in 1921, but it was 1922 before the pre-war promise fully turned into reality with over 1,700 runs and four centuries (although it must be pointed out that one was against Scotland for the M.C.C. after the openers had started with 212 in just over two hours). He was the most brilliant and most dangerous batsman in the Nottingham-shire team and saved all his centuries that year for his county for Trent Bridge, including a fine 103 in 105 minutes in the defeat of Lancashire. He hit with great power, particularly in his driving, and in the game against Northamptonshire — a team he regularly punished — he hit five sixes in a run-a-minute 99. Like every other hitter in the game, he took advantage of the Scarborough festival spirit at the end of the season when he played for the Gentlemen against the Players. In his innings of 65, scored in 50 minutes, he hit six sixes and five fours. All the sixes came off Frank Woolley, the first three coming in five balls, the others coming later off successive deliveries. Carr made full use of the supporting wind to bombard the houses at the southern end of the ground while Frank Mann hit five more sixes, one of them almost making the long journey to Trafalgar Square.

Carr had a marvellous season in 1925 when he hit eight centuries, two of them against Sussex, one coming in 48 minutes at Hove. In that game he finished with 124 in 70 minutes and hit five sixes and 12 fours after telling Arthur Gilligan, the Sussex

captain, before the match that he had never felt less like cricket in his life. He hit vigorously to score an unbeaten 107 in just over two hours at the Oval, and took the same time over 104 against Sussex at Trent Bridge. "Carr drove very hard and jumped right in to the pitch of the ball," wrote Gilligan. "One of his full-blooded shots from one of Tate's best deliveries sent the ball right over the stand on the left of the pavilion and it dropped just at the entrance gate. I believe this is one of the biggest hits ever made at Trent Bridge. Carr was a great sportsman who did not play safety-first cricket."

It was in that summer of 1925 that Carr created a record for the number of sixes hit in a season, 48. Six came against Kent, three against Lancashire, and his biggest innings was at Leicester where eight sixes and 24 fours went a long way towards his 206 scored in 225 minutes. He finished off the season quite beautifully with another bit of holiday hitting at Scarborough with two sixes out of the ground.

This period was the peak of Carr's performances. He captained England against Australia the following year and had the rather extraordinary experience of playing in the first four Tests and batting only once. That would not have been so bad if he had not had one of those awful days that overtakes us all, during the third Test at Headingley. He won the toss, which is a pretty good start, and then put Australia in to bat. He dropped a catch at slip when Charlie Macartney was two and then watched, wincing no doubt with every run, as the Australian hit a century before lunch, one of three Australian hundreds in the innings. Carr was long remembered for that. And coupled with his decision to field first was the choice of the team and the decision to leave Charlie Parker, regarded as the best left-arm spinner in the country, as twelfth man. Parker, it might be remembered by those with an eye for such detail, had dismissed the seventeen-year-old Carr for one and nought on his debut sixteen years earlier. Carr asked to stand down for the final Test when England won and recovered the Ashes under Percy Chapman. Carr was a popular man and sympathy was shown for him when he went in to bat on the first day of Nottinghamshire's match with Lancashire at Old Trafford in August. He was given a tremendous ovation when he stepped out of the pavilion, the spectators got to their feet, and the applause lasted for some time after he reached the wicket. When he returned to the dressing room after scoring 67 he said: "I'm glad I made a bit of a show. I felt a little overcome by the reception they gave me." He played only two more Tests, against South Africa three years later and finished his international career with hardly an innings to speak of.

At least Carr was able to devote his energies almost entirely to Nottinghamshire who stayed among the leaders in the championship and came out on top in 1929. Among the more stirring Carr displays in 1928 was a century in two hours against Learie Constantine and the West Indies, a quite colossal six off Fred Root at Trent Bridge, some spectacular hitting in Fred Barratt's benefit match against Lancashire, also at Trent Bridge, and 81 in 45 minutes at Bournemouth. The championship arrived the following year and with it two more Tests, against South Africa. His best innings was played outside the championship with 194 for Notts against the South Africans, including seven sixes and 20 fours.

Carr was a lover of horses and a keen rider. He was also a fine captain. Fred Root was playing for the North of England against the Australians in 1926, the week before the first Test, and when the Australians were collapsing against Root's leg theory, Carr made certain they would not follow-on and so get another look at Root's bowling. Root made his Test debut, again under Carr's captaincy, a few days later, and was supplied with pages of written information about the opposition by Carr. "It proved to be remarkably accurate," wrote Root.

Carr was also temperamental; Herbert Sutcliffe, who thought highly of him as a captain as well, told a story about him in the Nottinghamshire v. Yorkshire match of 1932. It was played at Headingley, the game in which Hedley Verity took all ten second innings wickets for ten runs. Nottinghamshire had scored 38 without loss before lunch on the last day, then lost all ten wickets for 29 runs after. Carr did not get a run in the match, caught Barber, on the boundary edge off a straight drive, bowled Verity in both innings. Two or three yards more, and each shot would have been worth six, reported Sutcliffe. This "pair" was the last straw for Carr who went back to the dressing room after the second dismissal and threw all his gear to the other players, telling them to help themselves. This sort of story has been pooh-poohed since. Seems Carr did it quite often, but then got it all back again.

His last match was in 1934 when a heart attack prevented him playing again. He died shovelling snow at home in West Witton, Yorkshire, in 1963, just short of his seventieth birthday.

7 LEARIE CONSTANTINE

As a boy in Nelson I was brought up on Learie Constantine. I never saw him, I did not even know anybody who had shaken him by the hand. But he was the biggest thing that had ever happened to the small Lancashire mill town. We all wanted to be Constantine in the school yard, we all wanted to smack the ball over the church spire. After all, wasn't that what Constantine did? In those years he was one of the biggest, most attractive names in cricket, a hard-hitting batsman, quick bowler, an electric, exciting fielder. A complete entertainer. When he was once sent a slow, high full toss, he turned to face square leg and hit the ball for six over the sightscreen behind the wicket.

Constantine played comparatively little first-class cricket and scored only five centuries, none of them in his eighteen Tests between 1928 and 1939. But he played some remarkable innings, the most thrilling probably coming in this country in 1928 when the first Test series was played between England and the West Indies. Jack Hobbs said of him: "As a batsman Constantine was a firework. He could hit like a prize-fighting champion. English crowds took Constantine to their hearts. Once or twice he played wholly to the gallery. Small wonder that whenever he appeared the crowd 'sat up' just as they had done in the days when Jessop came to the crease." C.L.R. James wrote: "Nobody, not a single soul, had ever seen Constantine bat in the West Indies as he batted in England in 1928. This was the biggest explosion so far. He had changed. Constantine had revolted against the revolting contrast between his first-class status as a cricketer and third-class status as a man." Constantine was twenty-five, a strong young man regarded more for his quick bowling than for his batting. In the second game of the tour, in fact, he batted at number ten, but in the next, played against Essex at Leyton at the beginning of May, he batted at number eight after opening the bowling. The score was 183 for six, in reply to Essex's 369, when Constantine batted, hitting so fiercely that in an hour and a half he had scored 130. He drove and pulled powerfully to hit three sixes and 14 fours.

His outstanding performance, however, was reserved for Lord's where his father, Lebrun, had scored the first century in England by a West Indian in 1900. The West Indians had laboriously reached 79 for five in reply to Middlesex's 352 for six declared when Constantine went out to bat. In less than an hour he had hit 86 out of 107 including one extraordinary square cut off Gubby Allen that soared high into the top balcony at one end of the Father Time stand. His innings was brought to a close when he was deceived by an Ian Peebles googly and the West Indians were 122 behind on the first innings. When Middlesex batted a second time Constantine, opening the attack as usual, tore through the team with seven for 57, hitting the stumps five times and leaving his team to get 259 for victory. Five wickets fell for 121 runs and the West Indians looked as good as beaten when Constantine batted again. This time he put on an even more astonishing display of hitting with 103 out of 133

in an hour with two sixes and 12 fours. He hit with ferocious power and one straight drive hit Jack Hearne on the hand and so badly damaged a finger that he did not play again that season. Peebles described it as the greatest all-round performance he had ever seen. So the West Indians won by three wickets after what was probably the outstanding achievement of Constantine's career. He came close to matching it at Northampton at the end of the month when he took 13 wickets for 112 runs, including the hat-trick, and scored 107 in 90 minutes with five sixes and 12 fours as the West Indians walked away with victory by an innings and 126 runs.

Constantine played another astonishing innings at Leeds a week later when he hit 69 in 28 minutes with four sixes and six fours before being teased out by the fifty-year-old Wilfred Rhodes. He also hit 70 in 40 minutes against Warwickshire, 50 in 25 minutes against Leicestershire, 62 in 45 minutes against an England XI at Folkestone and 50 out of 56 in 20 minutes against Leveson Gower's XI at Scarborough.

The West Indies lost all three Tests by an innings and Constantine was a big disappointment with only five wickets at more than 50 runs each and totalling 89 runs in six innings. Jack Hobbs recalled one hit of Constantine's in the Old Trafford Test which went higher than he had ever seen a ball go. "Freeman (the bowler) looked round to see if anybody would tackle it and found that he had to go for the catch," Hobbs wrote. "It went through his hands on to his chest and nearly choked him. In addition he had the mortification of reading in the papers next day that he had dropped an easy catch." Freeman, oddly enough, had a similar experience playing for Kent against the West Indians at Canterbury when Constantine skied a ball over Charles Marriott at mid-off. Freeman, who dismissed Constantine five times in five matches in 1928, rushed to take the catch himself and dropped it. Constantine laughed and laughed at the bowler's distress.

The tour as a whole — his only complete season in English county cricket — was a great triumph for Constantine with 107 wickets and 1,381 runs in first-class matches with three centuries, at Leyton, Northampton and Lord's. His own favourite innings was played at Sydney two years later, a little gem, 59 runs in 35 minutes with four sixes and four fours. One ball was hit halfway up the Hill, another bounced off the Paddington Stand roof and on to the show ground, and a third landed high on the roof of the Sheridan grandstand. It was on this tour that Constantine scored the fastest century ever by a West Indian, reached in 52 minutes at Launceston in Tasmania. He got 65 of the runs in 25 minutes before lunch and claimed his 100 out of 128 added with his captain, George Grant.

As he wanted a part-time job that would enable him to study law, Constantine took the position as Nelson's professional and helped them win the Lancashire League seven times in his nine seasons with them. He delighted the crowds which flocked to see him, losing many a ball in the surrounding streets. His move into the league meant he played only just over 100 first-class matches with a poor record in his eighteen Tests with 641 runs at an average below 20 and 58 wickets at 30 each. He played in just one Test in England in 1933 but his all-round brilliance on his home ground in Trinidad in 1935 brought West Indies victory over England by 217 runs. He scored 90 and 31 and took five wickets for 52 runs in the match, including that of Maurice Leyland that gave the West Indies a thrilling victory with one ball of the match remaining.

Constantine's outstanding Test innings in England came in the Oval Test of 1939 when he scored 79, the last 78 coming in 57 minutes, as he drove the fielders back to the boundary edge. He played an astonishing shot in this innings, one he regarded as one of his best ever, playing back to fast bowler Reg Perks and driving him over the long on fence. Said Neville Cardus: "Constantine drove with a ferocity and power quite terrifying. From the Press Box I looked down on this fury of primitive onslaught, beautiful if savage and violently destructive." And ..." I remember that as I watched this innings from the Press Box's altitude, I actually (but only temporarily) decided that there were not enough fieldsmen available. Nine were ridiculously inadequate to assist bowler and stumper. There was no excess of muscular effort in Constantine's swift plunderings. It was the attack and savagings of a panther on the kill, sinuous, healthy, strong and unburdened."

It is as a league cricketer, though, that people in the North remember him. Fred Root, an experienced county player, played for Todmorden in the Lancashire League while Constantine was with Nelson and remembered one game when his wicket-keeper, Tommy Carrick, appealed for lbw against the West Indian. Constantine jumped round, glared at Carrick and howled: "Not out!" Carrick was frightened. "I don't fancy appealing any more," he said to Root at the end of the over. "I thought he was going to bite me." Root bolstered Carrick's confidence enough for him to try another appeal a few balls later, producing exactly the same performance. Carrick pointed to the umpire and faced up to Constantine. "Thee shurrup," he said. "I'm not asking thee. I'm asking th' umpire."

Frank Dennis, the old Yorkshire bowler, recalled facing Constantine in a Bradford League match during the war, Baildon Green v. Windhill. "I think he got five wickets, then opened the batting," Frank wrote. "I opened the bowling to him and had one over and two balls — he was caught on the extra cover boundary for 32! The over from the other end was a maiden. One six off me was a length ball from off stump over fine leg."

Constantine qualified for the bar and returned home after the war to become a cabinet minister and then Trinidad and Tobago High Commissioner in Britain. He was raised to the peerage as Lord Constantine of Maraval and Nelson and died in 1971 aged sixty-eight.

8 PERCY FENDER

One of my greatest joys in nearly twenty-five years of being attached to first-class cricket came on 15th September, 1983 when I took Steve O'Shaughnessy to Horsham to meet Percy Fender. Two days earlier O'Shaughnessy, the Lancashire batsman, had scored a century in 35 minutes against Leicestershire on the last day of the season to equal Fender's world record. When he went in to Old Trafford the following morning there was a telegram waiting for him: "Congratulations on equalling my 63-year-old record, Fender." It seemed a good idea to bring the two of them together. It turned out to be an hour of pure delight in which two cricketers bridged generations of cricket by their joint record. O'Shaughnessy was twenty-two at the time and Fender ninety-one but the huge difference in age and playing eras was immediately forgotten as the young bombarded the old with a barrage of questions about his playing techniques, his memories, in particular his own century in 35 minutes, scored at Northampton in 1920. There were three plaques on the wall bearing testimony to world records. I assumed they had been presented. "Oh no, I had them made," said Fender. One of them read: "1920 World Record in first-class cricket. Fastest Hundred. Surrey v. Northants (August) in 35 minutes." Fender maintained, as apparently he had done often, that his century had taken 34 minutes. The Surrey scorer told him that, and in any case he had taken notice of the time himself. How funny. O'Shaughnessy, too, had looked at the clock when he reached the wicket and also believed he had taken under the recorded time of 35 minutes. Incidentally, I also noted the start of his innings as nearer 3.10 than 3.05 and as his century arrived on the stroke of tea at 3.40 his time was not much more than half an hour. Officially though — they were both 35.

Fender was an habitual fast scorer, a dashing batsman who loved to attack the bowling and averaged a run-a-minute through his career. He cared nothing for his own figures and played with a total lack of selfishness and brought flair and unorthodoxy to his years as captain of Surrey. Life was one long adventure for him. He was an airman in both wars, flying bi-planes against Zeppelins in the First World War, he invested in musical shows, gambled to some tune, even fought a fencing duel with a Belgian army officer over a girl. His appearance was full of character with the extra-long sweater, the Hitler-type short black moustache and the horn-rimmed spectacles. "For sheer entertainment," wrote R.C. Robertson-Glasgow, "I doubt if any modern cricketer has surpassed P.G.H. Fender."

Fender's first taste of county cricket was with Sussex in 1910 but by 1914 he had joined Surrey, the county he was to captain from 1921 to 1931, and with which he performed the double of 100 wickets and 1,000 runs six times. He was an outspoken man with a strong mind of his own and this quality might have been responsible for him having played only thirteen times for England. And if anybody ever should have captained England, but did not, it was Fender.

He was twenty-eight when he hit his record century in 1920, beating by five minutes Gilbert Jessop's record time for Gloucestershire against Yorkshire at Harrogate in 1897. The time and the details of Fender's innings have been analysed and chewed over ever since. Mathematicians, statisticians, bores and magicians have pored over every shot and dot in the score book, but it stays the same, 35 minutes and a world record. And if it was 34 or 33, what the heck? It was still pretty fast.

Fender hated to let any ball go through to the wicketkeeper. It was there to be hit and he had the ability to hit it to any part of the ground. His most remarkable shot at Northampton came after he had driven Jack Murdin twice through the covers and was expecting a bumper next ball. It was certainly pitched short but instead of rising, it shot through. Fender, already on the back foot, went through with his shot and hit the ball back over the bowler's head and the sightscreen and on to the football field. Another extraordinary hit followed at the Oval two years later when Godfrey Bryan, the Kent medium-paced bowler, sent down a half volley wide of the off stump which Fender hit in the direction of the gasworks. He hit the ball as it rose and it pitched out of the ground over extra cover's head and into the street behind the scoreboard. The hit was measured at 132 yards which made it probably the biggest hit ever in the direction of extra cover.

Fender would slash mightily at any ball wide of the stumps and once cut a ball at Lord's over point's head into the top tier of seats in the grandstand below Father Time. Although a good straight driver and fierce offside hitter, he particularly enjoyed hooking and pulling and most of his sixes went in the direction of mid-wicket. In one innings of 185 against Hampshire at the Oval in 1922 he scored his last 154 runs in 90 minutes, mostly with shots in front of square leg. That was a good year for Fender who did the double and captained Surrey to thirteen championship wins and third place in the table. His 143 wickets were 83 more than the next Surrey bowler and his 1,114 runs, averaging almost 40, included probably the two most astonishing displays of hitting that summer.

"There has been nothing like his play in these two matches since Jessop was in his prime," judged *Wisden*. "Nearly all through the season Fender played in glasses, but as he hit just as well when, now and then, he took them off, there could not have been much amiss with his sight." Both innings were played at the Oval, the first coming in the match against Hampshire in the middle of May when he scored 185 in 108 minutes while most other cricketers were still rubbing the winter sleep out of their eyes. Pelham Warner's magazine, *The Cricketer*, declared unequivocally that "No more astonishing innings has been played on the Oval since G.L. Jessop got his historic hundred for England against Australia in 1902." He did hasten to point out that Hampshire's bowling, of course, was not of the same class as the Australians and while the wicket in 1902 was dodgy, it was perfect for the county game, which already takes the innings down a notch or two in history. But ... "those who were fortunate enough to see Mr Fender's innings will never forget it." He was dropped at cover when he was 22 — the sun was in the fielder's eyes — and in the deep at 92, but it was still a sensational display. "His driving on both sides of the wicket was tremendously powerful; he cut square and late superbly and at one period of his innings he seemed able to hit the good length ball round on the on-side whenever he liked. Amongst the many beautiful strokes was one we shall never forget, and that was when he hit a good length ball of Kennedy's with apparently a mere flick of the wrist over extra cover's head against the top of the scoring board, with that lovely sound to a cricketer of leather striking wood. It was in every respect a most astonishing stroke." Fender hit three sixes, three fives and 25 fours and after completing his hundred he hit 52 runs off 14 consecutive balls. He went in at 164 for four and left at 455 for nine and followed with five wickets in the innings victory.

Eleven weeks later Fender was the subject of another eulogy as he took 137 runs off the Kent bowling in an hour and a half. More than 47,000 people paid for admission on the first two days and at lunch on the second day Fender was 29. It took him only half an hour afterwards to complete his hundred and apart from his huge hit over extra cover off Bryan, the feature of his innings was the way he repeatedly pulled good length balls from Frank Woolley to the mid-wicket boundary. There were five centuries in the match, three of them coming in Kent's second innings as they overcame a first innings deficit of 329. But again there were qualifications — "Both sides are somewhat deficient in effective bowling on hard wickets and that heavy scoring should have been seen hardly came as a surprise," wrote the po-faced *Cricketer*.

Fender won the match at Leicester that season when Leicestershire, after following-on, declared at tea and set Surrey to get 150 in 80 minutes. Three wickets fell for 42 runs but Fender hit 91 not out with all but 11 of his runs coming in fours and sixes. He scored 28 of the last 29 runs in eight minutes and finished off the match in grand style with a straight drive into the pavilion.

That is how Fender should be remembered, a man who played to win, brilliant, inventive, at times dramatic and outrageous. O'Shaughnessy and I, however, will remember him for his charm, a lovely old gentleman who gave us both a lasting memory. His sense of humour was still sharp at ninety-one and when it was time to leave he held on to the bat O'Shaughnessy had used and had taken to Horsham with him. "Thank you," said Fender. "It is very good of you to come all this way to give me a bat." O'Shaughnessy blanched. Fender's eyes twinkled: "I think I had him worried then, didn't I?" he said to me. Less than two years later he had died, in an Exeter nursing home.

9 GILBERT JESSOP

Gilbert Jessop handed me the ball. It was more than eighty years old, pink and brown, worn and badly knocked about. It was engraved and bore the date. "Father hit two centuries before lunch in the match against Yorkshire at Bradford in 1900," said Jessop junior. "This was the ball used in the second innings." The ball was a reminder of just one of the many eventful innings played through a celebrated career by his father. He scored 104 in 70 minutes in the first innings, but the second was even more impressive, a century in 59 minutes, 139 runs in all with seven sixes off Wilfred Rhodes, six of them clearing the football stand. I went to Bath, to see Gilbert Jessop the younger, seventy-eight years old. "I doubt if there is very much I can tell you," he had replied to my request to see him. Perhaps there is not for a man whose deeds have been so well chronicled, whose every innings has been analysed, every massive, marvellous six recorded and recounted. C.J. Britton even produced a book in 1935 which contained every innings Jessop had played — more than 800 of them. Still, just to see the ball which had sailed so many times over the Bradford football stand was something. After the ball came a bat on a small plinth to commemorate if not his best, certainly his most important, influential innings, his century against the Australians at the Oval in 1902 when England won by one wicket. "I don't know who presented that," said Mr Jessop junior.

England had been left to score 263 to win —" don't think there were a great many of us who really fancied our chances and if there were I am quite sure that the number dwindled considerably when our third wicket fell with the score at ten," Jessop wrote twenty years later in his book, *A Cricketer's Log*. "Personally, I was most uncomfortable, for I had embarked foolishly the night before at dinner at the Great Central Hotel, which one or two of us had made our quarters for the match, on a wager which bordered on the ridiculous." A glass or two of what Jessop described as "Pommery," the sound of rain which had dogged England through the series, and Jessop offered to take ten to one that he would make 50, and twenty to one he would get a hundred. The offer was snatched up immediately leaving Jessop, as he said, "most uncomfortable," particularly when he went in to bat at 48 for five with 215 runs still needed and the Australians looking certain of winning. In an hour and a quarter he scored 104, straw boaters were flying through the air and Yorkshire's George Hirst and Wilfred Rhodes were the last batsmen who safely saw England through. That century still stands as the fastest for England in Test cricket. The *Bristol Evening News* of 13th August, 1902, said Jessop had fallen in the hour of his triumph "to a very simple spoon of the ball on the legside". Then added: "As he turned to depart Jim Kelly, the Australian wicketkeeper, turned to pat him on the shoulder and all the Australians applauded him." The day after the Test match Jessop was at Cheltenham and was cheered all the way to the wicket before hitting 42 out of 46 in 40 minutes against Yorkshire.

Mr Jessop junior later produced his father's own cuttings book including the chart of the innings of 93 against South Africa at Lord's in 1907. This, said C.B. Fry, was Jessop's best innings. Jessop, who regretted never having hit a ball over the Lord's pavilion, landed one on the roof that day and the following year hit the iron scroll work on the offside, about four feet higher than the centre part of the roof.

Gilbert Jessop was born on 19th May, 1874, the eleventh child of a Cheltenham doctor and named Gilbert after another Gloucestershire doctor fairly well known in cricket circles, William Gilbert Grace. Jessop was twenty years old when he first played for Gloucestershire, against Lancashire at Old Trafford when, it has been suggested, W.G. tried him hugely by sending him in when Arthur Mold had a chance of a hat-trick. Jessop's first over from Mold produced three "fourers". In any case, said his son, that was his position in the batting.

Between then and his last match in 1914 Jessop scored at an average rate of 80 runs an hour. He rarely batted long. He was at the wicket for three hours only twice and for two hours about ten times — and that in a career which produced five double centuries and 48 single centuries. His first game at Old Trafford gave him a taste for Lancashire and Cec Parkin recalled playing against him in his last match at Old-Trafford, in July 1914 when he was forty years old. "He opened Gloucestershire's innings and soon hit Harry Dean for three sixes," wrote Parkin. "I took the next over. The first ball came flashing back past my nose and thudded against the sightscreen and the next one he clouted into the pavilion enclosure. I saw A.H. Hornby, our captain, laughing at me, but with my fifth ball I bowled the great G.L. who, as he passed me on his way to the pavilion, very kindly said to me: 'Well, bowled, boy.' He had scored 31 off 11 balls in seven minutes. I was glad when he was out. I was frightened to death of his fireworks, and felt that if he stayed he might hit me straight back and kill me!" Parkin exaggerated a little. Jessop hit only one six in his innings, plus four fours before he was first out after hitting 31 in a stand of 35.

Somerset's Len Braund once announced, on the eve of the 1904 game with Gloucestershire at Bristol, that he had invented a ball to get rid of crouchers. He was brought on to bowl just before lunch and Jessop, with a smile, hit him for 28 with two sixes and four fours.

Gilbert Jessop, by all accounts, was a gentle creature, a pleasant, friendly, popular man who never lost his composure. Hardly ever, anyway. One instance occurred at Old Trafford in 1905 when he and Lancashire fast bowler Walter Brearley clashed. William Howard, the dressing room attendant at the time who spent fifty years at Old Trafford, recalled in his reminiscences that in all that time he could recall only two unpleasant matches, both against Gloucestershire and the first involving W.G. and Archie MacLaren. The second, he regarded as more unpleasant. "Before the game started a lot of chaff had been going on between G.L. Jessop, the Gloucester-shire captain, and W. Brearley," wrote Howard. "Mr Jessop did not appear to be in his usual amiable mood that morning; some difficulty arose in fixing up our side owing to injuries, and he displayed a little irritation in waiting for the list of Lancashire players before tossing. In my recollections of this famous cricketer, this was not characteristic of him; he was a charming man and agreeable at all times. A small wager was made that the Lancashire fast bowler would hit Mr Jessop for four. When Mr Brearley went to the wickets, he hit a ball to the boundary (which the

Gloucester captain had simply rolled down the pitch after the over) and called out: 'I've won that half-crown, Jessop.' This bit of fooling was not appreciated by Mr Jessop, who made some bitter comments on the Lancastrian's action at the close of the innings. Gloucestershire, on going in to bat, fared badly against the bowling of Mr Brearley, and it was evident that when Mr Jessop went to the wickets to try to knock him off his length there was going to be a combat between them. Running down the pitch, he hit the fast bowler several times to the boundary, and called to the other batsman to adopt the same methods. It was the bowler's turn to become enraged and, receiving no objections from his captain to his intentions, he started bowling full tosses at the batsman's head to try to make him stay in his crease. It was the most thrilling tussle between batsman and bowler I have seen, although I have no desire to witness another of a similar kind. To see the ball hurtling past the plucky batsman's head, compelling him to duck to escape being hit, was to my mind not the kind of cricket one likes to witness. There was a feeling of relief when Mr Jessop was dismissed after playing a daring innings of about 40 runs; I admired his pluck." In fact, Jessop scored 57 in 41 minutes and he and Jack Board, in four overs, hit Brearley for 57 (12, 18, 12 and 15). Several deliveries had been so high they had gone straight into the wicketkeeper's hands standing back and Jessop, in protest, suggested to the umpire that some balls were so far over his head they should have been called wides. Two more, he maintained, were within inches of his forehead.

"He (Jessop) was in a terrible rage when he came in the room," William Howard continued, "and expressed his intention of not taking any further part in the game, as he considered it was a disgraceful action on the part of the bowler. I never witnessed such a display of passion over a game of cricket; R.H. Spooner seemed much upset, and, being of a peaceful temperament, he had an abhorrence of disagreements taking place among the players. If he had been skippering the side, I think a change in the bowling would have taken place. At the finish of the match the conversation was not complimentary. Mr Jessop was unable to control himself and said some hard things both to Mr Brearley and Mr MacLaren. The two combatants were the best of friends again in the following season. Mr Jessop was too good a sport to bear animosity against an old comrade; he was a jovial man and possessed an abundance of courage." Nevertheless, Jessop did not play against Lancashire again until 1911 when he scored 80 in 95 minutes. Brearley, it was said, bowled at a great pace. He missed the game in 1910 after being "seized with a severe chill earlier in the week" and, in fact, played only once against them in the five years after the Brearley incident.

When Jessop died in 1955, a few days short of his eighty-first birthday, *The Times*, in a leading article, referred to him having "added gaiety to the nation". When word got about that Jessop was batting at lunch, people would flock to the ground in the afternoon to see him. Jack Hobbs said it was difficult to bowl a ball from which he could not score. "He made me glad I was not a bowler," he said.

"Father often decided before the ball was bowled what shot he was going to play," his son said. "George Brown, the Hampshire bowler, pitched outside off stump and was hooked for six. So he pitched outside leg stump and was hit over cover for six — he was quite annoyed about that. He was different from other hitters in that he would go down the pitch to them, force them to drop short, then cut and hook. Nearly every side sent fielders to the boundary, all except Kent who maintained the usual field which annoyed Father, who expected fielders to go out. He got so upset, he hit when he shouldn't and tended to get out early."

Jessop went to Beccles College, then Christ's College at Cambridge University and played for the Varsity side in the closing years of the nineteenth century. A fellow student said it was not uncommon in the summer term, when two or three college games were being played in adjoining fields for word to go round: "Jessop is batting." Immediately "tools were downed" everywhere else. "The men would leave their own fields of action and crowd over the fences to share the excitement. They would see the 'Croucher' hitting balls all over the field to the utter consternation of the fielding side. It is a memory that lingers."

Jessop was known as the "Croucher" for his position at the crease. He crouched low over his bat as he grounded it, catapulted himself into a sort of rapid dance towards the pitch of the ball and flung his bat at it. His rapid dance was seen at its best one September day in 1907 when he scored 191 in 90 minutes at Hastings, an assault that included 30 fours and five sixes. He was playing for the Gentlemen against the Players of the South and after reaching his century in 42 minutes gave the only semblance of a chance at 158 when Frank Woolley ran from third man to short square leg in an effort to reach it, which gives an indication of the field placings with third man being the nearest fielder for a catch close to the wicket.

Hastings was one of Jessop's favourite grounds. He averaged 56 there over 33 innings and enjoyed the so-called "Holiday cricket". His conception of games where full tosses and half volleys were there for the asking was quickly shattered when he realised from his first Festival match that players approached the games with the same eagerness as in the championship. Except, he said, at one game at Hastings in 1899, the Home Counties v. the Rest of England when he batted on the last afternoon, a Saturday. He was into the 30s just before tea when he ran out to a ball from Digby Jephson, missed it and tried to get back though yards up the wicket. He reckoned he was still two feet from his crease when he was stumped, but umpire Bob Thoms squeaked: "Not out, not out" and muttered: "Sixpenny crowd, Saturday gate, can't disappoint 'em, near thing, near thing, but not near enough for the occasion." Jessop went on to an "undefeated" century!

Another hundred presentation to Jessop had come in 1898, also at Hastings when he played for the Rest of England against A.E. Stoddart's team that had been to Australia. "In my early days when a batsman climbed to within a few runs' reach of his century it was sometimes a kindly custom to present a long hop or a full pitch from which to complete the feat," he wrote. Jessop's highest score that season before the Hastings match was 65. It was his first visit to that ground and Tom Richardson "saw to it when I hove within sight of my century that I should not fall short by a miserable few runs". He finished with 112 not out.

Dicky Barlow, the Lancashire and England player, who was an umpire through nearly all Jessop's career, wrote of the game at Harrogate in 1907 when Jessop hit 89 out of 111 in 45 minutes. In one over Jessop hit 20 runs off George Hirst who turned to Barlow and said: "Well, he's a regular devil. The better I bowl, the better he hits 'em." He asked Barlow how he would have bowled at him in his best days. Barlow replied: "I would give it up." Likening Dr E.M. Grace as the nearest approach to

Jessop, Barlow also recalled a game at Nottingham in 1904 when Jessop made 206 in two and a half hours "which so delighted the spectators that they almost went wild."

Mr Jessop junior suggested that the biggest hit his father made came at Bristol with a hit over the stand away from the pavilion. "In those days there was a football ground on the other side," he said. "The seats in the stand could be turned round and people in the stand marked where the ball landed. It was measured at 150 yards. Crawford hit a ball over the Bristol pavilion. Father said that was the biggest hit he ever saw." I asked the younger Jessop, who played for Hampshire in 1933, if he ever tried to emulate his father. He smiled, a rare smile. "I couldn't do that," he said.

C.B. Fry said of Jessop: "No man has ever driven the cricket ball so hard, so high and so often in so many different directions. No man has ever made cricket so dramatic an entertainment." A Lord's spectator who watched Bill Woodfull dithering about against Hedley Verity in 1934, was heard to remark: "Give me ten minutes of Jessop and you can have as many hours of this sort of thing as Tommy Lipton owns tea leaves."

Jessop was also an outstanding quick bowler and fielder and Archie MacLaren maintained he was worth his place in the side for the runs he saved in the covers. He went out of the game in 1914 with a bang, smashing the clock on the county ground at Bristol with a prodigious hit against Somerset. He lived on for forty-one years, and when he died in 1955, the *Daily Telegraph* put his death notice alongside the report of a friendly match between Northamptonshire and Lancashire in which Denis Brookes had taken 40 minutes over his first run. He deserved better than that.

10 CLIVE LLOYD

I have my own memories of Clive Lloyd. Lots of them. Fine memories of a distinguished, honest cricketer who has arguably provided more entertainment for Lancashire supporters than any other player. He has hit as hard and as far as any batsman I have seen; just a twirl of his bat and an entire bar is emptied. Nobody dozes, drinks, knits, pours the wine, attacks the crossword, when Lloyd bats. Without even scratching below the surface of my brain, I recall a 50-minute century at Nottingham, a World Cup final whirlwind of an innings, six sixes against Surrey shortly before a double cartilage operation, a massive blow at Nuneaton that cleared a benchful of supporters, a square cut six at Hove and a huge hit out of the Oval and across Harleyford Road.

My first sight of Lloyd was when he first came to this country as professional for Haslingden in the Lancashire League, a small mill town in the heart of industrial Lancashire. His Test career was underway with a series in India and a home series against England which included centuries at Port of Spain and Bridgetown. A good friend, Ian Brayshaw from Western Australia, was the Bacup professional and the clash of these two was too good to miss. Brayshaw was a well-above-average medium paced bowler — he had taken ten for 44 against Victoria only a few months earlier — but Lloyd savaged him. An auction barn at one side of the small Haslingden ground attracted Lloyd who lost quite a few balls in that direction. "You know, you're costing this club a hell of a lot of money," said the groundsman every time the ball failed to reappear.

Lloyd hit his third Test century that winter, (Australian summer), which included 100 between tea and the close of play at Brisbane. Real, vintage Lloyd. Yet depression set in with three and a half series, four and a half years and twenty-three Tests without a century. But at least the hundreds were coming for Lancashire.

I did not have the pleasure of seeing Lloyd's debut for Lancashire in 1968, his qualifying year when he could not play in the championship but was able to turn out against the Australians in a washed-out match which allowed time for just 70 overs and for Lloyd to get out for one. It also enabled Lloyd to play alongside Brian Statham for the only time in his career. But I did see the man make his championship debut in 1969, immediately after the end of the short West Indies tour here. The tour finished at Southampton and after the party, Lloyd made his way to Bristol for Lancashire's game with Gloucestershire. Lancashire won the toss and Lloyd, batting at number four, padded up. Opener David Lloyd laughed at him: "Have you no confidence in us?" he said. "You can get off to the pictures." Lloyd had scored 80-odd in the game at Southampton, was in good form, and determined to make his county debut one to be remembered. He scored nought and two!

He did not get a century that year but helped Lancashire win the new John Player League. I particularly remember the game that clinched the title, against

Warwickshire at Nuneaton when Lloyd hit one or two massive blows on the small ground. The chrysanthemums and dahlias in the nearby back gardens are quite used to their yearly battering but one hit had everyone searching the sky for the dot of a ball. I remember a man had just reappeared from the bar with a pint in each hand and was just sitting on a bench when Lloyd let fly. Six men perched on the bench watched the ball soar and leaned back to watch the flight. Back and back they went until the bench toppled over and left them floundering like upturned turtles. The man with the beer clung to the glasses and got to his feet with a beaming smile. He had hardly spilled a drop.

When Lloyd's first century did arrive for Lancashire, in 1970, it was a little beauty. It was the second game of the season, at Dartford, and the houses at one end of the ground were so bombarded with sixes that a dear old lady called the police in an effort to stop it. The innings of 163 lasted only 145 minutes and included seven sixes. It seems that Derek Underwood, Kent's left-arm spinner, had boasted to teammate John Shepherd that he had a plan not only to restrict Lloyd's scoring shots, but to get him out. Every time the ball soared out of the ground off Underwood's bowling Shepherd, the West Indian all-rounder, would go up to him and say: "Is that the special ball you had for Clive?"

Lloyd brought joy into Lancashire cricket that year with 44 sixes, 25 of them in first-class matches. He hit another century at Oxford and his first at Old Trafford was 102 in two hours against Gloucestershire. The John Player League suited him down to the ground and his 134 not out against Somerset — still Lancashire's top score in this competition — took 94 minutes with four sixes. To make the season complete he also played for the Rest of the World in the series against England and got centuries at Trent Bridge and Edgbaston.

It was 1973 before Lloyd was hitting centuries for the West Indies again and it was in the middle of the 1970s that his attacking flair was seen at its best. One of several centuries for Lancashire in 1974 included one in 50 minutes and 50 balls in a Sunday game at Trent Bridge. Lloyd went into the last two balls of the innings against Nottinghamshire needing seven more runs. He hit the first for six and the last for a single. When I went into the dressing room Peter Lever told me to ask Lloyd why he had played for himself at the end. I duly asked Lloyd, from a decent distance, and he eyed me. "That guy Lever put you up to this, didn't he?" Lever broke into laughter from the far corner of the room.

Only three months later Lloyd was in Bangalore, hitting a Test century in 102 minutes against India. He went on to 163 with two sixes and 22 fours, an innings that is still the fastest century on record in West Indies Test matches. In that same series he achieved his highest score, 242 not out in a West Indies total of 604 at Bombay, an innings recalled by Indian batsman Sunil Gavaskar as "unforgettable". "He flogged the bowling about and twice hit Bedi deep into the Garware Stand." But it was 1975 that provided something special, a World Cup year, a brilliant summer in England, and six centuries for Lancashire, four of them in successive matches. Four of his hundreds were reached in 130 minutes or under and the slowest, against Hampshire at Liverpool, was barely over two and a half hours.

Lloyd's first century that year was against Surrey at the Oval when he scored 109 not out in 146 minutes and contained the biggest hit I have ever seen. The pitch had been laid towards the gasometers and Lloyd was at the Vauxhall end facing Robin Jackman who dropped one short. Jackman later claimed he had slipped, Lloyd said it was an attempted bouncer, but whatever it was Lloyd hooked it over the traffic in Harleyford Road and into the grounds alongside Archbishop Tenison School. David Lloyd, then Lancashire's captain, recalled the shot in Clive Lloyd's testimonial brochure in 1977 — "all of 140 yards (I measured it)" he declared. A few minutes after the shot I went to the point where the ball had departed the ground and where one spectator was still in raptures about it. "I thought at first it was going to land in the seats," he said. "Then I thought it might hit me, but it just kept on going, over my head." He maintained the ball had cleared Harleyford Road and landed on the lawn between the school and Stoddart House. Some years later I asked the Oval groundsman, Harry Brind, about it. He had no doubts about it being the biggest hit at the ground in his years there and estimated it at 150 yards — "easy" he said. From the wicket to the edge of the grass, he said, was 95 yards. "Work it out for yourself," he said. I did and reckoned another 40 yards to the railings on the other side of Harleyford Road and as it landed well beyond there, it seemed that 150 yards was about right, which must make it one of the longest hits ever. Certainly, of those I have asked who witnessed it, none has seen anything bigger. Clive himself rates it his biggest hit. "You know when you've hit a ball right from the moment it leaves the bat," he said. "I knew I'd got that one but even so I was surprised at the distance it went."

Lloyd's fastest century in 1975 came in 118 minutes against Nottinghamshire at Trent Bridge, but his most spectacular came in a freak of a game against Derbyshire at Buxton, his last before joining the West Indies team for the first World Cup. He scored 167 not out in 167 minutes, the last 67 runs coming in 37 minutes as he finished with eight sixes and 15 fours before Lancashire's innings closed at 477 for five on a lovely, sunny Saturday. It snowed the following Monday — 2nd June! — and Derbyshire were bowled out on the Tuesday for 42 and 87 to lose by an innings and 348 runs to Lancashire — and an innings and 38 runs to Lloyd.

One of his finest innings ever came in the World Cup final when he scored 102 off 82 balls against Australia. He returned to Lancashire and in August hit 751 runs (average 107.28) with scores of 82 not out, 102, 1, 112, 44, 135, 100, 82 and 93 not out. His 102 was in 129 minutes against Warwickshire at Old Trafford, 112 in 169 minutes against Hampshire at Liverpool, 135 in 158 minutes against Nottinghamshire at Trent Bridge, and 100 in 127 minutes against Yorkshire at Headingley. That season he hit 44 sixes, 29 in the first-class game and eight in John Player League matches where he scored two centuries in 98 and 80 minutes. He went to Australia that winter and Western Australia suffered a few months later when Lloyd's century took only 78 minutes.

The heavy duty of the West Indies tour to England in 1976 was relieved by a brief visit to Torquay where Lloyd hit a ball into the railway station and another into a duck pond during his innings of 145 against the Minor Counties. More fun came at Swansea where Gilbert Jessop's seventy-three-year-old record of a double century in two hours was equalled against Glamorgan. There has been lots of mighty hitting at Swansea, several clouts into the surrounding roads or towards the Bristol Channel. Lloyd had seven sixes and 28 fours, reaching his century in 80 minutes and scoring his third 50 in 15 minutes and his fourth in 25.

Lloyd was having trouble with his knees about this time and operations were inevitable, coming in 1977 soon after one of his most stunning innings. Both knees were dicey and he shifted the weight from one to the other while hitting six sixes in a Gillette Cup match against Surrey at Old Trafford. I can still see the ball pinging its way around the pavilion. He was in such agony and his movement was so restricted that he went up and down the stairs from the dressing room one step at a time.

Another of Lloyd's centuries for Lancashire, against Glamorgan at Liverpool in 1978, took only an hour and a half, and a John Player hundred against Middlesex at Old Trafford in 1981 is still recalled by those lucky enough to witness it. Lancashire were 68 for two towards the 219 needed for victory and 87 for five when Jack Simmons joined Lloyd. Victory looked out of the question but Lloyd greeted Simmons by saying: "We can win this." Simmons contributed 24 to a stand of 94, simply giving the strike back to Lloyd who drove the fielders back to the boundary edge and then still drove the ball between or over them. Simmons recalled one six in particular, a flat powerful drive off Wayne Daniel that smacked into the sightscreen before long off and long on could move. Mike Brearley, the Middlesex captain, was unable to control Lloyd who so finely timed the victory run-in that a boundary off the last ball gave Lancashire their three-wicket win.

Another single shot that is often recalled is a square cut at Hove which cannoned off the scorebox and bounced through the open window of one of the flats on the edge of the ground. The ball returned, so they say, draped in plant leaves, trailing ivy behind it.

Clive Lloyd — it has been great fun watching you.

11 FRANK MANN

Frank Mann stands alongside Charles Thornton, Albert Trott and "Big Jim" Smith as one of the biggest hitters to play for Middlesex. And none of them could have got the pleasure that Mann appeared to take in bombarding the steps and the balconies of the pavilion. We can discount Trott, anyway. He just hit the ball over the top. Mann could well have been as mighty a hitter as any of them and there is no question that he got the right height, if not quite the desired route, to clear the pavilion more than once. Wilfred Rhodes, great though he was, was frequently tonked for sixes, sometimes two or three an over, and not unnaturally hated it. I occasionally wonder what he would have done with the sixth delivery if the first five had been hit out of sight. He was once on the receiving end of an assault from Mann which resulted in the ball trying to find a way into the pavilion three times. No doubt the steward was taking hasty evasive action instead of seeing to his duty as the door opener. Rhodes's fellow Yorshiremen got great delight out of the attack and the bowler, his eyes ablaze, demanded angrily: "What the bloody 'ell are you laughing at?" They were probably amused at their fellow man's discomfiture. The crowd, too, would be laughing, or at least smiling, enjoying what is probably the game's most entertaining moment, the sight of a ball sailing high over the fielders and into the seats. Pelham Warner recalled the number of sixes off Rhodes as four, two consecutive hits landing on the top balcony. The year was 1924 and in describing the innings *The Times* said Mr Mann "showed the spirit of other days when it came to dealing with the half volley". Their correspondent was in no doubt that one of those two hits that landed on the top balcony would have cleared the pavilion if only he had got a little more under it.

Mann was a strong, obviously powerful man, a great character, solid yet mischievous. He had the bearing of the guardsman he was during the First World War, the build maybe of a bull, or of a sandbank as Warner once described him. His cricket background was distinguished, four years at Malvern, three years in the Cambridge University team, into the Middlesex team in 1909 when he was twenty-one. He joined the XXth Hussars when war broke out in 1914 and served with them in France before transferring to the Scots Guards. Mann, a captain, was severely wounded three times which might have accounted for one description of him as being a bit slow on his feet. Certainly, his hitting was generally fast-footed although he would make occasional ventures down the pitch as he did when attacking Rhodes.

The war took away some of Mann's best years. By 1913 he had got into his stride. He had been denied his first century in 1911 when he ran out of partners and was left on 97 against Surrey after some brilliant hitting. When that first hundred did arrive, two years later and in his fifty-fifth game, it was the sort of innings that was to be a feature of Mann. It was played in adversity when the runs were needed. Middlesex had lost five wickets for 39 runs against Worcestershire when he went in to bat. They had totalled 238 when he was last man out after scoring 135 in 165 minutes with two

sixes, a five, and 18 fours. Edward Mignon, the last batsman, did not let Mann down, staying 40 minutes as he contributed only ten to a partnership of 68. After referring to the experienced batsmen *Wisden*, in its review of the 1913 season, said: "Of the other batsmen who appeared in the XI F.T. Mann was far and away the most interesting. His record does not, in these days, look much on paper, but in scoring 750 runs he gave some glorious displays of hitting. Very few men now before the public can drive with such splendid power."

Some of the splendid power was evident in the first innings Mann played that season, against Sussex at Lord's when he was top scorer with 71. But it was in August that he really shone, starting with a brisk 68 at Southampton and 58 at Eastbourne where he went in with Middlesex 301 for four and shared in a partnership of 120 in 70 minutes with Patsy Hendren. He failed at Sheffield and Liverpool, but hard hitting at Trent Bridge brought him 50 in the first innings and 71 in 40 minutes in the second. The century against Worcestershire was Mann's last for several years as war broke out on 4th August, 1914. Warner, the Middlesex captain, gave up cricket as soon as war broke out and Mann was among other players to follow his example. So decimated were Middlesex that Yorkshire were told on 8th August that they would not be able to go through with the game at Sheffield two days later. They reconsidered later that day and sent a much-weakened team that made Yorkshire fight for their two-wicket win.

Mann became captain in 1921 and scored two centuries as he helped Middlesex retain the championship. When they scored their record 612 for eight declared against Nottinghamshire at the beginning of June, he punished the worn-out bowling with 53 runs in 19 minutes in 14 hits, four of them sixes. He won the match against Kent at Lord's when 314 runs were needed in 255 minutes. He joined Hendren at the fall of the fourth wicket and 136 runs were put on in an hour and a half with Mann hitting 80 of them, including three sixes. He gave chances, but he was blazing away so fiercely that the fieldsmen had little chance of holding on to the ball. He scored 112 at Trent Bridge with two sixes and 15 fours in a great display of driving, and 101 against Hampshire at Southampton. Once again he had to thank the last man, this time Frank Clifford, playing his only match for Middlesex when he was nearly thirty, for sticking it out so he could secure his century.

Mann was only 62 when Clifford went to the wicket but he hit powerfully to reach 101 with five sixes while his partner stayed unbeaten — without scoring. Middlesex had been in an unhappy position at 118 for seven but Mann had also found another valiant, rather more active partner in Harry Murrell, the wicketkeeper, who hit a half century in quarter of an hour. Mann had enjoyed his first year as captain and had played some stirring, invaluable innings. He was now regarded as the biggest hitter in English cricket, emphasised with three successive sixes off Maurice Tate against Sussex at Brighton, and a drive out of Lord's and into St. John's Wood Road. The hit that was considered by many to be his finest ever was achieved in 1920 when a straight drive off George Macaulay against Yorkshire at Lord's, pitched on the covered stands by the sightscreen and bounced 20 yards into the practice ground at the Nursery End. Warner said he could not remember seeing a longer drive. It was against the wind and was still carrying when it hit the roof of the stand.

Middlesex could not make it a hat-trick of championship wins in 1922 — they finished seventh — but Mann still played some memorable innings, two of them against Essex. Despite a bruised hand he scored 97 in 90 minutes at Lord's with three sixes and 11 fours in a brave but vain effort to secure victory. And his only century for his county came at Leyton where he hit two sixes and 13 fours in his 100, including one hit over the pavilion. Mann was one of the most popular players of the period but even he was capable of arousing the wrath of a crowd. In that same match at Leyton, Claude Ashton dropped the ball while delivering it and it rolled slowly towards short leg. Mann went out to it, hit it for four and some of the spectators were so annoyed and protested so noisily that Johnny Douglas, the Essex captain, had to go to the boundary to rebuke them. Warner, Mann's former captain, came out on the side of the spectators. "There is little virtue in hitting an accidental sitter to the ropes," he wrote.

Like many players before, and after him, Mann took advantage of the end-of-season game at Scarborough, to hit another hundred, this time for the Gentlemen against the Players. The last day was bitterly cold but Mann warmed everybody with five sixes, one of which almost found its way into Trafalgar Square. That winter he led the M.C.C. to South Africa where he played in all twenty-two matches including five Tests, the only ones of his career. He averaged only 21 through the tour but managed to indulge in some big hitting, particularly against Northern Districts and in the third Test at Durban. Probably of greater satisfaction was the comment in *Wisden*: "No captain of an England side beyond the seas has ever been more popular than F.T. Mann."

Mann continued to captain Middlesex up to 1928, when he was aged forty, delighting spectators with his hitting right to the end. One hit, in the closing games, was against the new ball delivered by George Hunt of Somerset who turned to see the ball bang against the terracing near the sightscreen and finish up in one of the arbours in the Nursery ground. He also hit a century at Headingley which included four sixes and shared in a stand of 202 with Patsy Hendren, a match for Percy Holmes's benefit and remembered by Frank Dennis who bowled against Mann and "came in for a certain amount of stick". "Mann was a very powerful hitter," said Dennis, "and one hit landed on the roof of the old pavilion which is pretty high and a long way from the wicket." Probably Mann's most famous partnership with Hendren had come in 1925 when Middlesex set a world record by getting 502 to win after Nottinghamshire had declared at Trent Bridge. The runs came in 375 minutes with Mann and Hendren sharing in an unbroken seventh-wicket partnership of 271 in 195 minutes.

The biggest innings Mann played must have been one of his slowest, 194 in five hours to save a game against Warwickshire. But the value of his batting right up to 1931 when he retired was not shown in figures. As the great book said: "His best innings were always played in a crisis."

Mann was seventy-six when he died, in Wiltshire, in 1964. His son George also captained Middlesex and took a M.C.C. team to South Africa, in 1948-49.

12 KEITH MILLER

I never saw Keith Miller play — not in the flesh, that is; just those lovely old Movie-tone News snatches at the pictures on Saturday afternoon, sandwiched between Buster Crabbe and Errol Flynn, which was not all that bad a position to be I reckon. It was his bowling, of course, that got him on to the screen, in harness with Ray Lindwall and making life a misery for those dear English boys. Brylcreem was all the vogue in those days but nothing could stop the bobbing and blowing of his hair as Miller charged up to the crease. I am sorry I never saw Miller, who will stay in history as one of the finest all-rounders the game has known, certainly in the top five.

However, I got to know Miller the journalist, as unpredictable in his writing as in his playing and captaining, a man who could form quick opinions, often from the poorest positions. When England toured Australia in 1970-71, Geoff Boycott was involved in one of those bat-flinging incidents after being run out during the Adelaide Test. Opinion was fairly sharply divided. I know my first reaction was that Boycott was nearer the sightscreen than the crease when the wicket was broken, but that was because of the ease with which he attempted to take the single. Miller was equally firm in his opinion when I found him. "From where I was standing he was definitely out," he said. He was standing at the bar underneath the stand.

Miller the man is a joy. As the England team were leaving for Australia in 1979, he was at Heathrow, setting off for home. He was casually dressed in a sweater and open-necked shirt, like a man who had been walking in the park, and carried nothing but his ticket and a round cardboard box fastened with string. He had been to London for a few days, just to take part in a "This is Your Life" programme for Freddie Trueman. A friend had asked him to bring back a bowler. "Dennis Lillee?" I asked. Miller tapped the box. "Six and seven-eighths," he replied.

He was a fine sportsman and one story that stays in my mind is of the last day of the final Test, at Sydney, in March, 1947, when Miller's bold batting had helped seal the game and a 3-0 series win. Colin McCool made the winning hit of three runs and Miller, before turning for the third run, seized a stump at the bowler's end. The stump was not for himself but was handed to Denis Compton.

But it is his batting he is here for, batting by a swashbuckler who seemed to hit sixes and score hundreds and send stumps flying as the whim took him. He scored 42 centuries, the first on his debut for Victoria when he hit 181 against Tasmania at Melbourne in February, 1938. He was eighteen years old. By the time he got his second century, two years later, war had started against Germany, an interruption that denied Miller what would probably have been his first tour of England, due in 1942. As it was, we English had to wait until 1945 to really get to know the man. Miller, named after two famous Australian airmen, Sir Ross and Sir Keith Smith who were creating history with the first flight from England to Australia when he was

born, fittingly became a pilot during the war and played for the Royal Australian Air Force team. The end of the war produced a Victory series between England and any Australian servicemen that were in the country and names like Cristofani, Pepper, Sismey, Hassett and Miller became familiar.

In the first match at Lord's he scored a circumspect 105 in 210 minutes which included only six boundaries. His second century also came at Lord's, a little faster this time with less than three hours spent over his 118 runs. In other games that summer he hit two sixes in an innings of 81 not out at Trent Bridge and three sixes into the Bramall Lane pavilion at Sheffield when facing the left-arm spin of Arthur Booth. But it was back to Lord's for the finest innings of a summer we all loved and enjoyed and threw ourselves into, the first for six years free from war. Any excuse for a cricket match was accepted and this one, played near the end of the season, saw England take on a Dominions team which included South Africans, New Zealanders and Australians, all led by a West Indian, Learie Constantine. Walter Hammond scored two centuries in a match for the seventh time, Martin Donnelly hit 133, but it was Miller, now known and respected throughout the game, who outshone them both. Flying Officer Miller scored 185 in 165 minutes with seven sixes and 13 fours. He had started peaceably enough with 61 of his runs in an hour and a quarter on the second evening. The following morning, in an hour and a half, he hit the remaining 124 and at one stage he and Constantine put on 117 runs in 45 minutes. It was the most electrifying innings and partnership in cricket's first post-war season. His biggest six was his first, crashing into the seats on the top tier of the pavilion between the towers. Another big one, the following morning, was off spinner Eric Hollies and landed on top of the broadcasting box over the English players' dressing room. With the game slipping, Hammond gave the ball to James Langridge whose first over yielded three enormous sixes, two from Miller, one from Constantine. The correspondent of *The Times* said he had never seen hitting like it in sixty years' experience at Lord's. How the spectators, starved of top-class cricket for so long, must have loved it. Certainly, the Englishman took Miller to his heart, even when he did destroy us.

Miller himself regards the best six at Lord's came on the first evening. "Eric Hollies, I'm sure, was the bowler," he said in a letter from his home at Newport Beach in New South Wales. "The six went to the upper deck of the members' stand and was a longer hit than the one the following morning. I went closer to clearing the stand with that one. Rex Alston was broadcasting on B.B.C. when I hit the six on to the broadcasting box roof — 'Miller hits, an enormous hit. It's coming directly towards the broadcasting box' — silence, then all the listeners heard was the great thud on that little roof."

On the way home to Australia, by ship in those days, the Australian Services team stopped off at India to provide more cricket, more entertainment, more joy from Miller who, in a game at Calcutta, hit the first four balls from Vinoo Mankad into a pond. He scored centuries at Bombay and Colombo and continued the frolic in Perth when the Services team arrived home, hitting a brilliant 80. The festivities just would not stop. The Services team played all round the country and then Australia went on to New Zealand where Miller scored another century in the first match.

In his first match for Victoria in the 1946-47 season Miller flogged the South

Australians for 188 runs. He scored two centuries against New South Wales, hitting Ernie Toshack for three sixes in one over at Melbourne, and then hit three more sixes in his 206 not out at Sydney. The sixes at Melbourne went over the leg fence and were hit with one hand. Bill Ponsford said the strokes were the most powerful he had seen. He hit one Test century, a hard-hit 141 not out against England in fierce Adelaide heat including a six off the first ball of the fourth day.

Miller moved from Victoria to New South Wales the following season and his first century for his new state was memorable, a century in 88 minutes, 170 in three hours against Western Australia, and that as opening batsman. He hit two sixes, one a colossal straight drive, the other to the top deck of the ladies stand. He returned to England in 1948 after a three-year absence and after hitting three sixes in the traditional opening match at Worcester he hit a double century at Leicester. He hit sixes at Bradford and Southampton — three of them off Charlie Knott — and hit a century at his beloved Lord's against the M.C.C. with three sixes, one of them to the Tavern.

He went to South Africa for the first time in 1949 and in a heart-warming innings of 131 at Port Elizabeth he hit six sixes, one of which cleared the grandstand. The Englishmen were in Australia the following year and soon heard that Miller was still at his entertaining best when he started the season with five sixes in his 201 against Queensland. The return match soon followed and when New South Wales were set to make 225 in 131 minutes for victory, Miller scored 138 not out in two hours and shared in an unbroken opening stand of 225 with Arthur Morris. The M.C.C. faced him just three days later and got first-hand experience as he hit 214 in five hours including three more sixes. Miller hit five centuries that season, one of them in the Sydney Test.

He went to England again with the Australians in 1953 and the first game was at East Moseley, a country club on the Thames that was celebrating its centenary. Tagg's Island was 140 yards from the crease, standing in the middle of the river, and £600 was offered to anybody who could hit a ball on to it. Miller failed by ten yards. Not surprisingly, one of his four centuries was in the Lord's Test, a responsible innings which went on a long time and did not threaten the spectators on the pavilion steps. He enjoyed himself more against the Combined Services at Kingston where he scored 262 not out and shared in a stand of 377 in 205 minutes with Jim de Courcy.

Miller toured England three times and on each visit the first two matches were at Worcester and Leicester. He scored 50 not out and 220 not out at Worcester, 202 not out, 42 run out and 281 not out at Leicester, an average of 795 from his first two games on the three tours! "And they reckon I was a bowler," he wrote.

His own choice of big hits, to go with those for the Dominions side at Lord's in 1945, came at Sydney in Test matches against England. One was in 1950 when J.J. Warr took the new ball. "I hit him directly over his head into the alleyway where the roller is, between the Noble stand and the Paddo Hill, now the site of the Bradman stand," Miller recalled. The other had come in 1946, against Alec Bedser. "This was at the other end of the ground, again a straight hit over the far sightscreen close to the wall," he said. "That was a good number one wood that Jack Nicklaus would have been proud of." Miller also remembered another big six at Sydney while playing for Victoria against New South Wales soon after the war. "I was over the 100 mark when Arthur Morris came on with his little left-arm spinners. I recall hitting him on top of the Members' pavilion (where the players' dressing rooms are) near the big clock. That wasn't a bad one."

Miller retired in 1956 but continued to play festival cricket, and in preparation for a few matches for M.C.C. after being made a member, he scored his last first-class century. Happily, it was in England, but oddly for Nottinghamshire against Cambridge University. "A county was able to invite an outsider to play against the Universities, so in I went," said Miller. "I was with the *Daily Express* at the time, in 1959, and naturally I had no cricket gear. Reg Simpson, who was a good mate and ex-R.A.F. wartime pilot, was skipper of Notts and said I could use his batting gear. In those days English batsmen did up their pads with the buckles on the outside while Australians always had theirs on the inside. We reckoned a ball hitting the buckle or strap could sound like a snick. I was putting my pads on Aussie style when Reg said I should pad up with the buckle on the outside. He said that when you were running between the wickets you would tear the inside of the pads. I said that was rubbish, that we all, including Don Bradman, wore the buckles on the inside. Arthur Jepson, then a Notts pace bowler and later an umpire, heard all this and said: 'Here Keith, use all my stuff and stick it on anyway you like.' So I used his pads, gloves, bat, the lot, and got a century."

So twenty-one years after scoring a century on his first-class debut, for Victoria, Miller scored a century in his first — and as it turned out, his only — match for an English county.

13 MIKE PROCTER

Mike Procter is arguably the most exciting, the most entertaining of the overseas players to have sampled English county cricket. And not just of recent years, but of all time. All sorts of names might easily spring to mind, but how many could match this man's all-round skills? How many could — just could — hit a century before lunch and follow it with a hat-trick? A few of them, I daresay, could have scored six centuries in six consecutive innings in first-class cricket — not that any did. Perhaps another overseas player has matched his thousand runs in a season at just short of a run a minute — not that I have heard. His six sixes in six balls from one bowler has been matched — just — and there have been hundreds of wickets, fastest centuries, inspiring captaincy. Through the years with Gloucestershire he maintained an unquenchable enthusiasm for a game that has been known to douse the spirit of many equally talented but less determined players.

Bob Willis got to the heart and soul of the man during a low period of his own in 1980. There was Willis, England's main fast bowler and captain of Warwickshire, in a slough of despair despite winning the John Player League. There was Procter, captain of Gloucestershire with nothing to play for, yet in a better frame of mind than Willis. "It truly is a huge uplift to be in this guy's company," wrote Willis in *Wisden Cricket Monthly*. "Robbed of Test cricket years before his time, he has thrown in his lot at Gloucestershire and produced performances out of thin air. His remarkable natural ability coupled with fierce determination against the odds, either playing against stronger sides or fighting off almost crippling injuries, makes him the perfect example for the young professional to follow."

Procter was robbed of years of Test cricket, of the chance to match, perhaps even eclipse, the mighty exploits of Ian Botham and Kapil Dev and Richard Hadlee and whoever else you might consider the best all-round cricketer the world has ever seen, by being South African. He did play Test cricket, sure he did. Seven matches, all against Australia, the last seven matches South Africa played before the international door banged shut on them in 1970. In those seven matches he took 41 wickets, a formidable striking rate. And each wicket, all Aussies, cost him 16 runs. His batting was gathering force when the South Africans were outlawed, the last series of four matches bringing him an average of 34.83 and the last Test producing 49 runs and nine wickets for 103.

Procter first played for Gloucestershire in the summer of 1968, hitting fiercely and scoring three centuries, and was in sight of the double of 1,000 runs and 100 wickets when his knee let him down. His hundreds are worth recording: against Hampshire when his team had dived to 49 for five, against Middlesex when he scored 134 in just over two hours, against Glamorgan on a dodgy Cardiff wicket. There was only one hundred in 1969 and that came from his bowling, 103 championship wickets to help lift his team to second in the table. He was an impressive sight when he charged in to

bowl, his butter-coloured hair streaming back as he charged up to the wicket, a heave of the shoulders, a whirl of the arms like a clock gone haywire, his legs seemingly at odds with one another, the ball emerging as if from a catapult. His approach to batting was just as pugnacious and few players hit the ball in the air quite as much. Many is the bowler who has had to twist sharply to watch the ball soar back over him, over the boundary, over the sightscreen. If he chose to turn back to the batsman he would see Procter's nose wrinkling and his cheeks, cheerful and chubby, lifting, breaking into a grin.

The grin must never have been off his face in 1970 and 1971. At home, playing for Rhodesia, he hit six consecutive centuries, the first five coming in the Currie Cup, the sixth arriving in a friendly match arranged against Western Province at the end of the season. Rhodesia lost three wickets for five runs in the friendly, but Procter took over the match to score 254 to equal the record of Bradman and Fry in scoring six consecutive centuries. In his seventh innings, for the Rest of South Africa against Transvaal he was out for 22. But the mood did not leave him. He was soon back in England and early in the season rescued Gloucestershire from 61 for four to 268 with a magnificent innings of 133 which included three sixes in one over from John Steele. He was at Lord's the following week where he scored 76 in the first innings, a little taster for the century that came in the second, the fastest of the season in 79 minutes. Procter took full advantage of a short Tavern boundary to hit six sixes and 11 fours and, but for the need for some late caution as he started to run out of partners, would have reached his century even faster. Procter hit his third century against Somerset at Bristol later that month, in under two hours, but produced probably his best in the four-wicket win over Yorkshire at Sheffield in July. Gloucestershire had been left 135 minutes in which to score 201 to win and at tea, with 85 minutes left they were 28 for three. Some players might have settled for a draw. Not Procter. Three sixes and 17 fours bounced off his bat and his 111 steered Gloucestershire to victory with two overs to spare.

In 1973, Procter hit four centuries in eleven days, two of them at Cheltenham, one at Worcester and the fourth at the happy hunting ground of all hitters, Swansea. As well as scoring an unbeaten 106 against Worcestershire at Cheltenham he took three wickets in four balls in his second over to spur Gloucestershire to a 138-run win. Warwickshire were the next to suffer in the Cheltenham — and Procter — week as he struck three sixes and 11 fours in his 118. He squeezed in a Gillette Cup semi-final century at Worcester before getting his highest score at Swansea on the opening day of the match with Glamorgan, his 152 in 140 minutes including six sixes and 17 fours. And just for good measure he hit 94 and took two for 27 in the Gillette Cup final win over Sussex.

The old knees, however, continued to play up and surgery was required in 1975. A measure of the man's determination was his ability to shrug off near crippling injuries and come back to take 100 wickets in a season again and produce more staggering feats of batsmanship. There was a century before lunch at Cheltenham — small beer, I guess, alongside his 13 wickets for 73 runs — in 1977, a double century at Gloucester and a spree of six-hitting at Guildford in 1978, a century before lunch and a hat-trick at Bristol in 1979, a. . . . but I go too fast. (Too many sixes, not enough quiet singles.) Procter's double hundred at Gloucester in 1978 was against Essex and was described by *Wisden* as being "generally regarded as the best innings seen on the ground since Hammond's heyday". By now, Procter was captain and his 203 in 165 minutes with four sixes and 26 fours lifted his team from the uncertainties of 70 for three. Four days later Derbyshire were plundered for 122 in not much over two hours and at the beginning of July, at Guildford, the Surrey attack was punished for eight sixes, 18 fours, and an innings of 154 in under two hours which included a century in 92 minutes.

The year of 1979 was a gem, and only the awful weather of May denied him the double. Still, there were 81 wickets and a host of marvellous, joyous innings which included the fastest of the summer, right at the end, in 57 minutes. Procter crammed a lot of living into those last few weeks of the 1979 season, starting with 122 in 104 minutes, including a century before lunch, and a hat-trick against Leicestershire at Bristol in the first game in August. This was only the second such double in England in forty-two years and it should not surprise anybody that the other one had been performed by Procter, too, seven years earlier. Procter did the hat-trick again in the next match, against Yorkshire, then hit a 76-minute century against Surrey at Cheltenham, five sixes and 15 fours bringing him 90 of his 102 runs. Procter had announced to his teammates that he was going for the season's fastest century and it almost arrived against Somerset at Taunton with 93 in 46 minutes, including six sixes off successive balls from Dennis Breakwell. Eight days later he thundered his way to 92 in 35 minutes against Warwickshire at Bristol — he scored 78 of a stand of 80 with Chris Broad — before stealing the Lawrence Trophy for the season's fastest century in that last match, against Northamptonshire at Bristol when his second 50 came in 16 minutes, and his hundred in 57 minutes. Teammate Brian Brain had some kind words to say about him at the end of the season and added: "The amazing thing is that he will play with any bat he picks up; he never seems to worry about the weight, balance or pick-up of a bat, he just goes out there and hammers it. He is a natural." In the last four matches of the season Procter had scored 512 runs in 349 minutes, a staggering scoring rate of 88 runs an hour. In all, in 1979, he scored 1,200 champion-ship runs at over 53 an hour, including 32 sixes.

His last century — at Cheltenham of course — was in 1980 when Middlesex went into the final day certain winners, only to run headlong into a brilliant 134 from Procter which turned the game inside out. He managed only six games for Glouces-tershire in 1981 — and that was the last that England saw of this great cricketer. South Africa was to get a little more out of him, despite injury. Word floated back to England, of a fine innings of 102 in Natal's 239 against the rebel West Indies, of ten wickets in the defeat of Northern Transvaal, plus an innings of 99 in 80 minutes with three sixes and 14 fours. How nice. Just a reminder of what we were missing. As Bob Willis said: "We will all miss this cricketing Colossus when he goes."

14 VIV RICHARDS

When Jack Simmons was preparing his autobiography he recalled facing Viv Richards in a match at Bath. Lancashire had worked out a plan to contain him, but Richards had plans of his own and one shot, branded on Simmons's brain, was a huge straight drive which hit a civic building at the end of the ground and bounced back to roll within three or four yards of Simmons's bowling mark.

Richards's hitting does not have the beefy belligerence about it that marks an Ian Botham innings. He has probably hit farther than his Somerset friend, but there is more a feeling of pureness about his hitting, the shot is so finely timed, he is into position almost before the ball is released. He is perhaps one of the sweetest hitters the game has known. Yet there can be a fury about Richards's game for he is a mood player and if he decides to dominate a bowler then watch out, the results will be worth remembering.

There are hundreds of instances of balls landing in the River Tone at the Taunton ground. It is said that Arthur Wellard used to love to hear the plop of the ball as it hit the water. He could clear the river, too, as did Richards in 1980 when he hit a six off Nigel Briers during a John Player League game with Leicestershire. He has cleared quite a few surrounding walls of other grounds as well, has hit 34 runs in one over, 34 off seven balls from one bowler and in 1977 hit 73 sixes in all matches.

It is always interesting to go back to the start of a player's career, for the first mention in the newspapers. The first notice of Richards in England came with the news towards the end of 1973 that "V.A. Richards from Antigua, has signed a two-year contract with Somerset". The Isaac part of his name was soon attached and Richards quickly made a mark by winning the Benson and Hedges gold award in his first game for Somerset for an innings of 81 not out against Glamorgan at Swansea. Simmons also remembered Richards's championship debut, at Taunton early in May, a game which also saw Ian Botham playing his opening first-class match. "Viv came in, smacked four fours in one or two overs and we all looked on him as something of a slogger," said Simmons. "Till we analysed it later and realised they weren't slogging cross-bat shots, but genuine ones. Maybe he wanted to impress, not only his teammates but the Lancashire side who were then one of the top teams in the country."

Richards's first championship century came in his third game, against Gloucestershire at Bristol, his second arrived three games later, a beauty against Yorkshire at Bath which included four sixes. He hit another century in the John Player League including 24 runs in an over and at the end of his first season, in which he was the only Somerset player to top 1,000 runs in the championship, only his captain, Brian Close, had hit more sixes. Richards was twenty-two at the time and his experience at Somerset helped him into the West Indies squad for the winter tour of India and Pakistan.

Another newcomer on that tour was Gordon Greenidge, a twenty-three-year-old opening batsman from Barbados and together, he and Richards, who were to form an important part of the developing new West Indies team, made their Test debuts against India at Bangalore. Greenidge immediately exploded into life with a second innings century after scoring 93 in the first. Richards, sadly, scored four and three. He held his place for the second Test in Delhi and there, with the entire Antiguan nation staying up all night to listen to the radio report of the match, he scored 192 not out.

Richards had arrived and 1976 was to see the flower in full bloom with a remarkable total of 1,710 runs in Test matches including 135 at Old Trafford, 232 at Trent Bridge, 291 at the Oval, 101 at Adelaide, 142 at Bridgetown, 130 and 177 at Port of Spain. During an innings of 175 against Western Australia at Perth he hit six sixes, a match which also included a century in 78 minutes by his captain, Clive Lloyd. Just before that he had played against Tasmania at Hobart, another game remembered by Simmons, the Tasmanian captain, who tossed one ball up to Richards after he had reached his century. He hoped the tiring Richards would attempt to slog from the crease and hit straight in the air. He does not remember seeing that ball again after it flew over the stand and the dressing rooms and on to the river.

It was at the beginning of the English summer of 1976 that England captain Tony Greig made his unfortunate remark about making the West Indies grovel. Richards was annoyed and in the first Test scored 36 runs in the first 20 minutes with two hooks and a straight drive off John Snow and a six off Derek Underwood as he swaggered his way to 232 with four sixes. When he had finished with England that marvellous summer — he averaged 118 in four Tests — he flew off to Queensland and, the day after arriving, scored 104 in 116 minutes, and broke two bats in the process.

Richards also damaged bats in other ways. In 1978 when Somerset lost the chance of two trophies — the Gillette Cup and the John Player League — on successive days at the end of the season, he was so disappointed with his own performance in the second game, against Essex at Taunton, that he smashed his bat to pieces in the dressing room. The following year, after being given out lbw in a championship match against Lancashire at Old Trafford, he returned to the dressing room in steaming anger. He threw his bat down, it bounced and took off like a Boeing to smash the window and startle the members sitting beneath. In 1983, after India had beaten West Indies at Lord's to win the World Cup, the teams met again in a Test series in India. Richards was given out lbw to Kapil Dev and a Delhi sports magazine reported: "There was no sign of dissent on the field, but Richards gave way to his real feelings in the dressing room. The cups and saucers took a knock from the jumbo bat flung in anger."

Richards had a great year for Somerset in 1977 when he averaged 86 an innings and 50 an hour with three double centuries and four singles and a host of sixes including five at Weston-super-Mare against Surrey. He hit 73 sixes in all matches, 44 in first-class games, a figure which had been bettered by only four players in history. He scored a century before lunch against Lancashire at Southport when he bombarded the houses with nine sixes in an innings of 189. He reached his 50, 100 and 150 with sixes, got his runs out of 308, and still finished up on the losing side.

David Graveney, the Gloucestershire left-arm spinner, was hit for 34 in an over in a John Player match at Taunton and in another Sunday game Derbyshire were hit for 104.

Richards has regularly shown himself a man for an occasion and one of the best examples came in the 1979 World Cup final against England at Lord's when he and Collis King shared in a stand of 139 in 21 overs. Richards himself scored 138 not out with three sixes and some breathtaking shots all of his own making. When the West Indies came to England again in 1980, Richards scored just one century, at Lord's, but made a lasting impression on Chris Clifford, a Warwickshire off break bowler, who was hit for 4-6-6-4-4-6-4 in seven consecutive balls in the game at Edgbaston. Graham Dilley, the Kent fast bowler, was also on the receiving end during the 1980-81 Test series in West Indies, being hit out of the ground at Antigua — where Richards duly scored a century in the first Test staged in his home country — and over the stand at Barbados.

The innings Richards himself rated highest came at Old Trafford in 1984 when the West Indies tour of England was launched with the first of three Texaco Trophy matches, 55 overs a side. Richards had played only two innings up to then, scoring 12 against Worcestershire and 170 in 162 minutes against Glamorgan, with three of his five sixes coming in one over against opening bowler Steve Barwick. The weather at Old Trafford on 31st May was beautiful, the ground was packed, the setting perfect for one of the most commanding innings ever played in one-day cricket. West Indies had started badly. Ian Botham ran out Desmond Haynes in his first over and had Gordon Greenidge caught at the wicket in his second. Bob Willis held a return catch from Richie Richardson and off-spinner Geoff Miller removed Larry Gomes, Clive Lloyd and Jeff Dujon, numbers five, six and seven, without too much trouble. Malcolm Marshall was run out by the wicketkeeper and a jubilant England left for lunch with West Indies 114 for seven and only one of the first eight batsmen having got into double figures. That, of course, was Richards, who had reached 50 out of 83 for four and was now 73. Eldine Baptiste was with him, only Joel Garner and Michael Holding were left to provide support. Yet from that Richards conjured an innings of 189, full of adventurous, ambitious shots as he dominated the remaining overs. Baptiste helped put on 59 runs for the eighth wicket but Garner went quickly, leaving Holding and Richards, the last pair, together at 166. England, we thought, could have them all out for 180 ... well, 190 if Holding's luck held. Yet in just under 15 overs, 106 runs were added for the last wicket, of which Richards hit 93. There were five sixes in his innings, one of them a straight drive which left the ground. West Indies totalled 272 for nine, with Richards 189 not out, and victory was duly achieved by 104 runs. Richards scored only three in the second match, at Trent Bridge, but hit 84 not out in the third at Lord's, with four sixes, three of them off Bob Willis.

There was more to come in 1985 when he hit nine centuries for Somerset and topped the English batting averages. He hit ten sixes in his 186 against Hampshire at Taunton in May including a special over extra cover, and eight against Warwickshire at Taunton where he hit his first triple century on the first day of June. An innings of 135 against Middlesex at Lord's included four sixes, while five more came against Lancashire at Old Trafford including a rather fierce attack against a fellow West Indian, Patrick Patterson, who was eager to make an impression. When Patterson tried to bounce Richards the ball flew over square leg and two overs brought 33 runs. Simmons, too, had to wait a couple of times while the ball was recovered from among the seats and then also had the misfortune to be set about by Ian Botham who hit him for three more sixes. That was Monday. On Thursday, down the road at Derby, Richards hit two sixes in a 109-minute century and on Saturday, back at home at Taunton, made it three in a week with 112 against Sussex (plus 66 not out in the John Player League on Sunday).

Richards hit 49 first-class sixes in 1985, which looks almost trifling alongside Ian Botham's 80, yet carried him alongside John Edrich with only Arthur Wellard and Botham having scored more in a season. He also hit 231 fours which gave him 1,218 runs in sixes and fours, an astonishing proportion out of his total of 1,836 in the summer.

And to think — there is still more to come and delight us from this thirty-four-year-old master.

15 "BIG JIM" SMITH

As a boy at Blackburn Grammar School, I was educated in the wondrous ways of cricket at the ground next door, Alexandra Meadows, home of East Lancashire in the Lancashire League. There was no greater joy than to sit with my back up against the school playground wall and wait, hopefully and expectantly, for the giant that East Lancashire employed as professional, to hit the ball screaming over my head and, perhaps, through a classroom window. Along with scores of other little boys I really went along and paid my sixpence just to see this man. They said he had played for England before the war; opened the bowling, the grown-ups said. We knew little about that. In any case we did not go to watch him bowl, high class though he was. We lived just for the moment when he strode from the pavilion, a match-stick of a bat in his hand, pads seeming to cover little more than his shins, ready to hit the other team into the playground or the tennis courts. His enormous feet dominated the crease, like warships in the village pond. There was no refinement to his batting. He would slog. For variety he would swoosh or slash or swish and if he could stay around for only 20 minutes he would send a hundred little boys home happy.

I knew little of Lancashire or Test cricket in those days and "Big Jim" Smith, late of Wiltshire, Middlesex and England, was my Hammond and Lindwall rolled into one. The purists might dismiss his batting, but if that was Test cricket — that was for me. When "Big Jim" retired from East Lancashire in 1948 to make way for the gentler, more subtle arts of Bruce Dooland, something went out of my life.

Cedric Ivan James Smith was born at Corsham near Chippenham in the corner of Wiltshire where it meets up with Somerset and Gloucestershire. He and his brother Walter opened the bowling for Wiltshire for many years before he was taken on to the groundstaff at Lord's where, he maintained, an administrative slip-up forced him to qualify for five years, playing for M.C.C. before he could first play for Middlesex in 1934. He was heralded as a "new Jessop" but it was an opening bowler Middlesex wanted and an opening bowler they got as he took 172 wickets to finish sixth in the first-class averages in his opening season. His swooshing was not quite so effective. He hit one half century, and although he often disappointed the young, excited boys in the crowd, he occasionally "caught her," and away she would go into the deep blue yonder. One hit at Lord's pitched in the pavilion and shattered a committee-room window. *Wisden* chose him as one of the Cricketers of the Year alongside Bill O'Reilly, Stan McCabe and Bill Ponsford, but understandably, although patronisingly, wrote off his batting: "Little need be said of his batting; he usually goes in and, standing fast-footed, hits hard at practically every ball." In my limited experience that was quite wrong. He always went in and, standing fast-footed, hit hard at *every* ball.

Smith was able to play only six seasons with Middlesex before the war brought its confounded interruption and, as it turned out, the end of his career in county cricket.

In that time he took nearly 700 wickets and scored 3,000 runs, averaging about 15. Yet it is the memory of Smith the batsman that lingers, vividly etched in the mind, and bringing him some immortality and a place alongside — well, fairly near — Gilbert Jessop. He hit 69 in 20 minutes against Sussex at Lord's in 1938 and ten days later, against Gloucestershire at Bristol, he scored 66 in 18 minutes — the first 50 coming in 11 minutes. And that time has been beaten only once when Clive Inman was fed full tosses for a declaration and got to 50 in eight minutes.

"Big Jim," however, needed no spoon feeding. Whatever the occasion, whatever the bowling, the barge of a boot would come bulldozing down the crease, the bat would descend from a great height at a fearsome pace and, if the length of the ball was just right, the bowler, umpire and backing-up batsman would leap in unison in their frantic efforts to get out of the way. If the ball was short of a length or Smith had started his swing too early the ball would take off vertically, breaking up any clouds trying to form and producing unbelievable panic on the cricket field beneath. The most spectacular miss off Smith must have been engineered by "Hopper" Levett of Kent who hardly needed to move in his role as wicketkeeper to get into position for the catch. Perhaps the ball vanished from sight of the human eye for a while, but whatever happened, Levett decided to move and once on the go nothing was going to stop him as he circled the stumps. By the time the ball was well within sight again Levett was in the wrong position. He lunged forward, sent the stumps and himself crashing to the ground. The ball was only a split second behind. And they did say that if everybody had stood still and let nature take its course the ball would have hit the top of the middle stump and Smith would have played on.

Smith hit one century, an 81-minute crawl at Canterbury in 1939, an innings that is the subject of a marvellous chapter in Ian Peebles's book, *Talking of Cricket*. Peebles had the great good fortune to be at the other end for all but the first four of Smith's runs. He watched fascinated and soon realised it was Smith's day when, after several balls in a good over from Watt had passed close to the stumps, the last flew over the big tree at square leg. Smith was away and the ball was given a terrible hammering as he moved towards his only hundred. He was in his 90s when left-arm spinner Claude Lewis decided to bowl over the wicket, crept one between bat and pad and almost bowled him. "I think I would have died if it had got him," said Claude. Les Ames was playing for Kent and was holding the record time for the fastest century of the season, 67 minutes against Surrey. "When Jim came in I never thought he'd be challenging me," he said. "The longer he stayed the more worried I became. But he mishit a lot and wasn't good enough to pinch the bowling." For all that, he still hit seven sixes, three over the tents ringing the ground opposite the pavilion.

Peebles was an observant teammate. He also recalled a game at Hove where Smith walked out to face a great England bowler, Maurice Tate, then nearing the end of his career. The Sussex captain had seen Smith before and asked Tate: "Do you want a man out for Jim?" Tate, who had never seen Smith bat, was greatly offended. "What? With the *new* ball?" "Please yourself," said the captain. So Tate bowled, Smith swung and, according to Peebles: "It met the very middle of Smith's thrashing blade and took off, due south, on a steeply rising flight path. It crashed on to the corrugated iron roof of the stand whence it shot into the road and was retrieved halfway to the beach, unrecognisable under its thick coat of rust, tar and sand. To add insult to injury, his skipper returned the ball to the bowler with an evil grin, holding it between finger and thumb by one of its several ears."

Hugh Bartlett remembered being in the field for Sussex during a Smith innings. "Jim hit the ball, a huge, high hit that was like a dot in the sky. I was at mid off looking up for it. I was seeing stars, the sky was shimmering and I missed it by ten yards. Ian Peebles said he would give me my Middlesex cap for that."

Some of Smith's most sensational batting came on his one M.C.C. tour, to the West Indies in the winter of 1934-35 following his successful first season for Middlesex. He turned on a remarkable display in Barbados when he shared with Walter Hammond in a last-wicket stand of 122 in 45 minutes. In that time Smith hit 83 runs with five sixes and nine fours. The tour provided Smith with a store of memories, especially his first Test match, also in Barbados, when wickets fell rapidly on a rain-affected wicket. West Indies were bowled out for 100, England declared at 81 for seven, West Indies followed with a declaration at 51 for six, and England needed 73 to win. Smith recalled the match for me when I saw him in 1976, three years before his death. "All eleven of us were padded up in the dressing-room ready for the start of our second innings," he said. "In the end I opened the innings and I went out and slashed at every ball. The first over from Martindale was a maiden and I was out in his second, for a 'duck'. That gave me a pair in my first Test match." Smith also hit Learie Constantine back over his head for six during that tour. "I can see it now," he said. "All these black men sitting in the trees watching us play and as the ball headed for one tree they fell out like a lot of monkeys."

Smith made some remarkable hits at Lord's, remembering particularly a rather special blow over Father Time, probably the hit that Bill Edrich recalled as the biggest he ever saw at Lord's and one of the three most tremendous blows he ever saw administered with a cricket bat. Middlesex were playing Lancashire and Edrich was nearing the end of an innings of 175 when Smith strode to the wicket, not just to bat, but to pass on a message: "Skipper says we've got to tread on the gas." Smith himself needed no second invitation and Edrich estimates, without exaggeration, that the ball flew at least twice as high as the statue of Father Time; a shot worth 12, never mind six. Said Edrich to Smith: "That was a nice one!" Said Smith to Edrich, sadly: "It would have been if only I'd middled it properly." The ball went over the grandstand, of course, and was never seen again.

Smith recalled, too, the shot through the committee-room window during his first season with Middlesex, another hit, one-handed, on to the pavilion roof off Yorkshire's George Macaulay, and one over the Tavern, across St. John's Wood Road, "and into a synagogue!" Another six at Lord's which he recalled with some pleasure was one that headed unerringly towards the members on the pavilion steps. "Oscar Asche, a well-known actor who was playing the lead in Chu Chin Chow in the West End, was there," Smith recalled. "He weighed about 22 stone and the cab used to have to drop him right at the pavilion, not the gate. He moved to get out of the way when he saw this ball approaching, fell off his seat, and it took four men to lift him back on."

Scarborough has been a happy hitting ground for many batsmen and it must have been a delight to have seen Smith in 1936 hitting 56 of the last 57 runs, nearly half the Middlesex total of 127. There were four sixes, three of them the reward for great hits out of the ground. But probably his two most spectacular knocks were scored in 1938, the first coming on 4th June, the Saturday of the Whitsun Bank Holiday, when he scored 69 in 20 minutes as Middlesex averaged 90 runs an hour in their total of 577 against Sussex. He went out to bat 20 minutes before the close and in his first five minutes at the crease scored five. In the next 15 minutes he hit six sixes, three of them into St. John's Wood Road, as he rattled up 64 more runs.

Twelve days later, on 16th June, he played an even more remarkable innings with eight sixes and two fours as he scored 66 in 18 minutes against Gloucestershire at Bristol, the first 50 runs taking 11 minutes. He hit three of his sixes off Reg Sinfield, the other five off George Emmett, whose solitary wicket — that of Smith — cost him 100 runs in 15 overs. Poor Sussex received a second dose of Smith-hitting in the August Bank Holiday match at Hove when he was promoted in the batting order as Middlesex threatened to falter in their hunt for 300 runs for victory. In 35 minutes he scored 57, including two sixes and six fours, and Middlesex were able to sail steadily on to a three-wicket win.

Age, I remember, brought little droop or shrinkage to Smith who still weighed 16½ stone when I saw him. In his pomp he weighed 17½ stone which had grown to 19 stone when he returned from the West Indies in 1935. "I couldn't bend down to fasten my boots," he told me. He wore size 14s and had cricket boots specially made, a pair a year. Even the slippers he was wearing were specially made. "When Lancashire came down to Lord's, Eddie Paynter would get my boots when they had been cleaned," said Smith. "He would put his own boots on, then step into mine, and would clop about the dressing-room."

"Big Jim" was a dear man. It was a pleasure to watch him, a privilege to meet him. I shall never forget either.

16 LIONEL TENNYSON

Lord Tennyson has come down through the years as one of cricket's most appealing characters. His immense love of the game is unquestioned. He was a splendid hitter of a ball, an autocratic yet kindly captain, a player who liked a fight. Some of his best innings were played in adversity, like his 74 not out against the fearsome pace attack of Gregory and McDonald and his 63 against them with a badly damaged hand. But what were a couple of Aussie fast bowlers to a man who had been wounded three times during the Great War? Forward he went, fearlessly, prepared to hit the shells back over the enemy's heads. He was woolly-headed, too, declaring in a Test match at Old Trafford when the laws forbade it, and once, in India, shooting the bait, a tethered goat, instead of the panther. He was a burly man, rising to 17 stones, and took advantage of every ounce in his assaults on the bowlers.

Lionel Hallam Tennyson was a grandson of the poet. He was not quite three when his grandfather died and his only memory, he told Raymond Robertson-Glasgow, was of a beard peering over his bed. The experience clearly was not enough to inherit much of the great man's poetic mind, although it has been recorded that he did write a poem in honour of A.P.F. Chapman's Test series win in Australia. He asked £100 from the London editor who suggested the idea, but when he was offered only £50 he published the ode himself. He succeeded to the title on the death of his father in 1928.

Tennyson was by nature a fearless adventurer, a characteristic he brought to his cricket with much gaiety and even more abandon. Any innings of any consequence was scored at the gallop. He dominated the batting, domineered the bowling, and if he batted for an hour it was bound to be to the accompaniment of "brilliant," "superb," "breathtaking". He hit the ball with such power that in 1921, during the game against Kent at Southampton, he drove a ball from Bill Fairservice over the pavilion and into a garden, a distance of about 140 yards.

He started his cricket life as a fast bowler good enough for Eton but not for Cambridge University, and was in his twenty-fourth year before he attracted any attention. He had joined the Army and had scored runs for the Household Brigade and Greenjackets before making his first-class debut for M.C.C. against Oxford University in July, 1913, when he and Meyrick Payne opened the second innings with a stand of 175 in an hour and a half. Both players were "favoured with plenty of good fortune," and Tennyson was dropped three times in his innings of 110. Still, it was good enough to alert Hampshire and a little over two weeks later he made his debut for them in the game against Worcestershire at Dudley. In only his second match, against Essex at Leyton, he scored 116 in 105 minutes out of 198 for six and did not even get a mention in the match report in *Wisden*. Two other centuries, by Lieutenant Abercrombie and George Brown, and their partnership of 325 in 210 minutes, took all the rave notices. Tennyson was never a man to be outdone. He

went to Trent Bridge for the next game, hit a magnificent 111 and shared in a thrilling stand of 132 in just over an hour with Edward Sprot. In his first four matches in first-class cricket, the Hon. Tennyson had scored three centuries. He got within one shot of making it four in five when he hit brilliantly for 96 in the next match against Yorkshire at Harrogate. He finished the season with 832 runs from 19 innings, and his average of 46.22 was the fifth best in England.

Tennyson was never to reach such heights again. The spirit stayed in his batting right to the last, more centuries followed and he could get runs when they were wanted. But he was never to average in the 40s again. He took over the captaincy after the Great War and his qualities of leadership more than atoned for any drop in average. When he was captain, there was no question of who was in charge as Jack Newman, the Hampshire bowler, discovered to his cost during a match with Nottinghamshire at Trent Bridge in 1922. Newman was being barracked by the crowd for what they considered was his wasting time as he set his field and when told by Tennyson "to get on with the bowling" he made what was described as an objectionable remark. In what was, up to then, an unprecedented move, Tennyson ordered the bowler off the field and as Newman made for the pavilion he kicked down the stumps. Newman later apologised to Tennyson and Arthur Carr, the Nottinghamshire captain, and was then allowed to play on what was the final day of the season. Tennyson captained Hampshire over 300 times. Neville Cardus said of him: "He would win the toss, then retire to a hot bath to perspire and exude last night's champagne."

Bill Edrich was only twenty-one when he went with Lord Tennyson to India. His description of his captain, recorded in his book, *Cricket Heritage,* is worth repeating: "He was a magnificent figure in the game — in more senses than one, as he advanced towards 17 stone! — and one does not see his like today (1948). He was one of the Corinthians; he played cricket for fun, and played it well enough to beat the professors at their own game, sparing neither time nor money to raise the standard of English and Hampshire play. They called him 'The Baron' because he was a man unaccustomed to mince words; but that was because he had a profound knowledge of the game and loved it, not meekly, but with a passion. That tour was one of the nicest I ever shall enjoy. It was made so partly by Lord Tennyson's kindness, and the firm, impartial and popular way he kept us all happy on and off the field."

The inspirational captaincy helped Hampshire up the championship table and produced some unlikely results, the most noteworthy being in the match at Edgbaston in 1922 when Hampshire were dismissed for 15, scored 521 in the follow-on and then beat Warwickshire by 155 runs. It took Tennyson back into the England team, too — he had played five times in South Africa in 1913-14 after his remarkable first season in county cricket — playing four times against Australia in 1921, three as captain. It was in that series, which England lost 3-0, that Tennyson displayed the pluck that was to be a mark of his play. He scored 74 not out in the Lord's Test, relishing the challenge of the extremely fast attack of Gregory and McDonald. He scored 63 and 36 at Headingly despite a badly-injured hand and got another half-century at the Oval after being hit over the heart and being nearly knocked out. It was during the Old Trafford match that he declared when he should not, although he had spent some time after lunch studying the rules. A long discussion took place in the dressing room when the Australians went in under protest. Tennyson, however, appeared unmoved.

That season of 1921 was a good one for Tennyson who led Hampshire into sixth place in the championship, a position they had bettered only once before. He scored three centuries, 152 against Leicestershire at Portsmouth with some tremendous hitting and a partnership of 259 in under two hours with Phil Mead; 131 not out, with superb hitting, against Lancashire at Southampton; and 101 in 110 minutes with three sixes against Yorkshire at Sheffield. His keen sense of sportsmanship was evident in this game which ended in a six-wicket win for Yorkshire but which finished with Ernie Oldroyd 99 not out. The game was over but Tennyson bowled another ball which Oldroyd hit for four to get his century. In a race for runs against Lancashire at Liverpool Tennyson hit 20 runs in an over off Cec Parkin and only narrowly missed his fourth hundred of the season when he hit "very brilliantly" to score 98 runs in the Whitsuntide match with Kent at Southampton.

His best innings in 1922 was his 94 in 75 minutes against Warwickshire although there was probably more merit in a brilliant little innings that turned the match on a spiteful Bradford wicket. After incessant rain on the first day, Yorkshire were dismissed for 56. Tennyson opened the innings himself and hit out at everything to score 51 runs out of 64 and give his side a lead of 57 and an advantage that carried them to a five-wicket win.

One of Tennyson's longest innings was played at Southampton in 1925 when he stayed 165 minutes and hit three sixes and 27 fours in his 184. His highest innings came in 1928. He could not get a hundred for Hampshire in the championship, yet against West Indies towards the close of the season he managed a double hundred. Hampshire were 88-5 when Tennyson, now a considerable size, went out to join Jack Newman. They were 399-6 when he left, having scored 217 in a four-hour stand with Newman that produced 311 runs. He was still a good enough player in 1929 to win a match for Hampshire by scoring 125 not out after half his team had gone for 106 towards the 280 needed for victory in three and a half hours. In his last year as captain, when he was forty-two years old, he still showed the ability to get quick runs when most needed. Hampshire inflicted one of only two defeats on Yorkshire who won the championship that season with Tennyson hitting 43 out of 65 in the first innings and 54 out of 68 in the second to play a significant part in the 49-run win. Hampshire moved from Leeds to Chesterfield where Tennyson, in the same vein, scored 69 out of 81 in 65 minutes and 44 out of 55 in 35 minutes to eke out a two-wicket win in a match which produced only 459 runs for 38 wickets. Again, his only century of the season came in a non-championship match, reached in two hours for the Gentlemen against the Players at the Oval.

He continued to play for Hampshire until 1936, when he was forty-six years old, and two years later sponsored and captained a strong team to India where they won three of five unofficial Tests. Tennyson played only one innings of any note, hitting two sixes and 13 fours in a century at Karachi. The game was played in stifling heat of over 100 degrees and after five batsmen had departed with a total of 32 runs between them Tennyson lumbered out to join Bill Edrich who was about 50 at the time. He hit two huge sixes and 13 fours but still had a lot of running to do to catch up with Edrich. At one stage they were each 92 and sweat was streaming off Tennyson like a brook. The twenty-one-year-old Edrich asked Tennyson, who was less than a week away from his forty-ninth birthday, if he would last out to reach his hundred. "I'll bet I reach my hundred before you do, my boy!" he grinned. "A pound on it, sir?" asked Edrich. They shook hands and Edrich, who was to bat right through the innings for 140 not out, lost out as Tennyson charged on to the last of his 19 first-class centuries.

One of my very favourite cricket stories concerned that tour when the team stayed as guests of the Jam Sahib of Nawangar, an independent state in the Bombay area. A ceremonial panther-shoot was arranged in their honour at three different lodges where a goat was tethered on the platform. Several goats had been sacrificed to lull the panther into feeling secure and another was there, the bait for the panther, when the party including Tennyson arrived. Rifles were at the ready and after about half an hour the panther arrived. It had been arranged that only Lord Tennyson would shoot and after what seemed a lifetime a shot rang out. The panther looked about, then vanished into the dark. Alf Gover, sitting just behind Tennyson, exclaimed: "Good lord, my Lord, you've shot the goat!"

Tennyson enjoyed sport of all kinds and loved to flavour it with a gamble. He loved to go to the races, and to the greyhounds, and once, after playing at Old Trafford, rushed off to Belle Vue where he backed the first three losers. The fourth scraped home by a neck and he finished up winning a large amount of money.

The third Baron Tennyson died at Bexhill-on-Sea in Sussex in 1952 at the age of sixty-one. His funeral took place while the opening Test between England and South Africa was being played at Trent Bridge. Play was stopped for a few moments as a tribute.

17 CHARLES THORNTON

Charles Thornton is probably the biggest hitter English cricket has ever had. Nobody hit the ball farther or over more pavilions and only he and Australian Cec Pepper have ever hit a ball over the houses at Scarborough and into the neighbouring Trafalgar Square. W.G. Grace said it was the biggest hit he ever saw, bigger than Albert Trott's that went over the Lord's pavilion.

The son of a rector at Llanwarne, Hereford, Thornton was an outstanding all-round sportsman who could putt the weight and throw the cricket ball with the best of them during his days at Eton in the middle of the last century. He played cricket for Eton and Cambridge University and also for Kent (from 1867) and Middlesex (from 1872). Like many of his day he regarded cricket purely as a game rather than a serious business. He indulged his spirit of adventure to the full on the cricket field and enjoyed opening the innings and taking the attack to the bowlers. He delighted in big hits, first ball or last, and it was seldom he scored a 50 without hitting at least one ball well over 100 yards.

There was great eagerness to measure drives in those days and it was not uncommon for Thornton to reach 140 and 150 yards. At Canterbury he hit the second ball he received over one of the tall flagpoles for four and then drove another "so hard, so high, and so very far, that it went clean over the spectators and into the adjoining road, and six was booked for that very hard thump". The hit was measured at 152 yards, a colossal drive and probably the biggest on that ground.

He drove the ball over the old Lord's pavilion while playing for Eton against Harrow in 1868, a shot he repeated with a big hit over the Oval pavilion, which was also later replaced. At Southgate he was dropped 100 yards from the wicket by Mr E. Rutter. The bowler, David Buchanan, glared at Rutter who was thoughtfully studying his fingers, probably afraid of looking up and meeting the bowler's eye. A similar hit, on the Lyndhurst ground, was caught by the Rev. E.S. Carter who was standing 120 yards away and who had watched an earlier shot sail over his head. By way of variation to hitting over the pavilion Thornton once threw his bat over the one at Fenner's. In those days it was a low wooden structure alongside the county gaol and Thornton flung the unsuccessful bat into the prison yard "for the benefit of its fellow sinners there".

Thornton's longest measured hit was at Hove while he was practising in front of the pavilion. The ball was lobbed up to him and finished in the road beyond the entrance gates. The Rev. James Pycroft, a cricket historian, who was about to enter the ground, marked the exact spot where the ball landed and measured the distance; nearly 169 yards. Thornton was a frequent visitor to Hove when he finished playing and Arthur Gilligan, the Sussex and England captain between the wars, said he never missed a Sussex-Middlesex match. At Hove he watched from the committee room, at Lord's he sat in his usual seat in the front row of the pavilion. Gilligan said

Thornton would tell of the days when they played on the old ground at Scarborough, right on top of the cliff. The wind would be so strong they had to use iron bails and when he hit a ball out of the ground it could go over the cliff and into the sea! Thornton, by the way, was also an avid film man and carried an enormous black wallet containing newspaper reports of every murder case for the past twenty-five years.

The Scarborough ground was Thornton's favourite and it was there he played probably his best innings and certainly his most famous, for the Gentlemen of England against I Zingari in 1886. The Gentlemen, 209 behind on the first innings, were 133 for five when Thornton went in to bat. Seventy minutes later, when the innings closed for 266, Thornton was left 107 not out, scored out of 133. He started with a six and in all hit eight of them, one the result of an overthrow, the other seven, of course, being hits right out of the ground. Lord Hawke said "his mightiest slog" came when he drove a ball straight over the sightscreen, so high that it hit a chimney on the roof of one of the houses outside the ground. Another six went through the window of an adjoining house, narrowly missing a lady who was knitting, and *the* hit into Trafalgar Square, according to Thornton himself, "sent the ball over the third chimney from the space between the houses, and it was off A.G. Steel. Mr Baker, the Scarborough secretary, and I measured it next day and we found the distance to be 138 yards ... not a record by any means." Thornton also described another hit in which the ball went through an open window on the second floor and was thrown back through a window on the first floor. "How it made the descent from one floor to the other — whether it rolled down or was taken down — we never ascertained." The occupant of number 45 Trafalgar Square wrote to the *Manchester Guardian* in 1899 to say that the first ball of an over smashed through the glass of the second-storey window of number 39. The next ball did the same and "the cricketer" suggested the window should be left open. "I also saw that marvellous hit when Mr Thornton lifted the ball clean over the same house — a four storey building — into the garden in the centre of the square," he added.

I have read several stories concerning Thornton's hit into Trafalgar Square, all with slight variations but all including a lady with little knowledge of the game. Arthur Gilligan, who was friendly with Thornton, wrote to *The Cricketer* magazine some years ago with his version of the sequel. Said the lady: "Mr Thornton, I hear you hit a cricket ball into Trafalgar Square. Was it from Lord's or the Oval?" Without hesitation Thornton replied: "It was from the Oval and it went via Westminster Bridge."

Thornton once hit nine sixes over the canvas with which the Tunbridge Wells ground was enclosed and at Canterbury hit each ball of one over — they were four-ball overs then — from V.E. Walker out of the ground. The Rev. Vernon Royle, one of Lancashire's earliest Test cricketers, once found himself on the receiving end of a Thornton assault. The first three balls were hit out of the ground and Royle responded by bowling the last delivery underarm and along the ground. "No one shall ever say he hit Vernon Royle four times out of the ground in one over!" he said.

Thornton, who himself bowled fast underhand grubs, treated the game lightly and with total enjoyment. Even in games that were regarded as first-class he could not resist taking up a challenge. He once invited Lord Harris to a duel, to see who could hit the ball farthest. Lord Harris hit a ball into the pavilion. In the following over Thornton hit the same bowler over the players' dressing room to win the challenge by quite a distance.

According to Sammy Woods, Thornton had to be watched when the coin was tossed. Thornton called "Woman" when the coin was spun, which could be either heads (Queen Victoria) or tails (Britannia) and before the other captain had come to his senses Thornton would have decided to bat. "He tried me at Cambridge when I was captain and nearly sucked me in," said Woods. "Only I happened to ask my old school captain what 'Woman' meant, and he said 'tails'. At twelve o'clock Thornton had two people ready to go in and so had I. 'Ain't you going to field, Sam?' asked Thornton. 'Yes, when you have got us out.' 'Well I'm blowed, I thought I'd won.'"

Thornton never wore pads when he batted, although Woods maintained he wore thin ones under his trousers when he faced him in a game in 1889; and did not bother with gloves until near the end of his career, and then only one. He just loved playing, no matter where he was. He enjoyed telling the story about being in the neighbourhood of a school and going to the cricket ground with the intention of watching. But one of the teams was a player short and the unknown spectator was asked if he would like to take part. Thornton was only too keen and hit the ball out of the ground thirteen times in a two-hour stay that brought him 188 runs. By the end of the match the teams knew that their stand-in cricketer was Charles Thornton.

Thornton was made a Freeman of the Borough of Scarborough where he organised several games and was largely responsible for the introduction of the cricket festival there. He was a keen motorist, very fond of travelling and went through Japan, Siberia and Russia. He was in Berlin when the First World War broke out and narrowly escaped being caught. He died in 1929 in London, aged seventy-nine.

18 ALBERT TROTT

Only one man has ever hit a ball right over the Lord's pavilion and into the tennis courts behind — Albert Trott, who played for both Australia and England. The hit was the fulfilment of an ambition and a spur for him to try to repeat the feat almost wherever he went.

Trott was born in Melbourne in 1873 and was twenty-one when he made an outstanding debut for Australia against England in 1894-95. In the Test match at Adelaide he scored 38 not out and 72 not out and took eight for 43 in the second innings. He played three times in that series yet unaccountably was left out of the party to tour England the following year. He was so disappointed that he left for England on his own and qualified for Middlesex, a qualification that also enabled him to play for England with two Tests in South Africa in 1898.

He was a powerful man who never tired, an all-rounder regarded by many as the best in the world. He was a good, hard-hitting batsman, a fine opening bowler and a brilliant fielder, particularly in the slips where his big hands seized everything. On two occasions he took 200 wickets and scored 1,000 runs in a season for Middlesex and is the only man to have taken four wickets in four balls *and* done the hat-trick in the same innings — in his own benefit match! He must have been something of a perfectionist for the story goes that a professional, having lost a match through careless fielding, was seized by Trott in the dressing room, laid across his knee and soundly smacked with the back of a hair brush.

Trott, as his ability to get 1,000 runs in a season shows, was no mere hitter. At his best he was a great deal better than that. But he did love to have a swing at the bowling and was too rash to do full justice to his natural powers and ability. Gilbert Jessop said of him: "About 1900 'Alberto' was a side in himself. Of very strong physique, he could bowl all day and every day without turning a hair. When he could succeed in checking his impetuosity he was a batsman fit for any team for he had his moments when his form was far removed from that of a hard-hitting batsman of haphazard methods. Dull cricket could never exist when A. Trott was playing in a match."

Trott, however, was an adventurer. He loved the spectacular, he thoroughly enjoyed swinging his heavy bat and seeing the ball take off. He hit eight centuries, six of them on his home ground of Lord's, the best being his 164 against Yorkshire in 1899 when he scored his last 137 runs in 90 minutes, and hit 27 fours, several of which would have been sixes today. He hit F.S. Jackson three times into the pavilion, two more hits landed on the top balcony of the pavilion, he struck the tavern, even found a way into the scorers' box, and drove so powerfully against the pavilion rails that the ball rolled back within a few yards of mid-on. He gave one chance in the deep towards the end of his innings when he hit the ball so high that Bobby Moorhouse, fielding substitute, had plenty of time to get into position. Moorhouse

watched the ball, let it drop on the ground five yards in front of him and threw it back to the bowler. When asked by his captain, Lord Hawke, why he did not catch it, he replied: "I didn't see her at first up against that blackboard (the score board) and then when I seed it up there and acoming to me, I says: 'Oh damn it!' and I leaves it." Moorhouse never played again for Yorkshire.

Earlier in the same month, when playing for M.C.C. against Sussex, Trott hit a ball from Fred Tate with such power that it hit the emblem of the coat of arms at the top of one of the pavilion towers. As the towers reach higher than the roof this hit was even bigger than the one for which he is best remembered and which followed a few weeks later.

It was July 1899, when Trott launched himself into his big hit, and he saved it for his fellow Australians, which must have given him added pleasure. He was playing for M.C.C. and was facing the bowling of Monty Noble who had been brought on in an effort to end Trott's frolic. Trott had already hit one ball just short of the pavilion rails and another on to the top balcony, both off Victor Trumper, both feelers for the shot that was to follow. Noble was brought on in Trumper's place and almost straightaway Trott hit his thundering shot, clearing the roof, striking the chimney, and bouncing away to finish up in the garden of the dressing-room attendant. All that for four runs. Trott had achieved an ambition but his desire for repeats, it was said, affected his batting which deteriorated.

Nevertheless, he had other memorable innings and shots, including an attack on the Somerset bowling in 1902 which brought him 136 runs in 70 minutes at Lord's. He once hit three balls into the River Tone on the edge of the Taunton ground, two of them off successive balls, and even cleared the river, too. He damaged the spokes of a hansom cab with a hit into the road at the pavilion end of Trent Bridge and at Headingley cleared the football stand to land the ball well inside the rugby ground. Another swinging, thundering hit was cut off in its prime when it landed in the stomach of the Sussex wicketkeeper, Henry Butt, who was laid out by the blow and had to be carried off.

Trott's powerful physique came in handy during a game against Surrey in the days when it was the custom in an important match for the man who captured the ball at the end to keep it. Jack Hobbs cut the ball to third man for victory and he and the other batsman, Tom Hayward, chased after it. So, too, did Trott. "While the other two were struggling on the ground for the ball I tried to hit it away," Hobbs recalled. "But Trott gathered it with his big hands and the trophy was his."

Trott toured South Africa with England in 1898 when Lord Hawke was captain and played in both Tests. He asked His Lordship to advance him some money for his brother in Australia. "It undoubtedly went to a bookie in Cape Town," Lord Hawke observed. The request was repeated in Johannesburg and Lord Hawke said he would send it himself if Trott would give him the address. He never received it. "Trott was droll and too apt to take his batting lightly," Lord Hawke wrote twenty-five years later. "Indeed, towards the end he degraded his magnificent hitting powers into blind swiping. Alas! He was one of those who, through too short a life, couldn't resist temptation. He resisted no temptation."

Trott, whose bowling brought him 626 wickets in one three-season spell, finished playing in 1910. He was a character with his large, droopy moustache, looking like something out of a Laurel and Hardy film. But he could be morose and in 1914, when aged forty-one, he shot himself in the head and was found dead in bed by his land-lady in Harlesden in London. He had been ill for some time and had been in St. Mary's Hospital under the care of Sir John Broadbent. He complained of the tedium and dreariness of hospital life and a week after going into hospital said he could not stand it any longer and insisted on going home. The hospital authorities tried to persuade him to stay but he insisted on leaving and three days later was found dead. He died in straitened circumstances and the only money he had was sixpence. "All the money I have in the world," he told his landlady.

19 ARTHUR WELLARD

Only men of deep imagination with an unending sense of fun could have brought "Big Jim" Smith and Arthur Wellard together in a Test match. The prospect was boundless. They might not take a wicket between them but they could have slogged England to a thousand in a day. It was Manchester in 1937; the war was looming; and light entertainment was welcome. Unfortunately, neither of them came off as a batsman, and reality faded back into a dream. Like Smith, Wellard was a bowler first, a big hitter second. And in a period rich with fast bowlers Wellard showed his immense talent by being chosen even for two Tests, the second coming in 1938.

Not even "Big Jim" could challenge Wellard as the most consistent hitter of sixes first-class cricket has ever known. Several times he hit more than fifty in a season and in all finished with over 500. He twice hit five in an over, both on the small Somerset ground of Wells, and on his home ground of Taunton he plopped many a ball into the River Tone. In 1935, the season that Harold Gimblett burst onto the scene, he hit 66 sixes, and many is the grandstand, bandstand, church and chapel, tea-room and toilet he bombarded through his colourful career. Nor could a Test match inhibit him. When England were in trouble against Australia at Lord's in 1938 Wellard took part in an eighth-wicket partnership of 74 with Denis Compton, hitting hard and mightily pulling a ball from Stan McCabe onto the grandstand balcony. But he was there to bowl, and the wickets in the match of Fingleton, Hassett and Badcock for 126 runs were not enough. His short Test career was over.

Wellard, born in Kent, did not start to play cricket, with Bexley, until he was about eighteen. He quickly became a valued all-rounder and in one match took eight wickets against Kent Colts. He headed the batting and bowling averages for three seasons for Bexley but it was not enough to persuade Kent of his worth. Somebody suggested he might be better suited for the police force. Instead, Wellard accepted a three-day trial with Somerset when he was twenty-three. He played against the New Zealanders that season, but he was twenty-six before he was qualified to play regularly for Somerset. He made an immediate impression with 131 wickets, including a hat-trick, and some raw, rustic hitting in his first season. He learned quickly. He added defence and more varied stroke play to his batting and three times he achieved the double of 1,000 runs and 100 wickets in a season. And all that without a day's coaching in his life. His record compared well with the great all-rounders of Somerset's history — more than 12,000 runs, over 1,500 wickets and nearly 400 catches by the time he finished after the war.

Wellard was the sort of player who could turn the course of a game quite dramatically as he showed in a match against Hampshire at Portsmouth in 1933. The match started with Somerset collapsing to 38 for six before Wellard, with four sixes and seven fours, pulled the score round by hitting 77 out of 94. In the second innings he hit two more sixes and seven fours in his 60, took ten wickets for less than 11 runs

each, and almost single-handedly carried Somerset to victory by 107 runs. This was one of his years of the double, and included 66 in 40 minutes with five sixes and five fours against Hampshire at Bath, 52 in 40 minutes against Essex at Taunton, 65 in 45 minutes with five sixes against Glamorgan at Weston-super-Mare and, in the last match of the season, 70 in 65 minutes with five sixes to lift him past 1,000.

Wellard's biggest innings came away from the more inviting grounds of Wells and Bath and Taunton and were scored at the Oval and Old Trafford. He hit 112 each time although the one against Lancashire, achieved in 93 minutes, was faster by nearly an hour. It was Lancashire's last championship match of the 1935 season. Rain interfered with each day's play and fast bowler Dick Pollard went down with tonsillitis. Lancashire scored 266 with Cyril Washbrook and Jack Iddon sharing in a stand of 119 in 90 minutes and half the Somerset side was out for 109 before Wellard started swinging his way to five sixes and ten fours. He scored his first 50 out of 67 in 35 minutes, his second 50 in 50 minutes as he got less of the bowling. Iddon was hit over the former ladies stand and almost over the Hornby stand; Len Hopwood was driven straight out of the ground into Warwick Road; and another six, off Frank Sibbles, landed near the railway station. But the most spectacular six, again off Sibbles, was the one to square leg which hit one of the pavilion's towers. Last man Horace Hazell was in before Wellard reached his hundred, achieved by moving from 90 with five singles and a six.

Yet Bill Andrews, Wellard's great friend and roommate, considered his best innings was played against Surrey, again at the Oval, two years later. Surrey scored 406 with centuries from Bob Gregory and Stan Squires, Somerset replied with 264 of which Frank Lee scored 130. Andrews took eight wickets for 12 runs — and that included a six that should have been a wicket — as Surrey were seen off for 35 in their second innings and Somerset were left needing 178 to win. In no time they had lost six wickets. "Then in came Wellard, strolling nonchalantly as ever to the wicket," wrote Andrews. "His 91 not out that day was his finest knock — and that's saying a lot. Watts and Gover simply could not bowl at him. They both had several men on the boundary." Wally Luckes went in at number nine and scored 19 and when an amateur called Paul Molyneux, batting at number eleven because of injury, went out, 29 more runs were needed. They got 17 of them before Molyneux was run out with Surrey winning by 11 runs and Wellard missing his hundred by nine.

Wellard and Andrews were good mates. They shared a room and a drink together, at times even a double bed to share expenses. Andrews got a fright in the early hours of one Sunday morning — when he felt something like a pin sticking into him. He turned on the light and felt down the bed to discover Wellard's set of false teeth; they must have slipped out during the night. "We always used to have an extra pint on a Saturday night," said Andrews with obvious fondness and relish. No John Player League in those days, of course. No silly Sunday cricket although how Wellard would have loved the challenge of a 40-over innings. And I daresay a two o'clock start would have fitted in with his extra pints and a few favourite pink gins on the Saturday night.

Several batsmen had hit four consecutive sixes before Wellard set the record with five in an over, the first time against Derbyshire at Wells in 1936. Somerset were 143 for five needing 274 to win when Wellard started batting, being immediately dropped in the deep off Tom Armstrong, the Derbyshire left-arm spinner. Wellard hit two sixes in the same over and Armstrong was taken off. But he soon returned to the attack and Wellard, after playing the first ball quietly, hit the next two into the car park. The fourth went straight out of the ground and was lost, and the last two were also hit out of the ground. Wellard hit 86 in 62 minutes with seven sixes and eight fours, and Somerset won an exciting match by one wicket. Two years later, against Kent, Wellard repeated his feat of five sixes in an over, this time off Frank Woolley who was in his last season. Wellard swept the first five balls for six, four of them clean out of the ground and three of them lost which brought an impassioned plea from the umpire, Alec Skelding, to stop it. They had only one ball left.

I have read that the fifty-one-year-old Woolley tossed the last ball up to Wellard, a generous gesture to help him make it six sixes in the over. I asked Les Ames, the Kent and England wicketkeeper at that time, if that was right. "Doesn't sound like Frank Woolley to me," he laughed. Anyway, Woolley bowled, Wellard did not quite get hold of it and Bryan Valentine almost took a catch near the sightscreen. The ball was dropped and Wellard took a single. He hit 57 in 37 minutes with seven sixes.

There was more good hitting that summer. He hit six sixes in an innings at Cardiff including four in two overs off Emrys Davies as he scored all but seven of the last 80 runs; and six more at Taunton to help Somerset to victory over Gloucestershire by one wicket in one of the most thrilling finishes of the season. Somerset had taken a first innings lead of 55 before Walter Hammond, with 140 not out, enabled Gloucester to declare at 338-7 and leave Somerset a winning target of 284. When Wellard went in, Somerset were 172 for seven and the chance of victory looked to have gone. In the next 40 minutes he hit six sixes and five fours in an innings of 68 and Somerset crept home in the last over of the day as Luckes hit two boundaries.

Wellard was chosen for one M.C.C. tour; the one to India in 1939-40 which had to be called off after the outbreak of war. But he had gone to India two years earlier with Lord Tennyson's team and in the second "Test" in Bombay hit a six still regarded as the biggest ever there. Amar Singh, India's fine all-rounder, had hit Wellard for six in a game at Jamnagar a few days earlier. Wellard vowed to get his own back and when Amar bowled in the "Test" he kept the ball pitched up in the block-hole. The half-volley eventually arrived and Wellard swung with all his might, hitting the ball back over the bowler's head and out of the Brabourne Stadium. Amar applauded the shot and said: "That's the greatest hit ever, Arthur." Bill Edrich, the Middlesex and England player, was sitting with Lord Tennyson at the other end of the ground and exclaimed: "Good heavens! That one's gone right over the top." Tennyson declared that nobody could do it and laid a pound that Edrich was wrong. Edrich took the bet, the pound and then measured the hit. It was 97 yards from the wicket to the edge of the turf where the sight-screen stood. Then there was a cinder-track, a series of terraces and the stand, over 60 feet high. Wellard had cleared the lot.

Wellard was proud of his hitting ability. Many times the ball went bouncing down the street bordering a ground; he even landed one on a church — not one of your towered or steepled churches of course; and regularly flushed the blackbirds out of the trees on the edge of the ground at Bath. Nobody can have plopped as many balls into rivers as Wellard — to be fair, a few other people have taken advantage of the temptations of the Tone behind the Taunton ground — and Alan Gibson remembers a shot from the river end at Taunton which bounced on the bridge and "alarmed several negotiating farmers in the cattle market". Wellard would have a go at any bowler, and even Harold Larwood was hit over the Weston-super-Mare pavilion. Larwood clearly did not take kindly to that sort of liberty. The next ball looked identical, the shot certainly was, but it was the leg stump this time which took off like a Spitfire. Wellard continued swinging during the Second World War and in one game at Hayes he hit 50 in eight minutes.

Hugh Bartlett, the Sussex batsman who played at the same time as Wellard, described him as a good, selective straight hitter. Les Ames agreed that Wellard "picked them out pretty well". He added: "Taunton is a very small ground and he could mishit one and it would go for six. The same stroke at Lord's and he would be caught on the boundary. But he was a magnificent hitter and he didn't just slog. I think he was the best I've seen, I can't think of anybody better."

Wellard served in North Africa and Italy during the war and when it was over he was forty-three, but still fit, and able to give Somerset four more full seasons and take 331 wickets. He went into league cricket and coached at the Alf Gover School before dying in his sleep on New Year's Eve, 1980, aged seventy-eight. Ron Roberts, writing in 1952, said Wellard had told him he intended playing until he was sixty-five, that he would never tire of cricket. They do say he was still running up to bowl when he was approaching seventy. And still trying to clear that damn church tower, too, I'll bet.

20 FRANK WOOLLEY

In his fourth match for Kent, while still only nineteen, Frank Woolley scored 116 in an hour and a half on his home ground of Tonbridge. In something around his 750th match for Kent, while in his fifty-second year, he scored a century before lunch . . . on his home ground of Tonbridge. That was his 144th century. The 145th, his last, followed ten days later at nearby Tunbridge Wells, 162 in 220 minutes against Sussex with two sixes and 18 fours.

When I was asking Claude Lewis, another Kent player, about people who could hit the ball, properly hit it, it did not take him long to get round to Woolley. "Frank was a fine striker of the ball," he said with some enthusiasm. Claude witnessed both Woolley's last centuries in his closing season of 1938, the near end of a career that brought over 50,000 runs, most of them at a fair old pace. The achievements might just have surprised the man who wrote in Woolley's opening season of 1906: "His physique at present hardly suggests a capacity to stand the continuous strain of strenuous cricket." Ah me, I can remember writing lots of similarly fatuous stuff.

Woolley's batting, they say, was all grace and timing and unruffled dignity. It all came so naturally to him. Yet he hit the ball just about as hard and as far as anybody. "His off drive goes like a cannon ball and feels like a lump of lead," wrote Arthur Gilligan. Bob Wyatt described his straight driving as "devastating". "I have never seen anyone hit the ball harder back over the bowler's head," he declared.

Woolley made the biggest hit Herbert Sutcliffe had ever seen, pulling a ball which, he said, "looked at one time like bursting one of the Oval gasometers. It carried the wall and, I believe, the road, but fell short, of course, of the gasometer towards which it flew." But of course. The grace, rather than the power, was expressed by Sutcliffe, who referred to the beauty of his hitting. "Woolley, you know, never appears to hit a ball: he just leans on it and away it flies." Ian Peebles, too, referred to the way Woolley hit the ball beautifully on the leg side with a full, rhythmical swing of the bat. Peebles recalled a game at Tonbridge when Walter Robins and himself were rather pleased at themselves for getting a couple of early wickets. Patsy Hendren, their Middlesex teammate, indicated Woolley approaching the crease. "Here comes the lion-tamer," he declared. Woolley set about the bowling and Nigel Haig worked out a plan which involved Harry Lee dropping further and further back from square leg until he was on the boundary edge for the fifth ball of the over which would be dropped short. "To a point the plan worked out," wrote Peebles in his biography of Woolley. "Nigel dropped the ball short and Frank slapped it away straight in the desired direction. However, it bisected the line of the fielder's upturned eyes about eight feet above his head and 'thwup' into a tent behind, so that the structure tugged at its moorings and shimmered like a belly-dancer."

Woolley was never afraid to hit the ball in the air. Open spaces invited him and

he was not frightened to hit the ball over a fieldsman. Charles Barnett recalled Woolley's strokeplay. "When he came forward it was either through the covers, *over* mid-off, or *over* the bowler or mid-on. Anything short went *over* mid-wicket; very few deflections, just beautiful, flowing stroke play."

Bob Wyatt spoke of the ease with which he played, and the power of his shots. "He never looked to be really forcing and yet the ball travelled like a rocket. He used to hit the ball back over the bowler's head harder than anyone I ever saw." E.M. Wellings knew all about being hit back over his head. During an innings of 95 inside an hour at Oxford Woolley drove Wellings back over his head — and over the pavilion's head, too.

Trying to pick out individual Woolley centuries is not easy. Not out of 145 it isn't. To get an idea of the consistency of his scoring rate, consider that in 1934, when he was forty-seven and considering reaching for his slippers, he scored ten centuries for Kent at an average time of around 107 minutes for each. Put it another way. Those ten centuries averaged out at 126 an innings in 135 minutes. His best, I suppose, must have been his century in 63 minutes against Nottinghamshire at Dover which earned him the first trophy — plus £100 — awarded by Sir Walter Lawrence for the fastest century of the season. He was quite happy with 104 runs in Kent's six-wicket win, and hit three sixes and 14 fours. That was his second century that summer against Nottinghamshire and followed his 176 in 160 minutes at Northampton. He gave nothing like a chance and hit four sixes and 22 fours.

Another century that season that deserves more than a passing mention was his dazzling 101 in 100 minutes against Nottinghamshire's Bill Voce and Harold Butler at Canterbury. He started with 52 in 33 minutes and he and Bill Ashdown opened with a stand of 109 in 55 minutes, of which Ashdown got 24! That was the year when Kent scored their record 803 for four declared at Brentwood, with Woolley hitting 172 in a bit over three hours, and still being outscored by Les Ames (202 not out) and Bill Ashdown (332). In addition that summer Woolley hit 124 in 125 minutes against Gloucestershire at Tunbridge Wells, 122 in two and a half hours against Hampshire at Folkestone, and sundry other centuries including one at Taunton where Ian Akers-Douglas, with his only century of the season, had the effrontery to eclipse Woolley by spending only 65 minutes over it.

But back to the beginning, to the very first, scored at a gallop against Hampshire at Tonbridge. The lanky, teenaged Woolley was at home for the first time, showing his neighbours what it was all about, this county cricket. Kenneth Hutchings, who burst on to the scene with such brilliance that summer of 1906, was playing his first match of the season, in the middle of June. The two rising stars, Woolley and Hutchings, shared in a sparkling fifth-wicket stand but it was Woolley who stole the day with an innings of 116 in an hour and a half. Some of Woolley's more prodigious hitting came at Gravesend and the first fine example of it came in 1908 when he and Hutchings were together again, belting out 296 runs in 170 minutes with Woolley scoring 152.

Woolley approached the First World War with his best season yet in 1914 including a couple of particularly fast-moving centuries at Catford and Maidstone. He hit six centuries but *Wisden* was not all that impressed. "The fact must be pointed out that five of his six hundreds were obtained against Gloucestershire, Leicestershire and Worcestershire. In the big matches his scoring was not so heavy." The medical examiner was not too impressed with Woolley, either, when he presented himself ready for active service. He was turned down because of faulty eyesight and teeth.

His highest score for Kent came in 1923 when he spent only 260 minutes getting 270 runs against Middlesex at Canterbury, including three sixes. Yet he finished on the losing side. Woolley, in common with many other fine hitters of the ball, enjoyed Taunton where he frequently hit the ball into the river. In fact, when he went there in 1924 John Daniel, the Somerset captain, was quick to point out that "that blasted Woolley" had lost nine balls in recent visits, most of them in the river. On this day he scored 98 in 65 minutes with 13 fours and three sixes, the first of which landed in the churchyard, and presumably was recovered. He hit four sixes off the South Africans in an innings of 176 at Canterbury, three of them huge hits to square leg.

Dear old Gravesend came in for another bombardment in 1925 when Woolley took advantage of the short boundaries of the Bat and Ball ground to hit eight sixes and 27 fours in an innings of 215 in under three hours. He played some splendid innings in 1926, his fortieth year, particularly his run-a-minute 114 against Harold Larwood and Nottinghamshire and, a week later, 137 against Ted McDonald and Lancashire. He hit 217 in 160 minutes at Northampton, with three sixes and 29 fours, and scored a breathtaking 172 not out in 125 minutes also against Lancashire, that season's champions.

Woolley again mauled McDonald and Lancashire in 1928 when he scored 151 and I remember Len Hopwood, the Lancashire all-rounder, recalling that game and Woolley's innings. "Ted had some theory about pitching short and getting him caught at square leg," said Len. "'I'll get him, I'll get him,' he kept saying. And when Woolley was eventually out he turned to us triumphantly. 'There, I told you I'd get him, didn't I?'" Still, Lancashire did win comfortably enough, by an innings, with McDonald taking 15 wickets.

Despite *Wisden's* doubts about the quality of opposition for the big innings, Woolley repeatedly did well against Yorkshire who were always considered to have one of the best attacks in the country. He averaged over 37 against them and hit five centuries, one of them a truly majestic effort at Bradford in 1931 against an attack which included Hedley Verity and Bill Bowes. I mention those two particularly because they had rather more to remember of Woolley than anybody else. Woolley had never seen Verity before but was highly impressed and decided to take him on himself with rather startling effect. He hit him for five sixes, one of them clearing a tree on a hill at mid-wicket. Another enormous six came off Bowes, recalled to the attack to remonstrate with "yon chap from t'South". One ball was just short of a length and Woolley hit through it to clear the terrace at long on, zooming over wall and trees and gardens and out of sight.

So it went on, and through his forties, he was still playing remarkable cricket. When he was forty-six he scored 161 against Bill Copson and George Pope of Derbyshire with five sixes and 17 fours at Canterbury. At forty-seven — and this is worth repeating — he recorded the fastest century of the 1934 season, in 63 minutes, one of ten centuries with an average time of 107 minutes. When he was forty-eight, he scored 229 in 190 minutes with four sixes in Andrew Sandham's benefit match at the Oval, and at forty-nine helped Leslie Ames get the fastest century of 1936 with some specially fast singles. When he was fifty he scored 193 against Somerset at Dover and at fifty-one he scored that century before lunch at Tonbridge in his last season with Kent. And that, just by way of a throwaway, was Woolley's twelfth hundred before lunch, a figure exceeded only by Jack Hobbs and Gilbert Jessop.

Woolley, it must be added, played sixty-four times for England, scoring five centuries and averaging 36. In a career spanning thirty-three years he also took over 2,000 wickets and stands among the greatest all-rounders this country has known. He lived to the grand old age of ninety-one before he died in 1978.

THE MEN WHO WENT MAD FOR A DAY

1 TED ALLETSON

There is a pub in Worksop called "The Innings". Near the entrance, perched on a 12 foot pole, is the figure of a batsman in action on one knee and inside the front door is a plaque that explains it all. "Edwin Boaler Alletson was born at Park Lodge, Welbeck, 6th March, 1884. He played for Nottinghamshire C.C.C. In a match against Sussex at Hove in 1911 he hit 189 runs in 90 minutes, the last 142 of those being scored in 40 minutes, including 34 in one over. The name and theme of this house is based on that 'innings' and Edwin Boaler Alletson's connections with Worksop." The Alletson Bar is the games room and hanging on the wall is the bat that was wielded with such ferocity that in an hour and a half one of cricket's legends was created. A huge enlargement of the scorebook containing the innings stands alongside and a series of cartoons capture some of the highspots of his innings including, "Ted cut a ball over point and smashed the pavilion window and wrecked the bar — John Arlott." There is also a large photograph of Alletson, the familiar one of him in relaxed pose, the tie knotted at his waist. "Was he any good?" I asked a man at the pool table as I jerked my head towards the wall. "They say he gave it a bit of a crack," he replied.

Alletson was born in the Park Lodge on the Duke of Portland's estate and was brought up in the closing years of the nineteenth century in an atmosphere still bordering on the feudal. He was the son of a wheelwright; he himself became a forester on the Welbeck estate. He grew into a strong young man, over six feet tall and weighing 15½ stone and developed into a hitter of some power and a medium fast bowler. His bowling, however, became more of a sideline with 33 wickets in his career. He was regarded first and foremost as a batsman, yet scored only 3,217 runs for a career average of 18.47.

He scored two runs in three innings in his debut year, 1906, had a top score of 40 in 1907, did not play regularly in 1908, and had to wait until the following season for his first half-century, an innings of 81 against Leicestershire when the first 50 came in an hour. His first real impression as a hitter came that year when he scored 70 in an hour against Gloucestershire. The following summer, of 1910, Sussex was given a taste of what was to come twelve months later with some splendid hitting in his 70 at Hove. There was more "good slamming" in 50s against Leicestershire, Lancashire, Derbyshire and Yorkshire and he hit 46 in 40 minutes against Essex.

Gilbert Jessop, who knew a little bit about big hitting himself, wrote of Alletson in *London Opinion* in June, 1910: "Of all the English big hitters at the present moment, for pure distance Alletson of Nottinghamshire deserves to be placed first. It is not necessary for him to make his best hit to clear the majority of our grounds. He gets more distance with hitting in the direction of long on than he does in any other direction. When he has had a little more experience it will be no surprise to me to read of big scores as well as big hits from his bat."

The prophet was soon to be proved right. Alletson was into his swing and at the start of the 1911 season he exploded into action in a game he could so easily have missed. Nottinghamshire took twelve players to Hove for Sussex's first county match of the season, two of whom were not fully fit — Tom Wass and Alletson himself who had an injured wrist. If Wass had been fit, Alletson would probably have been left out. But Wass's injury was more serious so he dropped out, opening the way for one of cricket's memorable days.

Alletson scored seven of Nottinghamshire's first innings of 238. Sussex replied with 414, Alletson being allowed to bowl one over, and Nottinghamshire were 185 for seven, only nine runs ahead, when Alletson went out to bat on a grey day and in front of a handful of spectators. At the fall of the seventh wicket he gathered his gloves and bat and asked his captain, Arthur Jones: "Mr Jones, does it matter what I do?" Jones said it did not. "Then I'm not half going to give Tim Killick some stick," said Alletson as he set off to bat.

In 50 minutes up to lunch he scored 47 and shared in an eighth-wicket stand of 73. The ninth wicket yielded only ten runs before the real blitz came with Alletson and Bill Riley putting on 152 runs for the last wicket. Of those, Riley, who was killed by shell splinters six years later during the First World War, scored 10 not out. Alletson got to his 50 three minutes after lunch, his hundred arrived 13 minutes later and he was out for 189 just 24 minutes after that. Forty minutes of cricket after lunch had brought him 142 runs and in the first seven overs he had hit 115 out of 120. In all, he hit eight sixes — two of them over the stand — 23 fours, four threes, ten twos and 17 singles. And Tim Killick didn't half get some stick with a return of one for 130 in 20 overs. In one over that included two no balls he was hit by Alletson for three sixes and four fours and in another for 22 runs. George Leach was punished for 34 in two overs and the man on the scoreboard swore the steel numbers became red hot in the action of being taken up and down.

Only a handful of spectators saw the early-season game and one of them was Fred Root, the Derbyshire player who was recuperating from a strained back. "Sir Harry Preston was my companion," he wrote in his book, *A Cricket Pro's Lot*, "and he was converted by Ted's innings into a much keener cricket fan than ever he had been previously. He had always said the game was too technical and slow; but later he declared he had never enjoyed a sporting event with quite such a thrill. I remember Tim Killick fielding in the long field near me and when H.P. Chaplin beckoned him and asked him to bowl, Killick, who wore very large-lensed glasses, turned to me and said: 'He'll kill me Fred if I'm not careful; you know I can't see 'em very well.' His anxiety was justified. Ted's overtowering build dwarfed Tim's stature in almost grotesque comparison. He was punished for 22 in one over. The next over, in which he bowled two no balls, added 34 to the score of the mighty Alletson, the scorebook analysis reading 4-4-6-6-4-4-6 (in those days an over consisted of five balls). That finished Tim!"

Alletson, who had been bathing in the sea that morning, hoping it would be good for his injured wrist, lost five balls in the course of his innings. One was recovered by the sea a mile away, taken to the beach by a small boy who had picked it up in the street near the ground. Another was driven so hard into the soft wood of a new stand that it became embedded and could not be prised out. Most sixes were over long-on and at one time there were five balls on the roof of a skating rink outside the ground. Jones, the Nottinghamshire captain, reckoned ten or 15 minutes could be knocked off the time of Alletson's innings because of the time taken up looking for lost balls. There were two extremely difficult chances in the hour and a half, at cover when he was 25 and in the slips at 42, before he was caught on the straight drive boundary, the fielder leaning back with his head against the stand to take the catch. The Duke of Portland, it is said, presented Alletson with a gold watch and chain with an inscribed medallion as a memento and has also been credited with giving Alletson a cheque for £100.

On his next playing day, Alletson did a mini-repeat by hitting 60 in the last half-hour of the opening day against Gloucestershire at Bristol. A big crowd turned up the following day to see him continue. Dennett bowled with three men on the boundary in front of the wicket, and Alletson was lbw to the second ball he received. Still, it was all enough to earn him a Test trial two weeks later when he scored 15 and eight. Alletson, however, was never to come close to matching that great innings. That season, despite his 189, he finished with a batting average of 24 and *Wisden* said: "The disappointment of the team on batting was Alletson. At Brighton, it seemed for the moment that Notts had found a hitter of the stamp of Thornton and Bonnor but the early promise was far from being fulfilled."

Alletson played so poorly at the start of the 1912 season that he was dropped after six matches which brought him 103 runs. He recovered in 1913 with occasional displays of startling hitting, scoring 69 in 47 minutes against Sussex, 55 in 25 minutes against Leicestershire, and 88 in an hour against Derbyshire, driving Bracey for four sixes in two overs, the ball twice passing over the top of the scoring box. He even had the audacity to strike the great Wilfred Rhodes for three successive sixes at Dewsbury. He played two matches in 1914, scored 21 runs, and was finished. "It is a misfortune that he was always judged by the standard he set for himself," said *Wisden*.

Alletson lived to be seventy-nine, dying in Worksop in 1963.

2 CHARLES BARNETT

A friend once told me about the day he went to watch Gloucestershire play. He got there a few minutes late, just in time for the start of the second over. The scoreboard showed 20 for one, last man 20. He told me that Barnett had hit the first five balls of the game for four, then got out off the sixth. I never checked the story. I would have hated to disprove it. Anyway, even if it did not happen, it should have, it seemed typical of the dash and adventure that marked Barnett's play.

Barnett spent many years at Gloucestershire in the shadow of Walter Hammond, but regularly managed to break out to bask in the warmth of the sunshine of his own special brand of batting. He came from a county of giants, of Grace and Jessop and Hammond, and it is not easy to get up alongside players of that stature. But he came a good second, and there are many players would have been more than happy to have settled for that. He played twenty Tests and scored two centuries against Australia, getting within two runs of a hundred before lunch in one of them.

Among the 18,000 spectators at Trent Bridge that day in June, 1938, was Yorkshire pace bowler Frank Dennis who recalls Barnett having to watch Len Hutton play the morning's last over for a maiden when all he probably needed was one ball, one miserable ball, to get his hundred before lunch. "Then, after lunch — bang, first ball for four," wrote Dennis. "I don't think he hit any sixes, but he attacked anything a bit short outside the off stump from McCormick and didn't hesitate to drive O'Reilly past and over mid-off and mid-on. A fine innings."

Dennis is right. Barnett did not hit any sixes, which is probably unusual for anybody getting so close to a century before lunch. It had been regarded as something of a surprise that Barnett had been preferred to Bill Edrich to open the innings with Hutton for this, the first match of a series which England were to draw 1-1 and in which Hutton was to get his record score of 364 at the Oval. Hutton was still only twenty-one at the time of the Nottingham Test, Barnett was twenty-seven, and before that last over before lunch Barnett, two away from his century, told his junior partner: "Don't think about me. Just play for lunch." They had opened for England on a pitch described by *The Times* as "far too good to be true," and by Neville Cardus in the *Manchester Guardian* as "one of the easiest pitches ever known". "Rather than bowl on this Trent Bridge wicket, I would break stones," he wrote with his customary hint of over-statement. Ernie McCormick, though, had to bowl on it and in his first over saw Barnett dropped by Bill Brown in the gully. It was a difficult chance, hard and high to his left, but he did get a hand to the ball, a palm to be more exact for his fingers never came into contact with it. Fleetwood-Smith had to bowl on it, too, and Barnett sliced him carelessly over the gully. Bill O'Reilly was driven for four and Barnett reached his 50 out of 69 in an hour. He had started hesitantly, his life charmed, his wicket invisibly protected but likely to topple to almost any ball in the opening half hour. Then it must have dawned on Barnett that nothing was going

to happen and, like a soldier in battle who defies every bullet and shell, he launched himself at the Australian bowling. Don Bradman missed him at mid-off and Barnett galloped away to reach 98 at lunch with Hutton 61. And as Dennis recalled, Barnett hit the first ball after lunch for the runs needed for his century. He was bowled by McCormick for 126, a great innings for the 18,000 crowd who had paid £1,406 5s between them for the pleasure. And for those who stayed on there was another masterly innings to see, the 232 for Australia by Stan McCabe.

Barnett's most explosive innings was played at Bath in 1934 when he hit 11 sixes against Somerset and was caught on the boundary edge going for the twelfth that would have given him his 200. Gloucestershire had lost the previous match to Lancashire at Bristol with Barnett scoring a single in each innings, and taking 40 minutes over it the second time. The following morning Gloucestershire were ten miles away at Bath where they batted all day for 376 for seven with Barnett hitting 194 in 225 minutes, his highest score.

He drove the ball with tremendous power and none of the five bowlers Somerset used could do anything better than hit the middle of his bat. Horace Hazell was hit for five of the 11 sixes, one of which was brilliantly caught by a spectator in a high stand alongside the sightscreen. Seven of the sixes came during his third 50, all the result of perfectly-timed drives. Reg Sinfield made 48 of the opening stand of 174 in two and a half hours, Basil Allen managed 26 of the partnership of 85 with Barnett who was unable to resist the temptation of hitting Arthur Wellard for what would have been his twelfth six and his first double hundred. Unfortunately, Reg Ingle, the Somerset captain, held on to the catch.

Barnett first played for Gloucestershire in 1927 when he was only sixteen. In his second season he shared in a stand of 145 in an hour with Hammond against Glamorgan when Hammond was approaching greatness and Barnett was still finding his feet. But it was 1933 before Barnett got his first century, another product of powerful driving. Even Hammond had to retire to the shadows as he and Barnett put on 113 runs in an hour, much of it against Tich Freeman, the Kent leg-spinner who had taken eight wickets in the first innings. Barnett hit six centuries that season, played for the Players and for England, and went on the M.C.C. tour of India. The mid-1930s saw Barnett at his best, an aggressive, dominating batsman who was more than capable, as he was to show against Australia at Trent Bridge, of savaging the best attacks.

Yet, for too long, Hammond stole the attention. When Barnett got an amazing 123, including six sixes, against Glamorgan at Bristol in 1934, Hammond scored an unbeaten 302; when he scored 170 against Worcestershire at Dudley the same year, Hammond hit six sixes in an innings of 265 not out. But what a prospect watching them together, what a joy Gloucestershire cricket was in those days. In the game against Glamorgan, Barnett reached his century before lunch with a glorious six and at one time, out of 70 runs scored, Barnett had 60, Grahame Parker three, and extras seven. On that same day Hammond got 210 of his runs and in the benefit match for himself at Downend the following day he hit 125 not out with 12 sixes landing in the road bordering the ground, or going over the pavilion and into the gardens of houses some distance away. In that same season of 1934 Sussex travelled to Cheltenham from Hastings by road, arrived at 2 a.m. and then had to field as Barnett scored 189 and he and Hammond together put on 251 in 155 minutes in front of a 5,500 crowd who contributed £48 to Hammond's benefit fund.

Barnett scored 101 in 60 minutes against Hampshire at Southampton in 1937 but it was not enough to win him the Lawrence Trophy for the fastest century of the season. That went to Joe Hardstaff who took 51 minutes against Kent at Canterbury. If a player of such natural attacking instincts as Barnett was to bat through an innings it was bound to be a big score. He did it once, hitting 228 not out of Gloucestershire's 363 against Leicestershire at Gloucester in 1947. He batted six hours for those runs, a giant of an innings with only one other batsman, George Emmett, with 42, getting past 20.

Barnett played three seasons after the war before retiring in 1948, at the age of thirty-eight, and with twenty Test matches and more than 25,000 first-class runs behind him. Yet even in that final season he was still whizzing along to his hundreds, making 141 with "hurricane hitting" and sharing with Emmett in an opening stand of 226 in two hours. Gloucestershire, needing 389 in four and a half hours to beat Yorkshire on a turning Bristol wicket, won a famous victory with 45 minutes to spare.

Cardus once wrote of Barnett: "The batting after Barnett departed became heavily laden, careworn and not profitable." But perhaps Robertson-Glasgow put it much more neatly: "Of all cricketers, next to W.R. Hammond, I should like to be C.J. Barnett." How lovely.

Incidentally, even if Barnett did not get out in the opening over of a game for 20, he certainly came close in a match against Somerset when Gloucestershire needed 26 in their second innings. Barnett hit 20 in Bill Andrews' opening over and was out to the first ball of Andrews' next over. "I had Harold Gimblett to thank for that," said Andrews. "He had bet Charlie he couldn't belt me over the stand and Charlie for once picked the wrong ball."

3 HUGH BARTLETT

The distinction of having scored the fastest century against the Australians belongs to Hugh Bartlett, a tall, dashing amateur who reached his hundred in under an hour at the delightful Hove ground in 1938. The Australians were probably not feeling all that well. Only three days earlier they had lost the final Test at the Oval by an innings and 579 runs. And that cannot do much for your self-confidence. Len Hutton had scored 364, poor old Bill Fleetwood-Smith had been hit for 298 runs in 87 overs, Bill O'Reilly had taken three for 178 in 85 overs. Not surprisingly, neither of them was at Hove — at least not on the cricket field. The first seven players in the batting order in the Test played at Hove; it was the last county match and they were labouring under the heavy handicap of injuries, including Don Bradman and Jack Fingleton who were both hurt during the Test and had been unable to bat. In came Ernie McCormick, Frank Ward and Ernie White to provide the bulk of the bowling, and up came Bartlett to slaughter them.

The Australians batted first and with Lindsay Hassett and Bill Brown scoring 70s, they reached 336. Bartlett, batting at number four, met the ball with the middle of the bat from the start, and reached his hundred in 57 minutes and had been batting barely two hours when he was out for 157. He hit six sixes and 18 fours and in one over hit Ward, the best bowler with six for 184, for 21 runs. Each six seemed to out-distance the previous. One pitched on the grass immediately in front of the tavern opposite the main — now Tate — gate, a stupendous on drive. Jim Langridge helped him in a stand of 195 for the fourth wicket, and also helped him keep the bowling.

"The Aussies were whacked," Bartlett told me. "They didn't give anything away but I could see there was some zip missing. I scored five in the first 15 minutes, then reached 50 in half an hour and 100 in 57 minutes. At the end of the game I was given the gold cup that was awarded for the fastest 50 on the Hove ground. There was only one game to go after the Australian match and I didn't play because of a leg injury. But George Cox did, beat my 50 by a couple of minutes and there was a tannoy announcement to say I would have to return the cup."

The year of 1938 was a high spot for Bartlett. He did not play until the fourth game when he scored 22 and nine against Warwickshire at Hove, a high-scoring drawn game that went to the last minute. The Sussex players then had to travel to Leeds to play Yorkshire and on the journey the Sussex captain, Flight Lieutenant A.J. Holmes, said to Bartlett: "If you score a 50 I will give you your cap. A 50 against them is worth a hundred against any other county." Bartlett batted at number seven against Yorkshire who were playing their first match of the season at Headingley. Sussex were 106 for five when he went in to launch a fierce attack on the team who were in the middle of a hat-trick of championship wins up to the war. In an hour and a quarter he hit 94 runs with 78 of them coming in sixes and fours. He twice hit left-arm spinner Hedley Verity for three sixes in an over — "Verity was not happy

against left-handers" he said — and as well as a seventh six he hit nine fours in an innings marked by brilliant on-driving and square leg hitting. He was caught on the long off boundary, a fine catch by Maurice Leyland to hold on to a ball that was travelling like a shell and looked like giving Bartlett his century. Said Leyland as Bartlett went off: "Ay, Mister Bartlett, a foot either side and it were a six."

"I played a brassie shot," explained Bartlett. "He put his left hand out and it stuck. Later on Brian Sellers, the Yorkshire captain, said to me: 'You were a bit unlucky, weren't you?' I asked what he meant. 'That's the first catch he's taken this season,' he told me. I rated that innings my best, against Yorkshire in Yorkshire. They give you nothing and you work for everything. They were at home, early season and were looking for every point. You know, when I hit Verity for those sixes, Arthur Wood, the wicketkeeper, said to me: 'Anybody can hit slow bowlers — you've got to do it against t' quicks.'"

Bartlett, the amateur, did not play again for Sussex for nearly four weeks because of injury. He missed seven matches, none of which was won, and returned in mid-June for a game against Worcestershire at Worthing and played a significant part in a six-wicket win by scoring 76 and 64. A week later Sussex were in danger of their seventh defeat of the season after following-on 289 behind Kent until Bartlett hit three sixes and seven fours in an unbeaten innings of 62, which included 23 runs in one over against another left-arm spinner, Claude Lewis. What a very entertaining game that must have been with Frank Woolley scoring 162 in 220 minutes and Bryan Valentine 118 in an hour with four sixes and 13 fours. Bartlett was now playing regularly and enjoyed a rich vein of scoring which started on the small Mitchell and Butler ground in Birmingham where four sixes and six fours helped him to an innings of 71 and a stand of 147 in an hour and a half with Harry Parks. He hit 91 not out in the next match, a five-wicket win over Essex at Hove, and on the following day, fifty miles away at Lord's, he played his biggest innings of the season and one that Bill Edrich described as "one of the best I have ever delighted to watch".

Edrich was part of a particularly strong Players' team and Bartlett, of course, was among the misters in the Gentlemen's team. It was Bartlett's first appearance in the Gents, so to speak, and his 175 not out in 165 minutes of glorious stroke-making was the second highest innings ever for the amateurs. He started nervously, trying to make proper contact for 20 minutes and then relaxed himself with a fine off-drive to the boundary. Now he could settle down. Powerful on-driving brought him four sixes, two of them high into the Mound Stand, one off Peter Smith and another off Stan Nichols that landed on the highest part of the turret at the western end of the grandstand. He hit five fours in an over from Nichols and two fours and two sixes in the next over from Smith. In all he hit four sixes and 24 fours and Edrich, enthusing over the innings with words like magnificent and superb, said of one shot: "One of the sixes I thought was going right over the Mound stand. It was a lovely innings." That, perhaps, was the same shot Bartlett had in mind as he re-lived the innings for me from the depths of the Warner stand, a glass or two to keep out the April chill as a new season was launched. We looked out of the windows and he waved his arm airily in the general direction of the Mound Stand facing us. "One hit off Nichols was a big one, high up the stand there," he said. "Nichols watched it, hands on hips. 'There goes my chance of a place in the Test side,' he said."

In his next match at Northampton, Bartlett scored another century, sharing in a partnership of 132 in an hour with Bob Stainton. He followed that by scoring 72, in nearly two hours of unusual restraint, and 63 against Lancashire, providing the first part of a hat-trick for Leonard Wilkinson in the first innings. Wilkinson, who played three times for England the following winter, was rated by Bartlett as the best leg-spinner in the country, ahead of even Ian Peebles, Doug Wright, Peter Smith and Walter Robins. "You couldn't sort Wilky out," he said, then told me the story of Wilkinson in South Africa when somebody asked, one balmy evening, what the croaking was. "Those are frogs," said the manager. "Nay, Mr Ridgway," said Wilkinson. "Them's ducks."

Bartlett scored 27 and 16 against Middlesex before going to Hastings for the Festival week where he hit 114 in each game, against Northamptonshire and Kent. He hit three sixes and 14 fours in the first game, four sixes and 14 fours in the second and Sussex ran out handsome winners in both matches.

The runs dried up for a while. Five innings against Leicestershire, Hampshire, Derbyshire and Glamorgan brought him only 41 runs and led him into his last game looking a little out of touch. But this was the match against the Australians and it did not take him long to find it and 57 minutes of powerful, relaxed hitting, brought him the fastest century of the season and the Lawrence Trophy. With it came the gold cup for the fastest 50 at Hove but with Bartlett absent for the final match of the season on the ground, George Cox was challenged to have a go against Yorkshire. Cox beat Bartlett by two minutes and after the tannoy announcement had claimed the cup back from Bartlett, Cox hurtled on towards the fastest century of the season as well. He was 95 after 53 minutes — four minutes faster than Bartlett against the Australians — when he lashed out at a long hop from Leyland. For a few seconds the ball looked to be going for six but it dipped, pitched inside the boundary and was cut off for a single. In the end his hundred took him an hour.

Bartlett, with five centuries, 1,548 runs and an average of 57, had not done enough to play for England but was chosen for the tour that winter of South Africa, although again he could not force a way into Walter Hammond's team. He continued to play for Sussex after the war, in which he took part in the landings at Arnhem, but never again touched the form he displayed in 1938.

4 BERNARD BOSANQUET

The Aussies, God bless them, have honoured Bernard James Tindal Bosanquet in the most delightful way. They have taken his name — well, a bit of it, "Bosie" — into their colourful language. Bosanquet, of Eton, Oxford, Middlesex and England, invented the googly at the beginning of the century and the first he ever sent down at the Sydney Cricket Ground was good enough to bowl Victor Trumper. The Aussies took to the googly, adopted it with the name of "bosie," and still count it an important part of their bowling attack. How strange that the country where it was invented no longer has any use for it, that the leg-break and googly bowler is just a part of English cricket history. Bosanquet started to develop the googly while playing with Middlesex, having worked out the principle of bowling an off-break with a leg-break action when he was flipping a tennis ball over a table. It took him several years of practice before he dared use it in a first-class match and he required constant practice to keep control over the ball. Arthur Shrewsbury, a great English batsman, said in 1900 that such bowling was unfair. This was the year when Bosanquet unveiled his invention, the first victim being Sam Coe of Leicestershire, stumped at Lord's for 98 off a ball that bounced four times. Whether each bounce was a "bosie" has not been recorded. The great William Gunn was stumped — 10 yards down the wicket they say — when bamboozled by one the following month. The googly, the product of a parlour game with a tennis ball that bounced the wrong way, was out in the open. For a time, Bosanquet laughed it off as a mistake. But not for long.

In the winter of 1902-03 the twenty-three-year-old Bosanquet went to New Zealand and Australia with a team which should have been captained by Lord Hawke but who withdrew and handed the captaincy to Pelham Warner. The tour took in New York, San Francisco and Honolulu which left little time for Australia where, in three weeks, the Englishmen lost to Victoria and South Australia but managed to draw with New South Wales. It was March, 1903, in Sydney where Trumper first experienced the googly. He had scored 37 in 20 minutes when Bosanquet, after delivering two leg breaks, decided to try his pet ball and knocked back the middle stump. Seven months later he was back in Australia with the M.C.C. team, again under Pelham Warner who went on record as attributing victory in the fourth Test, at Sydney, to Bosanquet's bowling. Clem Hill, the Australian batsman, said after the third Test, at Adelaide, that Bosanquet would not get another wicket in Australia as everybody had discovered his secret. After the final Test he said: "It was the peculiarity of Bosanquet's bowling that won you the rubber." Well, it is a gentleman's prerogative to change his mind, I suppose. And the following year, in 1905, when the Australians were in England, Bosanquet won the Nottingham Test by taking eight wickets on the final afternoon.

But, and I had nearly forgotten, the man could bat a bit too. He was a dashing batsman, stiff armed yet powerful, with a good eye and great strength of forearm. He

was a rough, natural hitter who struck anything short with great power. He scored 120 in two hours for Eton against Harrow and first made his mark with Middlesex when he scored a century in each innings against Leicestershire in 1900. He scored 136 in 110 minutes in the first innings after being dropped at 0, 93 and 99; he was rather more circumspect in the second innings, taking 170 minutes to score 139. This time, he did not give the fielders a chance.

Starting in 1902, he spent two successive winters in Australia, the second with the M.C.C. for whom he scored 114 in under an hour and a half against New South Wales at Sydney. Pelham Warner said it was the best he ever saw Bosanquet play. This was one of his most brilliant all-round games, being top scorer in both innings, with 54 and 114, and taking eight wickets for 96 in the 278-run victory.

The tour must have toned him up beautifully for the home season of 1904 which was his best with 1,405 runs including four centuries and 132 wickets, the only time he did the double. He gave a brilliant display of hitting to score 145 for the Gentlemen against the Players at the Oval — he also took eight wickets — and hit splendidly to score 110 in 85 minutes in Middlesex's tied game with the South Africans. In a ninth-wicket stand that lasted only 25 minutes he and Cecil Headlam put on 79 runs. And he played with great dash for a faultless 126 in 115 minutes at the Oval before becoming the first part of a hat-trick by Digby Jephson.

Bosanquet indulged in some tremendous hitting to score 141 against Yorkshire at Sheffield and it was during this match that he and Richard More, who batted number ten and hit 120 not out, shared in a stand of 128 in 48 minutes. They drove fast and furiously and with More and Jack Hearne putting on 91 in 50 minutes for the tenth wicket, the last two wickets had added 219 runs in 98 minutes. In 40 minutes at the end of the day Bosanquet had three players lbw. "Pleasant weather prevailed and about 7,000 people visited Bramall Lane but a section of them, when three appeals for lbw were allowed, became very abusive of the umpire," said one report. The *Manchester Guardian* described Bosanquet as magnificent at the wicket and irresistible with the ball. "The umpires could not show mercy," it proclaimed. "That quality is not for umpires." That was a lovely year for Bosanquet who also helped Cyril Wells to put on 128 in an hour against Essex at Leyton and, when 64 were needed for victory on the last morning, he and James Douglas got them in 35 minutes.

He again scored 1,000 runs in 1905 but his wickets, 63 of them, were becoming more expensive, although he had a great triumph in the Nottingham Test with his eight for 107. He scored three centuries that summer, all at Lord's, two of them in the same match and both fine examples of the forcing, free-hitting batsman. Bosanquet played many fine all-round games in his all too short career which became interrupted by business, but the match against Sussex at Lord's from 25th to 27th May, 1905, was probably his best.

The Middlesex team, dominated by amateurs with the only professionals being Albert Trott and Jack Hearne at numbers ten and eleven, had lost the first two matches of the season, both at Lord's, by hefty margins. Gloucestershire beat them by nine wickets on an awful pitch, and Nottinghamshire won by 198 runs (when a brilliant innings of 93 by Bosanquet delayed the end). Edwin Field, who was available for only three games that season, came into the side for the match against Sussex and was top scorer in the first innings with 107 not out. *The Times* was not impressed. "Except for a really good innings by Mr Bosanquet who always played with confidence and hit very hard without taking unnecessary risks, the batting was not very interesting. Mr Warner played well, but Mr Field, although his innings, no doubt, was of great value to his side, was painfully slow." Such criticism could never be levelled at Mr Bosanquet. He struck the ball powerfully, particularly on the onside, and scored 103 at a run-a-minute. Sussex managed to save the follow-on but with a lead of 110 Middlesex were able to take risks as they went for quick runs and a declaration. They started the final day at 174 for two with Bosanquet and George Beldam adding 142 in 75 minutes and as soon as Bosanquet reached his century, the innings was closed.

Bosanquet had scored his unbeaten century in an hour and a quarter, being missed just once, when he was 72. Said *The Times*: "Considering the pace at which he scored, he made few bad strokes." Sussex went in to bat at one o'clock needing 427 to win, and were all out by quarter past three for 102. Middlesex had won by 324 runs with Bosanquet having scored 203 runs in the match in three hours for once out, and having taken eight second innings wickets for 53 runs for a match return of eleven for 128.

The Middlesex-Sussex game finished on the Saturday. On Monday Bosanquet was at Nottingham for the Test match with Australia. By Wednesday he had won that match, too. But Bosie was fading. Business was calling and the following year, in 1906, he played only three games for Middlesex. He still managed another century — 101 in 105 minutes in the second innings of the match against Somerset after scoring 87 in the first innings when he and Beldam put on 162 in 80 minutes for the third wicket.

He had one more good season, in 1908, when he played in nine games for Middlesex and averaged 50, hitting a century in 95 minutes against Lancashire — equal to anything seen at Lord's, enthused one report — and another against Somerset when he and Len Moon both scored 135 and shared in a stand of 227 in two hours. There was also a little matter of 214 in 215 minutes for England against Yorkshire at the Oval. "He appeared on a good wicket to have almost two strokes for every ball," said Pelham Warner.

Bosanquet played little more, although he made himself available after the First World War when in his fortieth year. During the war he served in the Kite Balloon section of the Royal Flying Corps. He died in 1936 shortly before his fifty-ninth birthday.

5 LANCE CAIRNS

When I asked Denis Compton about "Big Jim" Smith's only century, at Canterbury in 1939, he told me that the Middlesex players had always said that "when old Jim gets a century it's bound to be the fastest of the season". In the event, through mis-hitting and a shortage of the strike, it took Jim all of 81 minutes. Lance Cairns, too, had a few tasters with fast 50s before his first — and so far only — century arrived in 1980, in his ninth season in New Zealand cricket. His hundred, however, arrived rather more quickly than Smith's, taking 52 minutes and being the fastest ever in New Zealand.

Cairns, a strongly-built swing bowler, first played Shell Trophy cricket in the 1971-72 season when he was twenty-two. He was soon recognised as the finest hitter in New Zealand, a tail-end batsman with a good eye, strong muscles and a deep desire to hit the ball as far as possible. He first played for New Zealand in 1973 and two seasons later really captured attention with his batting as he hit five fast 50s, three of them from fewer than 50 balls. He started with one in 40, beat that at 37 and then hit another in 32 balls for the fastest of the season in domestic cricket. He played one Test match that summer, the third against India at Wellington, and in an innings of 47 he pulled one ball from Prasanna so fiercely that Sunil Gavaskar, fielding a few feet from the bat, took a frightening blow in the face and had to have an operation on a broken cheekbone. Cairns's prodigious hitting also brought him a six off England's John Lever on to the roof of the Dunedin grandstand, and 60 in 46 minutes in a Prudential Trophy match with England at Old Trafford. His Prudential Trophy innings was played in 1978 when England were coasting to a comfortable win with New Zealand 85 for six. Cairns hit 60 of the last 67 runs, reaching 50 in 37 balls and including four sixes. New Zealand still lost but it probably cheered Cairns up after giving away 84 runs in 11 overs during the England innings.

Cairns played an important part in New Zealand's first ever series win over the West Indies, in 1979-80, when some uncomplicated hitting helped bring victory in the first Test at Dunedin and a 1-0 win in the three-match series. That same summer, after several mediocre performances, Cairns produced his history-making century for Otago against Wellington at Lower Hutt. Bruce Taylor and Ewen Chatfield, both Test bowlers, had torn an enormous hole in the Otago batting which was on its knees at 42 for seven when Cairns went in. Soon it was 48 for eight and Cairns decided to throw his bat at just about everything. In 24 minutes to the close of the first day he faced 28 balls and hit 68 runs, hitting Chatfield on to the grandstand roof twice from consecutive balls, and twice lifting Taylor over the scoreboard in one over. And Evan Gray, said one report, "seemed to be for ever lofted on to the corrugated roof of the stand with a deafening bang".

Cairns just kept going in the same rich vein the following morning and the first ball he received again finished up on the battered, dented grandstand roof. He was

eventually caught in the deep off a massive hit that was held back by the wind, with 110 runs in the Otago total of 173, having hit nine sixes, 11 fours, three twos and six singles. His century had taken 45 balls and of the 90 runs produced for the last wicket in 31 minutes, his partner, Graeme Thomson, claimed an unbeaten four.

There was some discrepancy for a time over whether his century should be recorded as 48 or 52 minutes. It seems somebody wanted to knock four minutes off for the time it took to retrieve the ball all those times from the grandstand roof. If that had applied to some of the performances of old-timers like Gilbert Jessop and Ted Alletson their times would have been incredible. So Cairns had to be satisfied with 52 minutes, beating Dick Motz's century for Canterbury against Otago at Christchurch twelve years earlier by one minute. At the time Cairns's hundred was also the joint second fastest ever outside England, behind Algie Gehrs in Adelaide in 1912-13 (50 minutes) and equalling Learie Constantine's for the West Indians against Tasmania at Launceston in 1930-31. The boundaries on each side of the Hutt Recreation Ground were on the short side but as one spectator pointed out: "No difference. Most sixes were well in, or on, the stand on one side or over the large scoreboard on the other."

Cairns was often promoted in the batting order when the situation demanded, especially in one-day matches. When New Zealand, needing only 104 to beat Australia in the Test at Auckland in 1982, were dithering at 44 for three, Geoff Howarth sent in Cairns who hit enormous sixes off Bruce Yardley and Terry Alderman and brought victory close at hand with 34 runs in 21 balls. And when England, at the end of their 1982-83 tour of Australia, went to New Zealand for three one-day internationals, Cairns was among the first four batsmen in all the games. He hit Geoff Miller out of the ground twice at Christchurch and had innings of 19, 44 and 21 in his country's 3-0 win. England saw enough of Cairns that winter, for only a few weeks earlier in the three-pronged World Series matches in Australia he had scored 36 in four overs batting number three at Melbourne and 49 in 35 minutes at Adelaide. And all with that funny-looking, round-shouldered, hump-backed bat he had started using.

New Zealand lost 2-0 to Australia in the finals but Cairns had one more glorious moment with six sixes in an innings of 52 at Melbourne. A few months later he was in England for one of his country's greatest triumphs, when they won the second Test at Headingley to record their first win in England after fifty-two years of trying. Earlier that month, July, Cairns had hit four sixes and seven fours against Somerset at Taunton, his innings of 60 taking 29 balls. At Headingley, however, it was Cairns the bowler who did the damage with his career best return of seven for 74 in the first innings. But he could not resist putting the cherry on the cake by hitting two sixes off Phil Edmonds as New Zealand went on to win by five wickets.

Cairns played professional cricket in the North of England and in a game for Bishop Auckland in 1981 he scored 174 against Glostrup, a Danish National League touring team. His innings lasted 64 balls, with 15 sixes and 16 fours, his century having occupied 36 balls (38 minutes) and his 150, 52 balls (58 minutes).

6 CHARLES DE TRAFFORD

Charles Edmund de Trafford was a member of one of England's oldest families. He was born at Trafford Park in Manchester close to the cricket ground that was to become one of the most famous in the world. Not so surprising, perhaps, that his leisure was spent in cricket, a long-serving captain of the county where he settled, Leicestershire. He was a batsman, a dasher, a fierce, fiery hitter good enough to still be getting a century at faster than even time in his fiftieth year after being out of the game for seven years.

When Charles was born in 1864 his father, Sir Humphrey, owned the huge Trafford Park estate, including the cricket ground where Lancashire County Cricket Club was also in its first year. The estate had belonged to the family since 1016 when King Canute granted Ralph Trafford a portion of land at Stretford as a reward for his military exploits. In the nineteenth century, however, after Charles had been born, the de Traffords started to feel hemmed in. Ships were getting too close to the front door on their way up the Ship Canal, the docks and the city seemed to be closing in on them and in 1896, the 1,200-acre estate with its 880-year association with the family, was sold. Sir Humphrey had had enough. The industrial estate of Trafford Park soon began to form.

Charles, son of the second baronet, was educated at Beaumont College, Windsor, and while there he also played for Manchester, Cheshire and Trafford Park. He played for Lancashire against Derbyshire at Derby in 1884 but failed to score in his only innings and was not asked to play again. But he had houses in Leicestershire and Northamptonshire and after playing for M.C.C. in 1885 he chose to play for Leicestershire, making his debut in 1888.

He would hit from the first ball and was a great attraction. He seldom wore batting gloves and once drove R.J. Mee of Nottinghamshire for four off his hand. His favourite shot was the drive and, during an innings of 55 against Essex in 1890, he twice drove straight over the Leyton pavilion, and in 1895 put a ball through the committee room window at Lord's. He fielded in a businesslike way and moved about the field, it was said, as if keeping step to a military band.

He first captained Leicestershire in 1890, and took them out of second-class status into the county championship in 1895. He was then thirty-one years old and the High Sheriff of Leicestershire. He was a natural for the representative games, playing for M.C.C under W.G. Grace and for North v. South, which produced one of his greatest triumphs in 1893 in the game at Hastings. The South gained a first innings lead of 93 and then took three Northern second innings wickets for eight runs. The North were still 14 runs behind when the fifth wicket fell; Tom Richardson and Bill Lockwood, the South's opening attack, must have thought they would soon be on their way home. But the fall of the fifth wicket at 79 brought together de Trafford and Yorkshire's Ernest Smith who turned the game upside down in one of the most

furious attacks first-class cricket had ever seen. In 105 minutes they added 254 runs. As *Wisden* said at the time, to be echoed by its monthly magazine nearly a century later: "So far as we know, such a number in so short a space of time is without parallel in a match of importance." De Trafford, who had gone in at the fall of the fifth wicket after opening the first innings, scored 110 of the runs in an hour and three quarters with 16 fours. He was missed by the accommodating W.G. at point when he was 19 and was put down in the deep off the shot that brought him his century. Smith scored even faster, hitting 154 in 125 minutes, being missed once before he reached his hundred and several times after. The partnership enabled the North to snatch a 25-run win and Grace must have gone away quite distraught after being hit for 50 runs in five overs.

De Trafford led from the front in Leicestershire's debut year in the championship, scoring 70 out of 131 in the first game at Leyton and then, four days later, on an awful Leicester pitch, he "hit out in a style that was beyond praise" to score 92 out of a total of 131. The only other double figure score was extras with ten. Yorkshire, needing 122, were bowled out for 74. He continued to captain Leicestershire until 1906 when he was forty-two years old. But by then the game was becoming hard; the High Sheriff had more important matters of State to attend to. However, he took with him several impressive performances, like his 103 in 95 minutes just after his forty-first birthday.

De Trafford did not play again until 1913 when Leicestershire badly needed reinforcing and turned in some desperation to their former captain. They played on his sympathies, on his background, on his very name. Would he play against Lancashire, not at Old Trafford unfortunately, but at least he would not have far to travel. The game was at Leicester and he scored 64 in the second innings. But it was his second match that produced one of his most astounding displays when Leicestershire went to Chesterfield to take on Derbyshire. De Trafford had celebrated his forty-ninth birthday the previous month and was in only his second first-class match after a lapse of seven years. Yet in two hours he scored 137 runs — his sixth century — by clean, hard hitting. For the first time in his long playing life, hits over the boundary line counted six and de Trafford struck three of them to go with his 17 fours.

It was a remarkable display after Leicestershire had been 11 for four, then 41 for five. De Trafford was in great form. Bill Riley helped him add 84 runs before lunch but it was the later batsmen, Bill Shipman and Billy Astill, who followed de Trafford's example so well that Leicestershire ended with a total of 351. Shipman hit fiercely to score 60 in 15 minutes and Astill — with his highest score in county cricket — hit 75 in 80 minutes. De Trafford's innings, however, was the innings of the day despite the occasional chance. The wicket was good — de Trafford said he had never batted on a better one — but a disheartened Derbyshire lost six wickets for ten runs as they sank to an innings defeat.

Derbyshire's poor performance brought a good deal of barracking and drove the county captain, Captain Richard Baggallay, to lodge a formal complaint with his committee. The local paper seemed to come out on the side of the supporters as it wrote: "Derbyshire crowds are always free with their comments and generally express themselves fluently without regard for the tender feelings of the objects of their criticism." But there was nothing but praise for de Trafford: "The great feature of de Trafford's batting was his sublime disregard of the consequences and the best balls, which would have thrown the more orthodox player on the defensive, he hit to the boundary in all directions. The ease and vigour he displayed were amazing in a man who is enjoying his fiftieth summer, and although he treated our bowling in such merciless fashion it was nothing like as poor as it might appear."

De Trafford played eight games in 1913 and averaged over 29 for 14 innings, figures beaten only by two other players. Leicestershire called on him just once more, in 1920, when he was fifty-six. At short notice he took the place of Aubrey Sharp against Sussex at Ashby and although he scored only eight and 23 he went out with a bang, with 15 runs in two overs off Vallance Jupp including a straight drive for six against the sightscreen.

He was still to be seen sitting in the pavilion at Lord's when he was turned eighty, still with the silver snuff box presented to him to mark the game in 1888 against the Australians. He died at his home, Sibbertoft, Market Harborough, in November, 1951, aged eighty-seven.

7 HAROLD GIMBLETT

Nobody rated Harold Gimblett's 63-minute century on his debut as lightly as Harold Gimblett himself. When I saw him in the 1960s, more than thirty years on, when he was coaching at Millfield School, he was still playing it down, still preferring to talk of other innings, of other days. It was almost as if it was an embarrassment instead of the marvellous achievement it was, 123 in 79 minutes in his first match. "It was, I suppose, one of those days you dream of but I couldn't work it out," he told David Foot who wrote a marvellous book on Gimblett. "I took all the praise but Bill Andrews, who scored 71, was even faster in his scoring. I savoured the moment but loathed the publicity that followed." Maybe that was why Gimblett played it down. Maybe the sweetness of the moment turned sour on him and the pleasure of looking back on it left him.

Gimblett, of true yeoman stock, was the son of a farmer in Bicknoller, near Watchet on the Somerset coast. He hit his first six at the age of nine, a chip into "Jobber Jones's" orchard while attending Williton Church of England School. He scored his first century at eleven and played with the Watchet village team, cycling the seven miles there on evenings and after lunch on Saturdays. He was recommended to Somerset by the Watchet secretary, Bill Penny, and went to the county ground at Taunton for a two-week trial in May, 1935. But he did not match up to Somerset's requirements and was told: "You may as well finish the week. We'll pay you 35 shillings and your bus fare. Afraid you're just not good enough." Gimblett hid his disappointment by declaring he had had a wonderful time and "I have met all my heroes."

Gimblett was packed and ready to catch the bus home on the Friday night when Somerset learned that Laurie Hawkins had a thumb injury and would not be able to play against Essex at Frome the following day. Somerset, in some desperation, turned to the young man they had rejected. At least he was a good fielder, and his selection would keep old Billy Penny quiet. The Somerset secretary made sure that young Gimblett knew his way to Frome and arrangements were made for him to be met at Bridgwater by another of the players, Wally Luckes, and taken by car to the ground. Gimblett was up at half past five the following morning but missed the bus to Bridgwater and was forced to thumb a lorry. The driver asked the twenty-year-old Gimblett where he was going and why and was told: "To Frome to play cricket." "Who for?" asked the driver. "Somerset," said Gimblett. "Oh ah," said the driver.

They put Gimblett down to bat at number eight and when he went in at twenty past two, carrying Arthur Wellard's spare bat, Somerset were in something of a mess at 107 for six. Wellard himself was at the crease and as Gimblett left the dressing room, he was told: "Leave it to Arthur." Gimblett got off the mark with a single and when Peter Smith tossed a ball up to him he drove handsomely as if he were at Watchet and got his first four. In Smith's fourth over Gimblett hit two more fours

and his first six — on to the beer tent. Wellard was out stumped after being upstaged and somehow contributing only 21 to the stand of 69 and Gimblett raced on to his 50 in 28 minutes by pulling Smith for a square leg six. Gimblett had reached 72 when the new ball was taken but he played it just as confidently as he had the spinners and two fours in an over took him to 99. A two into the covers off Stan Nichols, and Gimblett had reached a memorable century in 63 minutes, with three sixes and 17 fours, and taken his place in history.

"Just how or why a whippet should achieve such heights I still cannot find an answer," wrote Gimblett thirty years later. "Is there, or should there be, one? I don't think so, for this is cricket. The glorious unexpectedness of that innings. Of the many memories, one in particular was the expression on Stan Nichols' face when I hit him straight and true over the sightscreen when he took the new ball at 200." Essex, after having Somerset by the throat at 107 for six, had lost their grip. Somerset totalled 337 and won by an innings.

Gimblett scored a half century in his second match, against Middlesex at Lord's, but averaged only 18 in the season. He moved up to opener the following year and a century against the Indians and 93 and 160 not out at Old Trafford against Lancashire, helped him scored 694 runs in 11 innings in May. That year he played for England against India, his first Test at Lord's — "a terrified lad so green in the arts of cricket I should not have been picked". He remembered, too, Hedley Verity fathering him the whole match, "truly a gentleman of cricket". Amar Singh made Gimblett look the novice he was in the first innings and Gimblett recalled walking round the ground feeling rather sorry for himself when Sir Jack Hobbs spoke to him and demonstrated with his umbrella the art of playing inswing bowling.

Although he was now an opener, Gimblett still batted with the abandon he had showed in the middle of the order. He scored a century before lunch at Kettering with six sixes, hit 143 against Northamptonshire at Bath with nothing but boundaries between 70 and 142, and a six off Jack Buswell went on to the roof of the pavilion. In 1937 he hit nine sixes in an innings of 141 against Hampshire at Wells, a century in 95 minutes at Bristol and 129 in just over two hours at Newport. "I just hate being tied down," he told David Foot. "Once I lose my adventurous style I may as well pack the whole thing."

He hit five centuries in successive matches and 905 runs in May 1939, the season in which he played his third and last Test, against the West Indies. The war arrived soon after and Gimblett became a member of the Auxiliary Fire Service and experienced some of the heaviest raids on Bristol and Plymouth. He escaped one incident in which two members of his crew were killed. There was still some cricket to play and Gimblett turned out for various teams, usually enjoyable games with not too many maiden overs. One of them, in June 1943, at Lord's, was for the Civil Defence against the Army when he scored 124 in 100 minutes. From a wicket pitched towards the grandstand, he hooked a ball from Stan Nichols into the Mound Stand, a hit of almost 130 yards and thought to be the longest hook on record in England. This has certainly been beaten at least once with Clive Lloyd's clearance of the Oval in 1977, a hit of anything between 140 and 160 yards.

Somerset had their best season ever the first year after the war, finishing fourth in the championship in 1946 with Gimblett, criticised by Robertson-Glasgow for being "too daring," averaging nearly 47 and, according to *Wisden*, "curbing his natural tendency to recklessness, showed defence worthy of an opening batsman, combined with powerful hitting". Nevertheless, the entertainment continued. His 114 against Cambridge University took 95 minutes and included six sixes. He scored seven centuries, was eighth in the English batting averages, but it was not enough to get him into the Test team against India or on the M.C.C. tour to Australia. He was chosen for another Test, against the West Indies in 1950, but was ill and unable to play. But he was also chosen for a Commonwealth team which played in India that winter and played in the five unofficial Tests.

Gimblett had his share of illnesses and despair and in 1951, after scoring a century at the Oval in May, he hit such poor form that in 26 innings he could not reach 50. He took a rest in July and returned refreshed and full of vigour and adventure to hit three centuries before the end of the season, including 174 not out against Worcestershire. He averaged nearly 40 in 1952 and 1953 with nine centuries but finished playing the following year.

Sadly, he ended his own life in 1978 when aged sixty-three.

8 DAVID HOOKES

A little item of news at the beginning of June 1975 recorded that "David Hookes, a South Australian, hit six sixes off an over from Bexley's Geoff Burton at Dulwich on 1st June." Hookes was just turned twenty at the time. Seven years later, a rather more prominently displayed article reported that David Hookes, the South Australian captain and Test batsman, had scored the fastest century ever by an Australian in first-class cricket. It had taken him 43 minutes and in terms of balls — 34 — is regarded as the quickest ever anywhere.

Until Hookes got going, only four centuries had been scored in under an hour in Australia. Two were by Australians, Victor Trumper and Algie Gehrs, one by an Englishman, Jack Crawford — all before the First World War — and the fourth by Learie Constantine. The majestic Trumper had taken 57 minutes while batting for New South Wales against Victoria in 1905-06 and had hit 18 fours and a six on to the pavilion roof of Sydney Cricket Ground. In one over he hit Herbie Collins for three fours and a three off successive balls as he swept along to a century that was to remain the fastest in the Sheffield Shield until Hookes cut loose 77 years later. Gehrs's time was not accurately recorded but was said to be "inside 50 minutes" as he batted for South Australia against Western Australia in the 1912-13 season long before Western Australia were accepted to the Sheffield Shield. He went on to reach 119 in an hour with 21 fours. Sandwiched between Trumper and Gehrs came the century in 53 minutes from twenty-year-old Crawford who was with the 1907-08 M.C.C. tourists. The South Australian attack had been savaged to the tune of 472 for five by the time Crawford went in to bat, the perfect platform for an all-out assault. After giving an unaccepted chance to the wicketkeeper he took 20 runs off one over from Wright and raced to his 50 in 24 minutes with a huge six. He and Len Braund put on 109 in 34 minutes and Crawford batted another five minutes after reaching his hundred, finishing with 114 in 58 minutes including three sixes and 18 fours. Constantine's hundred, scored in 52 minutes, came in the 1930-31 season when the West Indians were wobbling at 131 for five in reply to Tasmania's 184 in Launceston. He started with 24 runs in six minutes, then slowed down to reach 65 in 25 minutes by lunch. The pace slowed a little more after the interval but Constantine still reached his 100 out of 128 added with George Grant before being out to the next ball. He had hit a six, a five, and ten fours and it still stands today as the fastest century by a West Indian.

Hookes's feat was born, like many outstanding performances in sport, out of annoyance and frustration. He, as South Australia's captain, had become annoyed at a delayed declaration from Graham Yallop, the Victorian captain, which had left about 30 overs in which to score 272 for victory. Hookes, a happy middle-order batsman, promoted himself to opener and followed his first innings 137 with a furious assault on a Victorian attack which was restricted to three bowlers. One of

them, Peter King, opened the attack and after being hit for 38 runs in two overs, was taken off to leave the attack in the hands of Rod McCurdy and Sean Graf. Hookes reached his 50 in 17 minutes and charged along to his century as he dominated the strike to such an extent that when the first wicket fell at 122 Hookes's opening partner Rick Darling — who is no slouch himself — had scored 11! Hookes finished with 107 in 55 minutes including 18 fours and three sixes, one of them a colossal, furious hit on to the roof of the members' grandstand. All his sixes went in the same direction but his innings was noteworthy, too, for some fine driving on both sides of the wicket. Only two boundaries and two singles came from shots behind the wicket. McCurdy was hit for 88 runs in 12 overs, Graf for 67 in ten before the chase was called off with six overs to go and South Australia 206 for seven.

"Yallop left us a ridiculous target." said Hookes. "I can't see the point of declaring unless you leave a target. We could have just played out the overs but that's not my way of playing. So I said to Rick Darling: 'Let's give it a go.' We couldn't lose and I wanted to show the guy. It wasn't a slogging innings. With every shot the ball went where I intended, through the gaps and from the middle of the bat. It was a controlled innings, perhaps my best, and included the biggest hit I've ever made — on to the roof of the stand."

That was a wonderful summer for Hookes. Only two days earlier, in the first innings, he had scored 137, recording a century between lunch and tea and becoming the first batsman to make twin centuries in a Sheffield Shield match three times. He had started the season with two half-centuries at Brisbane and followed his blazing century by taking a 50 off the English tourists. The runs kept coming with 65 in 52 balls off the New South Wales attack and before Christmas had arrived he had hit his third century in a session, scoring 146 in a temperature of 100 degrees against Western Australia. His highest score came towards the end of the season, and not surprisingly it was against Victoria and Graham Yallop, as he scored 193 in around three hours in a seven-wicket win. He finished the season with 1,424 runs — more than anybody else — and an average of 64.72.

Hookes had come a long way from that day in London when he had hit six sixes in an over. "One of them was a catch, dropped over the line," he said. "All credit to the bowler who bowled a bit quicker but didn't try to pitch a couple of feet wide." He had not then played first-class cricket. That came a few months later when he returned home and went into the South Australian team in 1975-76 to score 55 and 44 in separate matches against the touring West Indies. He broke into first-class cricket with relative quiet, but really cut loose the following Australian summer with four centuries in successive innings, five centuries in six with an average scoring rate over 50 runs an hour. Not surprisingly he headed the Sheffield Shield averages with 78.80. His first century came in February, 1977, when he was twenty-one, helping South Australia recover from 100 for five and in the course of his 163 hitting Victorian leg spinner Colin Thwaites for 666.6.41 in one over. He got nine in the second innings but followed with 185 in 191 minutes and 105 in 101 minutes in a tied match with Queensland at Adelaide. South Australia's next match was also at Adelaide and Hookes scored 135 and 156 against New South Wales. His Test debut soon followed, in the Centenary Test against England in Melbourne that March when he scored a brisk 56 which included five boundaries in an over off Tony Greig.

He had done more than enough to get a place in Australia's team for England where his fourth first-class innings, against Somerset at Bath, brought him 85 not out in 90 minutes on the Thursday. He reached his century on Friday when he finished with 108 including four sixes and 15 fours. He averaged 31 in the five Tests — an unhappy tour for the Australians, most of whom were concentrating on the coming move to join Kerry Packer and World Series cricket — and saved his best innings for the last Test with 85 runs, all sweetly scored with the knocked-about bat which had brought him his five centuries at home a few months earlier.

In common with most other outstanding Australian cricketers Hookes played for Kerry Packer in the next two years and although he did pretty well, averaging 40 in twelve Super Tests, he was soon to fade out of the Test scene through injury and poor form. He was a natural first choice when Packer withdrew and establishment cricket regained control and went with Australia to Pakistan in 1980 where he did not score in either innings in the first Test in Karachi and was not seen again at Test level for two and a half years. At one stage, in 1981, he was almost forgotten, even in South Australia, and came into one game against Western Australia at the last minute — and as the third seam bowler. Yet the following year he was captain of South Australia and led them to success in the Sheffield Shield. He recaptured much of his old form and in one innings against Queensland he hit Dennis Lillie — apart from the slightly different spelling this Lillie was a slightly different bowler, a leg spinner — for four sixes in an over. "I hit the first four balls for six and blocked the fifth, on middle and leg," Hookes said. "I will always swing at a ball on the line of the leg stump but I blocked this one and I'll always regret it. I should have gone through with it and if that had been six I would have gone after the last ball. To have done that at first-class level — I would have liked that. But I was captain then and playing more responsibly. If I hadn't been captain I would have gone for it."

Hookes's return was highlighted with his record century the following season and he fittingly finished off the 1982-83 summer by going to Sri Lanka and scoring a century in Australia's first Test there. He scored 143 not out, hit two sixes and 17 fours, and scored a century between lunch and tea.

⑨ ALBERT H. HORNBY

This is not the famous Hornby of Lancashire, "O my Hornby and my Barlow long ago". That was his father, Albert Neilson Hornby, "Monkey" Hornby, captain of Lancashire and England, friend and contemporary of W.G. Grace, president of Lancashire through twenty-three years. Albert Henry was born in the middle of the 1877 season and first appeared for Lancashire in 1899, a marvellous bit of timing because it marked the end of his father's career and kept a Hornby in the Lancashire team for nearly fifty years. They played together once, at Leicester in July when Albert Henry opened the innings and scored 18 and was outshone by his father, then aged fifty-two, who went in at number nine and hit 53 in an hour.

No doubt Albert Henry had the same problems that all sons have who follow famous fathers. Comparisons are inevitable and it must have been difficult for the young Hornby to actually replace his respected and esteemed father in the side. Indeed, there were many who did not think he would make it as a first-class cricketer. Yet in the end, although he did not follow his father into the England team, he just about matched everything he had done for Lancashire. He played 283 times for the county, only nine times fewer than father, scored eight centuries to dad's ten, but when he finished in 1914 he actually had a better average, by two-tenths of a run!

The Hornbys were keen sportsmen and Albert Henry also had a great love of hunting. He was an enthusiastic cricketer, a magnificent captain who inspired players, an unselfish, charming man, a gentleman who made his mark through his own deeds. Like his father he went to Harrow. He was also at Cambridge University at the same time as Gilbert Jessop who recalled "Young Monkey" being allowed to play for M.C.C. against the University for the purpose of a trial.

Hornby, then twenty-one, opened the batting with Charles Wright, thirty-six years old, a Nottinghamshire county player and himself formerly of Cambridge University. Wright opened with a nice four and then in the next over came "the horrible happening". Hornby must have inherited some of his father's recklessness at running between the wickets and after playing a ball softly into the covers he committed Wright to galloping for a hopeless single. Wright finished up some five yards short of the crease and although the bails were off and the umpire was about to raise his finger Wright sprawled along shouting: "I'm in, I'm in, I'm in." His optimism was not justified and as he mournfully retreated he shouted at Hornby: "You wretched young thingumajig. Do you think I'm a blessed archangel with wings?" Strangely enough, a similar misunderstanding occurred in the second innings, only this time it was Hornby who was out.

After making his debut for Lancashire in 1899, he missed the next three seasons and it was 1904 before he scored his first century, in the match against Somerset at Old Trafford. After Somerset had been dismissed for 166, Archie MacLaren, who scored 151, and Johnny Tyldesley, 103, put on 187 runs in 105 minutes for the second

wicket. Hornby, batting at number seven, scored 114 in brilliant style and with Willis Cuttell, opening bowler and number eight batsman, contributing 101, Lancashire, for the only time in their history, had four century-makers in the one innings. Lancashire's eventual victory by an innings and 136 runs would have been even more convincing if MacLaren had not made some light-hearted experiments with his bowling on the third morning, including the introduction of Hornby, hit for 20 runs in three overs.

Lancashire, who were champions in 1904, were in irrepressible form at this stage of the season and three weeks later won for the seventh time in eight matches when they beat Essex by ten wickets. Their total of 411, scored in just over four and a half hours, included four innings of 86 or more, and seven of ten or under. Reg Spooner and Johnny Tyldesley put on 166 in 100 minutes for the second wicket after the early dismissal of MacLaren; Jack Sharp, the only century-maker with an unbeaten 107, and Hornby, 89 in 105 minutes, added 177, also in 105 minutes, for the seventh wicket. But Hornby could also defend when necessary as he showed against Yorkshire at Headingley when he scored 59 in 220 minutes.

It was the following year that Hornby played his most spectacular innings, a remarkable century in 43 minutes, a time that had been beaten only once before, by Jessop, of course. It was an achievement that was not recorded for many years and was not even part of his obituary in 1952. Yet that century was still the fourth fastest ever up to the start of the 1977 season, having been beaten only by Jessop twice — he had done it again two years after Hornby's effort — and by Percy Fender. Again, Lancashire were playing Somerset, who have had good cause to curse Lancashire a time or two in their history, not least for the record total of 801 with MacLaren's 424 against them at Taunton in 1895, and the victory at Bath in 1953 when poor old Bertie Buse's benefit match was over and done with in a day. Dear Bertie. He was still shaking his head about it when I saw him in Bath twenty-five years later.

Hornby's game started on Monday, 3rd July, 1905, in fine, but rather cold weather. It was Manchester, of course. Somerset had a bad time that season, winning one match out of eighteen, and finishing fifteenth out of sixteen in the county championship. Lancashire, on the other hand, finished runners-up to Yorkshire despite losing MacLaren, Spooner, Tyldesley and Walter Brearley to the Test matches against Australia. MacLaren and Tyldesley were at Leeds for the third Test when Lancashire played Somerset, but Brearley, who was not brought into the English team until the last two Tests, was at Old Trafford. And what havoc he created with nine wickets in the first innings, eight in the second, a return of 17 wickets for 137 runs and a match total that has been matched by only one other Lancashire player in a county game, Harry Dean. Somerset won the toss and batted. In an hour and a quarter they were all out. Walter Brearley and Jimmy Heap bowled unchanged, one taking nine wickets for 47, the other one wicket for 15. Some Somerset players attributed their failure to what they called the fiery state of the wicket. They even suggested Lancashire might find it difficult to equal their score of 65. By the end of that first day Lancashire had reached 424 for eight.

At ten minutes to six Hornby took guard. He had gone out to bat at the fall of the seventh wicket with Lancashire 285 and only William Findlay, later to become secretary of the M.C.C., and the triumphant Brearley to come. In the remaining 40 minutes of Monday, Hornby hit 93 runs out of 139, six of his shots clearing the ring, hits worth sixes today but only fours then. It was an astonishing display. Hornby and Heap added 40 in 12 minutes and in the last 25 minutes Hornby and Findlay scored 99 runs in an unbeaten ninth-wicket partnership. The innings continued on the Tuesday, of course. Hornby, who gave one chance at 14, took three minutes to get the seven runs needed for his century. He went on to reach 106 in 45 minutes and when he was out he and Findlay had put on 113 runs in half an hour. Hornby had hit 18 fours. His six hits "over the ring," if they had counted sixes, would have given him 12 more runs. He would have had 12 fours and six sixes, a total of 118, and would have reached his century on the Monday evening, probably in something like 37 or 38 minutes. And his partnership with Findlay? At least 125 in half an hour! Hornby's 43-minute century stood second only to Jessop's 40 minutes for Gloucestershire against Yorkshire at Harrogate in 1897. Jessop again beat it in 1907 with a 42-minute hundred for the Gentlemen of the South against the Players of the South at Hastings, but the only century to beat it in the next 70 years was Fender's record 35 minutes in 1920. It stood as Lancashire's fastest for seventy-eight years until Steve O'Shaughnessy took advantage of some obliging Leicestershire bowling in 1983 to equal Fender's record of 35 minutes.

Hornby got a second century just over a week later. Another brilliant display of hitting, this time against Essex at Leyton, brought him 111 not out in just over two hours and shored up the Lancashire innings. He showed the Leyton crowd that as well as hitting he could also defend by holding out in the second innings to secure a draw. *Wisden* referred to him incurring the jeers of a somewhat ill-mannered crowd at Leyton by playing a strictly defensive game. But then added: "Both as batsman and field he is now fully worthy of the famous name he bears." He was, indeed, a superb fieldsman. Neville Cardus recalled a catch, in 1906, near the offside boundary at Old Trafford when Hornby "ran yards like a hare to hold a really magnificent hit by E.W. Dillon of Kent". Dicky Barlow, by this time an umpire, put Hornby alongside such players as Jessop as "almost perfect examples of fielding . . . well worthy of imitation and of travelling miles to see".

Hornby usually batted at number seven or eight but when circumstances demanded he would open. In 1907 he and MacLaren dominated a match against Derbyshire with an opening stand of 182 in 105 minutes at Chesterfield. Hornby went on to score 125 in 135 minutes, his only century of that season. He was not a man for building big scores or for records and it is likely that the innings that gave him most satisfaction was one that could pass by unnoticed in the scorebooks — 55 not out against Nottinghamshire at Old Trafford in 1910. Joe Hardstaff and Jack Sharp scored centuries and Hornby's 50 was only one of six more in the game, including one from Ted Alletson who was to strike fame at Hove the following year. Hornby, by now captain of the side, twisted his knee on the opening day and did not bat when Lancashire replied to Nottinghamshire's total of 376 with 162. They were 214 behind but Nottinghamshire did not enforce the follow-on but chose to bat again and set Lancashire a victory target of 400 in 315 minutes, an average scoring rate of 76 an hour. Up to then, the highest score that had been achieved in a fourth innings for victory was 350. It was a tall order.

There had, incidentally, been a curious incident on the opening day, when play was temporarily stopped by Hornby who despatched Ernest Tyldesley, then aged twenty-one and the junior professional, with a message to someone sitting on the stand in front of the Press Box. Tyldesley vaulted the railings and crawled over the forms until he came to one where Mr A.N. Hornby was sitting. It was thought he was carrying some message of urgent importance to the Lancashire president from his son. But Tyldesley stopped before he reached the president, whispered a few words to another gentleman sitting near and returned. The gentleman instantly buttoned up his coat and tried his best not to look embarrassed. It turned out that he was wearing a rather nice holland waistcoat decorated with plain bronze buttons which were flashing in the eyes of one of the slip fielders, though they were well over 100 yards apart. "What could be more vexatious than to go to a cricket match sporting a resplendent, smart waistcoat and then be publicly forbidden to display it?" posed a newspaper the following day.

The last day of the game was a Saturday and about 7,000 spectators were present to see Nottinghamshire lose their last eight wickets for 47 runs and leave Lancashire their daunting target. The innings started at half past twelve and at lunch, after losing openers Alf Hartley and Bill Tyldesley for 50 runs, Lancashire were 100 for two. Sharp went on to score a magnificent hundred but in the same over was hit on the foot by the ball and dropped to the ground. Any feeling for Sharp must have been blurred by the sight of victory for while he was lying down and recovering, out went the waiters with refreshments to save the tea interval. Sharp and Johnny Tyldesley added 191 in 145 minutes; Ralph Whitehead, whose opening shots were six fours and two sixes, put on 80 in 40 minutes with Ernest Tyldesley. When Tyldesley was out, Lancashire were 327 for five; 73 were needed, and who should hobble down the steps but Hornby. He limped and was heavily padded, was clearly in pain, and the move was generally regarded as a blunder. Yet Hornby won the day after Lancashire had slipped to 364 for eight, leaving 36 needed in 40 minutes. When Harry Dean was eighth out, Lol Cook went in smiling and blocked out the rest of the over. He stayed over 35 minutes for three while Hornby, with 55 not out in an hour, carried Lancashire home by two wickets with two minutes to spare. He cut the ball through the slips for the winning hit and the crowd surged on to the field, seizing Hornby and carrying him to the pavilion rails. The match finished at 6.20 on the Saturday "amid the most intense excitement". The crowd lingered on for some time, shouting, singing, flinging hats in the air. They danced and whistled and wrung each others hands and whenever a player appeared on the balcony the renewal of applause was deafening. It was a match and an innings long to be remembered by those lucky enough to see it. There never was such a day before.

Hornby's best years came in his thirties and it was in 1912 that he got his highest score, 129 against Surrey at the Oval when Reg Spooner and Harry Dean were omitted from the Lancashire team so they could be fresh for the Test starting five days later. That season he and Jack Sharp shared in a partnership of 245 in two and a half hours against Leicestershire at Old Trafford, still a seventh-wicket record for the club today. He cleared 1,000 runs only once, in 1913 when he was thirty-six, and scored his last centuries that year, both against Gloucestershire, both innings of unusual restraint. At Bristol, where he scored 109 in 195 minutes, he wore a heavy sweater and thick scarf as he tried to ward off a very severe cold.

He did not play again after the First World War and created a sensation at the end of the 1918 season by condemning in public the Lancashire committee's policy of economy, forcing a special meeting of members to consider the matter. Unlike his father he never became president of the club and died at North Kilworth, near Rugby, in 1952 when aged seventy-seven.

10 KENNETH HUTCHINGS

Just south of the village of Thiepval, about five miles north-east of Albert in Northern France, stands the Thiepval Memorial, which commemorates by name more than 70,000 British soldiers who lost their lives at the Battle of the Somme and have no known grave. Among them is Lieutenant Kenneth Lotherington Hutchings, 4th Battalion The King's Liverpool Regiment, attached to the 12th Battalion, who died on 3rd September, 1916, and was among those the Army Graves Service were unable to trace after the war. He was thirty-three and had finished with first-class cricket after playing seven times for England and being a member of Kent's championship-winning team. He was the most illustrious cricketer killed in the Great War, a dashing, daring batsman who was greatly mourned.

Hutchings was a true man of Kent. He was born near Tunbridge Wells, in 1882, he went to Tonbridge School, and he could hit the ball over the lime tree at Canterbury. He played for Tonbridge for five years; the last three were dazzling with centuries against such worthies as the Band of Brothers and the Free Foresters and with a double century in there as well. He was nineteen when he first played for Kent in 1902 but, apart from the following summer when he scored a century at Taunton, he played and produced little until 1906 when he exploded over cricket like a thousand rockets on Bonfire night. He was the most brilliant batsman in the country that summer and as he made his runs quickly and in the most attractive way, the crowds flocked to see him. He did not come into the side until 18th June, yet scored 1,454 runs with four centuries. His batting was a relevant part of Kent's championship success which included eleven wins in a row. It was a revelation, too, and if there had been somebody for England to play against that summer he would no doubt have played Test cricket as well. As it was, he had to wait until the next tour, the 1907 trip to Australia.

Rather like Ted Alletson, who is best remembered for one innings, Hutchings is mostly recalled for one season, 1906. He did top 1,000 runs again, in 1909 and 1910, but did not again touch the particular brilliance of 1906 when he averaged 60 runs an innings. After a miserable time in 1912 he gave the game up, fed up of his form, out of cricket at the age of twenty-nine.

Anyway, to 1906, a year of achievment, starting fittingly enough in the town he knew so well, Tonbridge. In the second match there he swashbuckled his way to 125 in 135 minutes against Middlesex, followed by a more sober 97 not out in the second innings to save the game. Middlesex looked to have won the game when they had Kent 134 for six with 105 minutes to go but Hutchings found enough support from his partners, including Fred Huish, the last man, who was in such discomfort from an attack of lumbago that he needed a runner to help him survive the last 12 minutes. "The stirring finish aroused great enthusiasm among the company who assembled in front of the pavilion and called for Mr Hutchings," reported *The Times*,

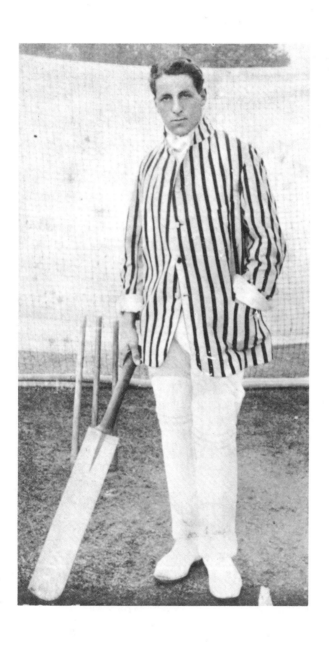

who also remarked on his unselfish attitude in sacrificing many runs so he could keep the bowling.

Kent then travelled to Sheffield where Hutchings played a gradely innings of 131 against the county champions, Yorkshire. He was dropped twice by Wilfred Rhodes, at eight off a hard return, and at 11, an easy chance to mid-off. He was a powerful driver and after surviving another difficult chance to Schofield Haigh when he was 33, he settled down to some fine hitting to make an attack, that also included George Hirst, look unusually weak. His third hundred was against another formidable foe in Lancashire and brought him the highest score in his eleven-year career, 176 in three hours at Canterbury. Lancashire had played at Manchester the previous day. They travelled to London that night, then to Canterbury in the morning, arriving so late the game could not start until 12.30. Hutchings made up for any lost time in front of a crowd of well over 13,000 people, a record for the ground, and helped Kent win both their Canterbury-week matches by an innings and over 100 runs. During the week collections totalling £136 were taken on the ground for the Kent professionals. The committee decided to give Fielder £30, Huish, Woolley and Blythe £15, Humphreys, Hearne, Fairservice and Seymour £12, Hardinge and Hubble £6 10s. Hutchings rounded off the season in grand style with 124 against Hampshire at Bournemouth when he reached his century in an hour.

He also scored four centuries the following season, in 1907, with another at Tonbridge, two gems at Worcester on his return to the side after injury, and a repeat century against Lancashire at Canterbury. Off he went to Australia with A.O. Jones's team where his only Test innings of any consequence was 126 at Melbourne during which he hit 71 out of 90 in an hour with Len Braund. There were centuries for Kent at Gravesend and Derby in 1908, but the high spot was 120 in 100 minutes for the Gentlemen at Scarborough (what a friendly, tempting ground Scarborough is for the hitter). There were three more in 1909 when Kent were champions again, including his fastest, scored in 50 minutes against Gloucestershire at Catford. But 1910 proved his last impressive season with nearly 1,500 runs, an average of 43, and five centuries, another of them at Scarborough. The other four were all for Kent and all had been scored by the first week in July with 104 in under 100 minutes at Northampton, 122 in two hours at Derby, 109 in 100 minutes against Leicestershire at his favourite ground of Tonbridge, and 144 at Hastings with a stand of 233 in 140 minutes with Frank Woolley. Hutchings was a fierce driver and his only chance at Hastings was to the Sussex mid-off who could not hold a ball that hurtled on to the boundary.

Hutchings also hit 57 in half an hour at Cheltenham when Kent rattled along to 607 for six declared in five hours on the opening day against Gloucestershire. In the half hour Hutchings was in, he and Humphreys put on 93 runs for the third wicket. But once again Hutchings had timed badly. There were no home Tests, no winter tour, and he had to take his form out on the Rest of England with top score in both innings for Kent in the four-day game in the middle of September. Only ten days earlier he had scored 114 in an hour and a half for M.C.C. against Yorkshire at Scarborough.

"Never since his memorable season in 1906 has he been so entirely himself," enthused *Wisden*. "While retaining all his brilliancy he exercised greater control than in 1909. Trusting more to his splendid driving he kept the pull in its proper place as an invaluable servant and did not allow it to become his master. ... with all his fine qualities he is not an England batsman of quite the same class as Jackson and MacLaren in their day. He has not their strength of defence and therefore inspires less confidence. Still, taking him just as he is, he stands out today one of the most commanding figures in the cricket field.''

Hutchings was then only twenty-seven. Two years later he was finished with the game. He had not reached 1,000 runs in 1911 and averaged under 30, and when he could muster only 178 in ten innings in 1912 he said farewell. How nice that his only century in 1911 had been one to remember, a typically powerful display that brought him 103 not out in 100 minutes after Kent had been 50 for three. War broke out in 1914 and in 1916, still three months short of his thirty-fourth birthday, he fell in battle.

11 KAPIL DEV

Tunbridge Wells in June is as pretty a spot as you could wish for. The blossom has given way to the rhododendrons and Kent, the fairest and most English of counties, is a picture. The oast houses disinguish it from any other county, the village greens and ponds emphasise the beauty and the peace. Big sport does not intrude; Tunbridge Wells has just a couple of Kent county games a year with neighbouring Sussex making a popular fixture.

In 1983 Essex, Kent's neighbours from across the Thames, played the first game of the festival week, a miserable match that was drawn. At least the peace and quiet were not disturbed. Sussex followed hard on the heels of Essex and were twice cheaply bowled out as Kent convincingly beat them. The game finished on the Friday, a pleasant day, and as Sussex prepared to go back across the border two more teams, from rather a few more miles away, arrived in town for an unlikely clash. It was the year of the World Cup and Tunbridge Wells had been blessed with a game between India and Zimbabwe, not the sort of encounter designed to set the town alight. There was no rush on the deck-chairs.

Zimbabwe had caught Australia cold in the opening round of games and pulled off a shock win but had then lost the next three matches. India had won two and lost two, the same as Australia, and could not afford to slip up. But slip they did, to 17 for five. Then came the most remarkable innings ever played in limited-over cricket, an innings of 175 not out from Kapil Dev, the Indian captain, which included six sixes and 16 fours. With the help first of Roger Binny and then Madan Lal, Kapil Dev got India to 140 for eight before really cutting loose in an unbroken ninth-wicket stand of 126 in 16 overs with his wicketkeeper, Syed Kirmani, whose contribution, 26, was modest but vital. India won — but not by much — and went on to beat the holders, West Indies, in the final at Lord's.

Sunil Gavaskar, who had been dismissed for a "duck," described Kapil Dev's innings as "unbelievable stuff". "His first 70 to 80 runs were really calculated in the sense that he pushed and nudged the ball and only hit those which he was convinced should be hit," wrote Gavaskar in his book, *Idols*. "After that he had enough confidence and when he saw he had partners who would stay with him he launched a counter-attack the like of which one had never seen before. He was hitting the bowlers as if at will and we were applauding each and every shot. Our hands became weary but each shot was absolutely thrilling."

Kapil Dev was just over twenty-one when he became the youngest player ever to have completed the double of 100 wickets and 1,000 runs in Test cricket and vied with Ian Botham, Richard Hadlee and Imran Khan for the title of the world's top all-rounder. Botham was the most genuine all-rounder while Kapil Dev, although capable of explosive innings, was a better bowler than a batsman. He had made his first-class debut in November 1975 when still two months short of his seventeenth

birthday, taking six for 39 for Haryana against Punjab, neighbouring states in the foothills of Northern India. Kapil Dev, himself a Punjabi, made much more impact as a bowler than a batsman in his early years with several outstanding returns while still in his teens, including eight for 36 against Jammu and Kashmir — that was a match return — seven for 20 against Bengal and eight for 38 against Services. It did not escape attention, either, when he played in a University match and scored 300 in a day.

Kapil Dev's Test debut was in Pakistan in 1978 when India lost the series but gained some consolation in "the emergence of nineteen-year-old Kapil Dev as an all-rounder of considerable worth. A clean and hefty striker of the ball he made some useful runs in the lower order." His most impressive innings was his 59 in 48 balls which included two sixes and eight fours in the third Test at Karachi.

A visit by the West Indians followed the trip to Pakistan and Kapil Dev strengthened his position in the side with some fine all-round displays, including his first century. Batting at number nine in the third Test at Calcutta he scored 60 out of 80 off 62 balls to help India from 220 for seven to 300. By the fifth Test, at Delhi, he was batting at six and took advantage of a strong Indian position at 353 for four to hit 126 not out. Kapil went to England in 1979, was the leading wicket-taker in Tests but throughout the tour played only one innings of real merit, 102 in 74 minutes — the fastest century of the season until the penultimate day — with a six and 19 fours. And he reached it in his first match, against Northamptonshire, the county he was to join two years later.

A benefit match in Bangalore produced a spectacular century in 33 minutes with ten sixes and eight fours but there was little to rave about on his next tour, to Australia and New Zealand, although he did produce one quite special shot during a one-day match at Brisbane where he hit New Zealand's Jeremy Coney over the Clem Jones stand and into Stanley Street. It was an enormous hit and forced Coney to wave his handkerchief in surrender. Kapil Dev's best innings in many a Test came against England at Kanpur in 1982 when, with nothing at stake, he hit a century off 83 balls in the final afternoon of the series, lovely entertainment that included two sixes and 16 fours. The entire morning session had been lost because of mist, before Bob Willis took three wickets in 18 balls to make India 207 for six. Kapil Dev scored 116 out of a 169 stand with Yashpal Sharma before being dismissed in David Gower's only over of the innings. Kapil Dev was now ready for his second tour of England, in 1982, better equipped and eager to take on Ian Botham for the "title" of the world's best all-rounder.

Many of Kapil Dev's finest and most exhilarating displays as a batsman have happened in England. In only his third game for his first county, Northamptonshire, in 1981, he hit 79 against Worcestershire, taking advantage of the small Stourbridge ground to thump six sixes and six fours. But the best came in 1982, spurred possibly by the head-on clash with Botham which produced some entertaining encounters through the summer. He scored a thoughtful 41 in the first innings of the opening Test — only he and Sunil Gavaskar got into double figures — but gave Botham a first-hand glimpse of his power by hitting 89 out of the 117 added for the last four wickets in the second innings. He hit Botham into the grandstand to reach 50 and hit two sixes off Phil Edmonds and was on course for the fastest Test century of all time when he was out after batting 77 minutes and facing 55 balls. England needed 65 to win but Kapil Dev showed his bowling talents, too, by removing Geoff Cook, Chris Tavaré and Bob Taylor in eight balls before the job was done.

In the second Test at Old Trafford he hammered 65 but saved the best till last, the final Test at the Oval, his final innings of the tour which saved India from following-on after England's 594. He went in at 248 for five and in the next 102 minutes hit a sparkling 97 which included two sixes — one into the Vauxhall Stand off Botham — and 14 fours.

When playing for Northamptonshire later that season, he rattled off a couple of whirlwind centuries in the half-dozen matches he played. He went to Eastbourne on 11th August and hit 103 on a pitch that was so bad it was reported as being unsatisfactory for first-class cricket. He hit three enormous sixes and 11 fours as Northamptonshire walked off with an innings win over Sussex. Northamptonshire's next match was against Derbyshire, over a weekend. On the Saturday, the opening day of the championship match, he scored 65 not out with four sixes and four fours. On the Sunday, in the John Player League he hit 75 off 48 balls with four sixes and eight fours. On the Tuesday, he tore the same attack apart again with an unbeaten 100 in 98 minutes in which time he and Robin Boyd-Moss added 182 for the fifth wicket.

India have needed Kapil's bowling more than his batting and when they went to Pakistan a few weeks later he was again their best bowler by a mile but scored only one half century in eight innings, hitting 73 of India's 169 in the second Test at Karachi. The Indians moved on to West Indies with Kapil Dev installed as captain at twenty-four years of age. Again he topped the bowling and his batting, greatly improved, included an unbeaten, explosive 100, helped by the West Indies taking the extra half hour at the end of the game which was no use to them, and which included three sixes and 13 fours.

He returned to Northamptonshire in 1983 after his great triumphs in the World Cup but played only seven games in the championship. His bowling was disappointing but he took the chance to bombard a new, unsuspecting ground with 120 at Weston-super-Mare. He got his runs out of 172 and hit two sixes and 16 fours in a stay of 38 overs. Kapil Dev moved on to Worcestershire in 1984 and scored his first century for them on the opening day of the 1985 championship season. He went in at 96 for five against Middlesex at Lord's, and walked out 75 minutes later at 223 for six after scoring 100.

By this time he had lost the captaincy of India to Sunil Gavaskar and had even had the ignominy of being dropped by his country during England's tour of 1984-85 for reckless batting during the Delhi Test. Kapil Dev had been heard to say to Gavaskar on the final afternoon of the match: "This match is safe. I'm going out to have a slog." Gavaskar disagreed and Kapil Dev then apparently said casually: "Slogging is my normal game." He was later reinstated in the side.

12 COLIN MILBURN

Dear old Colin Milburn was one of county cricket's great treasures. He loved to play, especially bat, and treated the game as great fun. He liked to thump the ball, was thrilled to see it flying about the ground and displayed the enthusiasm of a boy. Consequently he was a pleasure to watch, one of the game's real joys. Cricket suffered a great loss when he was involved in a car accident and lost an eye but he did at least leave behind more memories than most players who stay twice as long in the game.

Milburn himself, when choosing a memorable match for the *Wisden Cricket Monthly*, went for his second Test match, played at Lord's against the West Indies in 1966. He scored a century, one of two Test hundreds he was to make in his nine games for England. Milburn had made his debut at Old Trafford in the first Test and, after running himself out for a "duck" in the first innings, he made 94 in the follow-on before trying a big hit off Lance Gibbs and being bowled. The next Test was at Lord's and, after again going cheaply in the first innings, he opened the innings a second time after a Gary Sobers declaration had left England four hours in which to score 284 for victory. An hour was lost to rain and then England lost four good wickets, Geoff Boycott, Colin Cowdrey, Ken Barrington and Jim Parks for 67. In came Tom Graveney with a bruised hand and two hours to go. The two batsmen had a chat and decided Milburn should play his natural game while Graveney held up the other end. Milburn's natural game brought him 126 not out and the fifth-wicket partnership of 130, of which Graveney's contribution was only 30 not out, is still a record. Milburn, who never weighed less than 16½ stones, recalled that several Englishmen ran from the Tavern bar and tried to pick him up. He proved too heavy for them, much too heavy. "They failed miserably," said Milburn. Graveney recalled Wes Hall letting a bouncer go and shouting "catch it" as Milburn hit it. As far as Graveney could recall the ball landed about fifteen rows up in the Mound Stand.

Most people would probably have gone for another Lord's innings, played against Australia two years later, which so delighted John Arlott he was moved to write: "Milburn went on to play a heart-warming innings of simple power which argued convincingly that he should never again, in his active cricket life, be left out of an England team. He may not often be able to bat so magnificently; no one else in sight could do so at all." Cowdrey won the toss and England batted first. John Edrich was out at ten and after a heavy shower had held up play, Geoff Boycott and Milburn — batting at number three — played courageously to take England to 53 for one before another storm, this time of hail, flooded the pitch and held up the innings until the following morning. Milburn scored ten runs off Graham McKenzie's opening over, he hit Bob Cowper into the grandstand and he and Boycott scored at a run-a-minute until Milburn, after scoring a marvellous 83, hooked a long hop from Johnny Gleeson into Doug Walters's hands just inside the boundary.

Milburn's most explosive innings, however, came outside England when he went to play in Perth for Western Australia in 1968, a few months after his fine innings against Australia and a few months before joining England in Pakistan when Colin Cowdrey's fitness was in doubt. Western Australia had made a disappointing start to the season, losing by nine wickets to Victoria and only avoiding an innings defeat by two fighting half-centuries from Milburn. They hit back to crush New South Wales in the next match with Milburn hitting a blistering 93 in the innings win, including 15 fours and a six. Milburn's really outstanding innings came in the next match, a hard-hitting double hundred against Queensland at Brisbane that kept Western Australia at the head of the Sheffield Shield table. Milburn's innings was one of the best in Australia since the days of Bradman and took Western Australia to 615 for five, making their total of runs in two games 1,209 for the loss of 11 wickets. He roasted the Queensland attack with 243 runs — beating by seven the record held by a Western Australia batsman, Bobby Simpson — in 228 balls. He scored 176 of his runs in boundaries with 38 fours and four sixes and created a record for runs in a session by hitting 181 in the two hours between lunch and tea. He so overshadowed his partner, Derek Chadwick, in a stand of 328, that he had already passed 150 when Chadwick reached his half century. "Everything was right that day," recalled Milburn. "Every shot went between fielders and it was as if I just couldn't do anything wrong." One shot he particularly remembered was against Indian Test player Rusi Surti. "I went out to him and slipped and I was on my knees when I cut the ball for four. I was shattered after the game and Rodney Marsh and I nearly drank Brisbane dry that night."

Milburn was born in the mining village of Burnopfield in County Durham. There was always a suggestion of mining stock in his forbears. He was chunky with massive forearms and it could well have been a pick or a hammer he held in his hands instead of a bat. His father was a professional in the Tyneside Senior League so there was no lack of encouragement for a youngster who was keen on the game. By the age of thirteen Colin Milburn was in the Burnopfield first team and when he moved into the Durham Senior League to play with Chester-le-Street he made a remarkable debut with two centuries in three weeks with his forceful batting. He was only seventeen when the Indians toured England in 1959 and Milburn played against them for Durham, making an immediate impression with an innings of 101. He joined Northamptonshire after trials with Warwickshire, scored his first century against Cambridge University with some fierce hitting and during an M.C.C. tour of East Africa he enjoyed himself with five consecutive sixes off a leg-break bowler before being caught in the deep off the last ball of the over. Milburn had established himself as Northamptonshire's opening batsman by 1964 and two years later hit four sixes and 22 fours in an innings of 203 against Essex, hit three centuries before lunch including one in 82 minutes against Nottinghamshire at Trent Bridge, and also hit 126 against the West Indies in the Lord's Test.

Milburn's career was just gathering force. The century against Australia in 1968 was quickly followed by his 243 for Western Australia and the flight to Pakistan to score 139 for England in the riot-ruined Karachi Test of May 1969. He was looking forward to the visit of West Indies and New Zealand that summer when he was injured in a car crash in May and lost his left eye. There was something poignant in the presentation to Milburn some months later of the Lawrence Trophy ... for the fastest hundred for England during 1969, the one that was destined to be his last for his country, in Karachi.

Milburn played just one championship match for Northamptonshire that year before the accident, against Leicestershire at Northampton, where he had an innings of 158, which included five sixes, and was played against an attack which included three Test bowlers in Barry Knight, Ray Illingworth and Graham McKenzie.

13 C.K. NAYUDU

When English cricket teams used to go to India, in those far-off days before the Second World War changed everything, the trip was the thing. Fly the flag and all that. I love Colin Cowdrey's description, second-hand, of course, in his book "M.C.C.," of Raj cricket, pure Kipling stuff, when even packing priorities were different. "First came your white dinner jacket, then your black dinner jacket, then your tails. Fourth was your topee, fifth your sports jacket and sixth your rifle. After that, if you had room, you might cram in some cricket equipment. If there was no room it hardly mattered. You could borrow the lot from some nawab or maharajah. You stayed in palaces, not hotels. Test matches were things you played between tiger hunts. It was, without question, the most luxurious cricket ever played in all history." How lovely. Bill Edrich, I remember, recalled his visit there in 1937 with Lord Tennyson's team, staying as guests of the Jam Sahib of Nawangar and taking part in a ceremonial panther-shoot seventy miles away in the hills. The climax came when My Lord shot the bait, a goat, and the panther got clear away. The Maharajah of Patiala also honoured them and arranged a display of the State jewels. The entertainment was royal, the hospitality overwhelming, and it must have been just like that when Arthur Gilligan took an M.C.C. side to India in 1926, a team of nice blend with such good old established pros as Andy Sandham, George Brown, Maurice Tate and Jack Mercer and such presentable amateurs as the Rev. Jack Parsons, Peter Eckersley, and Major R.C. Chichester-Constable.

At that time, India were still six years away from their first Test match and a visit from the Englishmen was something to be savoured. As *The Times* of India reported in its issue of Wednesday, 1st December 1926: "The greatest cricket festival in the city of Bombay commenced on Tuesday morning with a two-day match between the M.C.C. and the Hindus. The nature and extent of the accommodation which has been erected on the Gymkhana Maidan and the widespread interest and enthusiasm which the M.C.C. tour has awakened throughout India and especially in Bombay almost justifies the description 'religious function' — the arresting phrase used by one of Bombay's recently-elected representatives to the Legislative Assembly when referring to the M.C.C.'s visit at a recent meeting of the Municipality. Certainly, the vast crowds which thronged the stands, tents and every possible vantage point both inside and outside the ground, had come prepared to worship at the shrine of English cricket as exemplified in the representative side under Gilligan's captaincy. To the Hindus, as winners of this year's Quadrangular Tournament, had been given the honour of being the M.C.C.'s first opponents in Bombay. If the intention was to regard the match as both a reward for and test of merit it is perhaps unfortunate that it was not fixed for later in the visit when the M.C.C. had had time to accommodate themselves to the peculiar conditions under which cricket is played in Bombay."

However peculiar the conditions they seemed to have no effect on Guy Earle, the

powerful Somerset hitter, who scored eight sixes and 11 fours in an innings of 130 in 90 minutes. Yet this marvellous exhibition was overtaken on the second day when C.K. Nayudu hit 11 sixes and 14 fours and scored his 153 in 115 minutes. What marvellous entertainment for Bombay's "greatest cricket festival".

Cottari Kankaiya Nayudu is one of India's more remarkable cricketers and characters, his love of the game spreading his first-class career over forty-seven years, right up to the age of sixty-eight! His debut came in 1916 when he was twenty-one, playing in the Bombay Quadrangular and announcing himself by hitting the first ball he received for six. Four years later he scored 128 before lunch with one hit for six off a leg spinner being acclaimed as the biggest ever at the Chepauk ground. Cota Ramaswami, who played alongside Nayudu in the M.C.C. match in Bombay in 1926, was at Cambridge in 1920 but kept in touch with events in India through letters from his eldest brother. In a recent letter to me he wrote: "I believe 'C.K.' straightaway captured the imagination and admiration of Madras crowd because, as one would expect, he hit a sixer among many others which sailed out of the Chepauk ground and landed in the adjoining ground near two palungra trees which must have been not less than 140 yards from the cricket pitch."

Nayudu was a long-serving, established cricketer by the time Gilligan and his men arrived in 1926 and the M.C.C.–Hindus match was enough to give him wider recognition and put him in the record books. Centre stage, however, belonged to Earle on that opening day. Not that many people would have known the identity of the batsman who was repeatedly clearing the spectators with his mighty hitting, for the organisers had underestimated the appeal of the game and were short on programmes. The numbers on the scoreboard meant nothing to many spectators and on those that were available, particularly at the start, the names were wrongly numbered.

Every seat was taken an hour before the start and Major Chichester-Constable chose to bat when he won the toss. It must have been quite an experience for the Major whose cricket, apart from one first team match against Essex at Hull in 1919, was confined to captaining Yorkshire's second team. Chandarana played for the Hindus despite suffering from fever and after having the satisfaction of sending down the first over against M.C.C. he also gave them their first boundary, four over-throws when he made a wild return when fielding to Ramji's bowling. M.C.C. were 105 for two at lunch but swiftly slipped to 124 for five, opening the way for the entrance of Earle. The batsman's reputation must have gone ahead of him for the fielders were soon on the boundary edge, watching bemusedly as Earle threw himself into the attack.

Earle's first boundary whistled through the covers like lightning and thwacked into one of the tents circling the ground. His first six soon followed, a big hit to leg off Godambe which resulted in a big search for the ball for a few minutes. An even bigger hit lifted a ball from Pardeshi right over the tents and into Esplanade Road, a gigantic hit. The crowd delighted in Earle's hitting and his 50 arrived with his third six, a mighty shot off Ramaswami which crashed through a window in the Gymkhana pavilion. The fourth and fifth sixes were not far behind, a high hit to the onside followed by a huge high-rise shot that lifted the next ball on to the roof of a tent. The fieldsmen now lined the boundary every time Earle faced the bowling and many big hits brought him only singles. A change of bats gave him another boundary and after an hour's batting he fittingly reached his century with another big drive over the sightscreen. By way of celebration he lifted a ball on to the Gymkhana roof, spurring Tate to emulate him with a six that disturbed the occupants of the ladies tent. When Tate was out, caught in the slips, he had contributed 50 to a stand of 154 in 67 minutes.

It was after tea before Earle was out, bowled by Ramji for 130, which he had scored in an hour and a half with the help of eight sixes and 11 fours. Such hurricane hitting had never been seen on the Gymkhana ground ... how astonishing that the following day an even more exciting exhibition of hitting was to be seen. The M.C.C. went on to score 363 in 282 minutes with the help, in all, of ten sixes. By the close of play the Hindus were 16 for one. At 84 for three the following morning, Nayudu, commonly known throughout the game by his initials, "C.K.," strode forward to start one of the most stupendous innings in Indian history. Bob Wyatt recalled the day nearly sixty years on. "Of course I remember it," he wrote, "if not in detail. C.K. Nayudu was a beautiful driver and I think he obtained most of his runs at Bombay by straight drives, some along the ground and some over the bowler's head." *The Times* of India had no doubts which of the two batsmen had played the finer innings. "It is not depreciating Earle to say that while he delighted the crowd, Nayudu sent them wild with enthusiasm and excitement. The tall, spare, lithe Hindu drove with great certainty, more accuracy and better judgment than were revealed by the equally tall, but burly and muscular European."

Nayudu's first scoring shot was a two. Then followed a six on to the pavilion roof and a four off successive balls from Stuart Boyes, who suffered even more in the next over when he was twice hit for four before being lifted over the Gymkhana, a stroke that had even the umpires clapping with great enthusiasm. Nayudu emulated Earle with a six into the Esplanade Road and his first 33 runs had come from three sixes, three fours, a two and a single. Then came an expensive mistake by Bill Astill who could not sight a skied hit by Nayudu off his own bowling because of the sun and dropped a catch that could have saved M.C.C. at least 120 runs. Nayudu reached his 50 with another mighty six out of the ground but was in danger of running out of partners when lunch was taken with the Hindus 154 for six. That soon became 175 for seven but the support Nayudu needed then arrived in the person of Godambe, who stood firm for two hours while his partner plundered yet more sixes off the M.C.C. attack. The next three all came off Astill as Nayudu reached the first century by an Indian against M.C.C. And it had taken him just 73 minutes. Not unexpectedly, the achievement was greeted with deafening applause, impartially led, no doubt, by the umpires. The Major and several of his players shook Nayudu by the hand but any hopes that the flush of success might go straight to his head and bring about his downfall were soon dismissed. Many more runs were to come, including 22 in one over off Wyatt consisting of two sixes on to the Gymkhana roof, two fours, one of which smashed against the scoreboard, and a two.

The M.C.C. were at their wits end. The Major, who must have been wishing he was back in Hull, had made several bowling changes before Geary persuaded Nayudu to mishit and Boyes, to the great relief of his teammates, took a skied catch at deep mid-off. In 115 minutes Nayudu had hit 11 sixes and 14 fours in an innings of

153, scored out of 187. The Hindus were 273 for eight and in the partnership of 98 Godambe had scored 12 runs. The Hindus went on to a total of 356, seven short of M.C.C. who finished the game at 74 for one in their second innings. Ramaswami, who was at the wicket when Nayudu reached his 50 with a six, wrote to me from his home in Madras shortly before his eight-ninth birthday. "'C.K.' was very cautious to begin with. As soon as he got his eye in he began his usual fireworks and hit boundaries and sixers all round the ground. Needless to say the cricket-loving public of Bombay went to ecstasies and throughout three days and nights they went round the city with loud trumpets and noisy drums and all sorts of musical instruments. Many rich millionaires presented extremely costly presents to 'C.K.'"

Nayudu dominated Indian cricket for two decades yet when his country went to England in 1932 to play their first Test match he was not appointed captain, or even vice-captain. The Maharajah of Porbandar was appointed captain, his second in command was K.S. Gonshyamsinhji of Limbdi. A tour of such importance had to be conducted by men by distinction. Only a prince could lead the side in England. But when it came to the Test match, Nayudu received his due and had the honour of leading All India in the country's first Test, the first real acknowledgement of their cricket strength. England were given a few scares before winning by 158 runs at Lord's at the end of June and Nayudu, despite badly damaging his hand when trying to catch Les Ames in the gully, was top scorer in the Indian first innings with 40. He had a marvellous tour with six centuries, 1,842 runs and an average of 40 in 34 matches, 26 of which were first-class. Two of his centuries came at Lord's, 118 not out against M.C.C. and 101 against Middlesex. He scored 125 in 165 minutes against Lancashire at Liverpool, 130 not out in less than two hours with three sixes and 16 fours against Somerset at Weston-super-Mare, 104 not out in 100 minutes against Indian Gymkhana, and a marvellous 162 in just over three hours with six sixes and 13 fours against Warwickshire at Edgbaston. *Wisden* paid their own tribute to "C.K." by making him one of the Five Cricketers of the Year.

Nayudu was appointed India's captain in the three-match series against D.R. Jardine's team in 1933-34 but the prized honour of leading his country in England again eluded him in 1936. The captain this time was the Maharajah Kumar of Vizianagram, by all accounts a poor cricketer but who still led his team in all three Tests. It was 1951 before England were able to go back to India after the Second World War and when they got to Nagpur in January of 1952 to play Central Zone it was to find the fifty-six year old C.K. Nayudu still good enough and fit enough to play against them and prove the best batsman with innings of 37 and 39. It was just a quarter of a century since his historic innings. What pleasure it must have given him turning out once more against the English tourists.

Two years later, having retired from the Holkar Army, he captained the newly-formed Andrha in the Ranji Trophy and hit 74 in 86 minutes with a six and ten fours. On and on he went, hitting 81 with two sixes off Vinoo Mankad, when he was sixty-two years old. His last first-class match, in November 1963, came when he was sixty-eight and played for a Governor's XI against a Chief Minister's XI in an Indian Defence Fund match at Nagpur. Just four years later, two weeks after his seventy-second birthday, he was dead.

14 TIMOTHY O'BRIEN

Cricket is not a game for the Irish. The all-bash sport of hurling seems to suit their nature much better, or rugby, perhaps. The climate does not help either and the grass is too green. Cricket has never really got a grip in Ireland or Scotland who were too busy warring to bother with a silly game that took all day, sometimes all week. They blame it partly on climate, and more than a bit on it being a game for the wealthy folks of leisure in its formative years. Not surprisingly then, the number of outstanding Scottish or Irish cricketers is quite low. Probably the most illustrious Irish cricketer was a man with the most Irish of names, Timothy O'Brien, born in Dublin in 1861, a baronet in 1895, England's captain in 1896 in the third of his five Tests. When he died two weeks before Christmas in 1948 he was eighty-seven and the oldest Test match cricketer in England.

O'Brien, always a quick, often a hectically fast scorer, learnt his cricket, it must be emphasised, in England and not Ireland. He went to a good Catholic school at Downside in Somerset, but it was the move to St Charles College in London's Notting Hill which allowed him to qualify for Middlesex, the county for which he played from 1881, when he was nineteen years old, to 1898. He did little for Middlesex in his early years. His first three innings brought him 11 runs and he toiled away without much success before deciding to go to Oxford and New Inn Hall when he was twenty-two to see if he could get some runs there.

The move was to prove astonishingly successful. It was 1884. The Australians, who seemed to be in this country as much as their own in those days, were in England for the third time in five years and when they went to Oxford for a game, Manley Kemp, the University captain, chose the freshman O'Brien for his team. In a famous University victory, O'Brien scored a brilliant 92 and as if to show that getting runs against the Aussies was easy he repeated his form for the M.C.C. a few days later when he hit 72. The fairy tale continued when the Lancashire committee chose the England team for the first Test at Old Trafford in July, a team of twelve that included five Lancashire players, among them Jack Crossland, a fast bowler, and Lord Harris. The choice of Crossland was a provocative one. He was a source of irritation to many players who considered his bowling action unfair. One was Lord Harris who had written to the Lancashire committee before their selection, expressing his feelings and throwing his considerable weight to the exclusion of Crossland. Still the Lancashire committee picked them both and then, and only then, considered His Lordship's letter. The club secretary was instructed to send the following reply: "July 7, 1884. Dear Lord Harris, My Committee have decided to play Crossland against the Australians, therefore we suppose under the circumstances the English team will lose your valuable assistance which we very much regret." So the team, when announced, did not include Lord Harris — who was to captain in the remaining two Tests — but brought in, instead, the Irishman.

The powerfully-built O'Brien, an expert at the pull and an excellent driver, got a "duck" in his first innings for England, bowled by the "Demon" Spofforth when he batted at number eight. He did much better in the second innings to help England fight off the threat of defeat, an innings that did not impress that solid institution of a newspaper, the *Manchester Guardian*. "A useful though not very good twenty from Mr O'Brien turned the scale."

The object of O'Brien's move to Oxford had been to gain a Blue. This he did, although he did not get a run in either innings in the Varsity match with Cambridge. But the fiery Irishman of the unpredictable temperament was on his way, hitting powerfully, a dashing player with a good physique and an urge to get on with the game. He scored a rather fine 119 against Gloucestershire and had a couple of hard-hitting knocks against Surrey as he at last found success at Middlesex. The Gentlemen, of course, selected him — twelve times in all — the Hon. M.B. Hawke chose him to go to Australia in 1887 and he played in his second Test in the home series of 1888. His finest moment was just around the corner.

The year was 1889, the month June, and Yorkshire, led by the now Lord Hawke, were at Lord's. The climax of the game arrived at about quarter past three on the final afternoon, Saturday the 22nd, when Lord Hawke's declaration left Middlesex with 215 minutes in which to score 280 for victory. The game was due to finish at seven o'clock and it was half past five before the twenty-seven-year-old O'Brien got to bat. Alec Webbe and Andrew Stoddart had opened the batting and both were out by the time the score had reached 35. The early run-rate was kept down to one a minute and Lord Hawke allowed the batsmen no liberties by putting an extra man on the offside at each end and so saving a lot of runs. The third wicket fell at 73 and when the hundred was reached Middlesex were left with 110 minutes in which to score 180 runs. At half past five, with an hour and a half to go, James Walker was out; Middlesex were 129 for four and, wrote the *Manchester Guardian* correspondent: "It was here that O'Brien came in and commenced his wonderful innings. From the first he played all balls with the greatest confidence and hit with all the vigour that made his name so famous in 1884. O'Brien scored a large majority of the runs and the rate of scoring greatly increased the spectators' growing excitement as there began to be the prospect of a good finish."

O'Brien lost his first partner, Evan Nepean, at 172, and his second, Ted Hadow, caught at the wicket, at 197. Eighty-three runs were needed in 45 minutes when George Vernon joined O'Brien and the runs were hit off in great style in 35 minutes. Said the *Manchester Guardian*: "O'Brien, who seemed nerved for a great occasion, hit at almost everything and never made a mistake." (A slight change of opinion after earlier saying that the only blemish had been a lofty drive when 87 which Louis Hall had misjudged.) "Vernon occasionally hit well but he knew O'Brien was well in and was quite capable of making the runs in time." Three beautiful drives along the ground against Bobby Peel brought O'Brien 12 runs, the first shot sending the ball as far as the Nursery. As the score increased, so did the excitement and Middlesex had an escape when Vernon played a ball from Lees Whitehead on to his stumps without removing a bail. "Mr O'Brien signalised his partner's escape by driving a ball from Wainwright on to the roof of the pavilion," said *The Times*. "Middlebrook was put on and Mr O'Brien placed his first ball to the square leg boundary."

O'Brien, who had scored 92 in two hours in the first innings, reached his century in the second innings in 80 minutes with a clever single towards point. It was greeted with "a perfect roar of applause". The score was now "647 all" and a single from Vernon won the match for Middlesex by four wickets with ten minutes to go. The *Manchester Guardian* was ecstatic. "Mr O'Brien played an innings such as would scarcely have been possible to any other batsman in England. We can hardly recall an instance of a man winning a first-class match against time and keeping up such a rate of run-getting for as long as 1hr 40min." (The excitement had extended O'Brien's innings by 20 minutes. It had lasted only 1hr 20min and included 14 fours and six threes). "The excitement of the moment never interfered with his hitting which was brilliant to the extreme. Needless to say that at the finish both batsmen were enthusiastically cheered." Said *The Times*: "There was a demonstration in front of the pavilion at the end of the game and cheer after cheer was given for Mr O'Brien. His hitting all round the wicket was of great brilliancy, his precision and skill in timing the ball being most remarkable. When at Oxford, Mr O'Brien played several remarkable innings, especially that against the Australians, but all of these were eclipsed by that on Saturday."

Lord Hawke, although on the receiving end, was just as complimentary when he recalled the match in his book, *Recollections and Reminiscences*, twenty-five years later: "Only the epithet 'superb' could describe the power and judgment of O'Brien's hitting. I put on every bowler and they each tried all they knew but we might have been Lilliputians flogged by two giants. At last it came not merely to the runs being made within time but whether Tim would get his century into the bargain. Both were accomplished seven minutes ahead of the clock and I believe the opponents were as admiring as the victors were pleased." In referring to O'Brien's early days in county cricket, Lord Hawke said he was first tried purely as a wicketkeeper. "This may have been the reason for his invariable habit, soon after he went in, of always standing behind the wickets and carefully making sure that the stumps were actually pitched in alignment with the other end."

O'Brien's highest innings for Middlesex was 202 against Sussex at Hove when he and Bob Lucas put on 338 in 200 minutes. He was one of the few men to hit a ball out of Lord's, playing for M.C.C. against Rugby School in 1886 when he cleared the old grandstand. His last game for Middlesex was in 1898 but he continued to play and in making 216 not out for Wiseton against Arthur Jones's team in 1906 he and his partner hit 70 off three overs from Jones. He captained the Gentlemen of Ireland in England and made a brilliant 167 against Oxford University and in 1914, at the age of fifty-two, was still good enough to score a first-class century. He was playing for Lionel Robinson's XI against Oxford University at Attleborough in Norfolk, part of a team which included several Test players but which was dismissed for 147. O'Brien, now Sir Timothy after succeeding to the baronetcy on the death of his uncle, Sir Patrick O'Brien, batted at number six and scored 90. Robinson's team followed on and O'Brien opened the innings to score 111 in 200 minutes to save the match.

Lord Hawke clearly had great admiration for the Irishman with the buoyant, playful, fiery personality. "What I liked about his methods," he wrote, "was that he never pottered nor was in doubt how to play a ball. He is not only a typical Irishman but the very best batsman the Emerald Isle ever produced. Tim was always 'agin the

Government' and had pretty strong dislikes, for instance at one period he was thoroughly antagonistic to everything at the Oval. But like Father O'Flynn, he had a 'wonderful way wid him' and no one ever felt annoyed for more than a few minutes. He expressed considerable impatience with the methods of present-day batting and only last summer (1923) in the pavilion at Lord's he remarked: 'In my day we waited for the full pitch and half volley but when they were served up to us we sent them to the boundary, thanking God for them. Whereas nowadays these are the balls treated with profoundest respect by modern batsmen.'"

Although known for his batting, O'Brien could also bowl — right hand or left and frequently practised when a wicket fell. "He thinks it rather hard luck that he can't get the Middlesex captain to believe in his powers," wrote W.G. Grace, "but consoles himself with the thought that a prophet has little honour in his own country; and with having got me out on one occasion at Cheltenham when the regular bowlers had failed."

O'Brien's fiery nature was seen during a match at Harston, near Cambridge, when he was batting with Charles Thornton and was given out caught to a ball that had hit him high on the sleeve of his shirt. He was furious and went to the umpire and said: "That was either a very ignorant decision or a downright swindle." The umpire replied: "I guess sir, it was just a bit of both." But like most Irishmen he had charm and Lord Hawke so enjoyed his company he took him on tours to Australia and South Africa. On one visit to South Africa most of the side sailed before Hawke who went with O'Brien and Herbert Hewett on the boat S.S. *Moor*. Hewett played a good deal of whist with the captain and could not stand him. Five days out of Cape Town a cylinder was blown off about one o'clock in the morning. O'Brien went into Hewett's cabin, roused him and said: "The ship is sinking. Which boat are you going in, the skipper's?" On one journey home, in order to enable two ladies to share a cabin, O'Brien, Hawke and Charles Wright were together in a three-berth cabin. One morning, after going up on deck early, O'Brien told Wright that Kirk, their attendant, had knocked a steward down. "Presently Kirk came down and Charles lectured him until he was thoroughly exhausted," related Lord Hawke. "Kirk stood unmoved and silent and then said: 'Mister Charles, it is the first of April and Sir Timothy has been having you. I ain't knocked no steward down.'"

O'Brien played jokes on W.G. as well. Grace had been bowling in a festival match and the umpire, Farrands, had persisted in turning down all the appeals for lbw, much to W.G.'s annoyance. That night at dinner, he received a long letter, apparently written by the umpire, stating how much he had been hurt by his honour being impugned through W.G. appearing not to agree with the decisions. W.G. was upset and in the smoking room he decided to write to him — until he was told that O'Brien was responsible.

His truculence showed through at Melbourne when Lord Hawke's team, who were staying at St Kilda, were invited to a concert in the city. "We had ordered cabs to drive us into Melbourne but, when the time came, the cabbies refused to drive us in because there was a ball at St Kilda's and they could make more money locally," wrote Lord Hawke. "This was too much for Tim O'Brien who put both his elbows through the windows of a hansom and there was nearly a fight between him and the cabby. Eventually we went by train."

O'Brien married, in 1885, Gundrede Annette Teresa, daughter of Sir Humphrey de Trafford, and was the father of eight daughters and two sons, the elder one of whom, Lieutenant Timothy John Aloysius O'Brien, was killed during the Great War.

Incidentally, a few days after O'Brien's first Test at Old Trafford in 1884, the Lancashire committee ordered the secretary to write to Manchester Hiring Company, the caterers, "asking them to inform the committee who ordered champagne for the players on the occasion of the Australian match". I wonder . . .

15 CHARLES OLLIVIERRE

The West Indies has given cricket a host of talented batsmen. Charles Augustus Ollivierre does not count among the more familiar and was not among the best, but he was certainly the first. Ollivierre hailed from St Vincent, one of the islands above the South American mainland. He came from a cricketing family that had made its mark in 1896 when another of the Ollivierres was involved in a match for St Vincent against the touring M.C.C. team captained by Lord Hawke. His Lordship was, in his own words, "a sort of glorified being" and the man who could bowl him was indeed a hero. Sure enough, Ollivierre, "a man of colour, shot my middle stump into the air before I had scored," wrote Lord Hawke. It must have been the most momentous happening on the small island since Christopher Columbus had discovered it four hundred years earlier. Ollivierre turned a somersault on the pitch and then both umpires and the players shook hands with him. The crowd were beating the ground with sticks, throwing hats in the air and embracing each other.

The next time an Ollivierre attracted attention was in 1900 when twenty-three-year-old Charles Augustus was chosen for the first tour of England by a West Indian cricket team. The team was chosen on a quota system stemming from the jealousy of various colonies and was made up of four from Barbados, four from Trinidad, three British Guiana, two Jamaica, and two, one of whom was Ollivierre, from the small islands. The M.C.C. would not recognise any of the games in England as first-class, a sensible enough decision it seemed as London County, Worcestershire, Warwickshire and a weak M.C.C. team shouldered them aside without too much trouble. After beating the Minor Counties, the West Indians, poor old souls, ran headlong into Gilbert Jessop who hit them for 157 in an hour.

Pelham Warner, West Indian born, decided it was time to help out and played in the next match against Leicestershire. He took Ollivierre with him to open the innings, and saw him score a magnificent 159 as he showed himself the finest bats-man in the touring team, finishing the summer at the head of the averages with 32.70 from 883 runs. His form attracted the attention of Derbyshire, a county forever grovelling in the depths of the championship table and in sore need of strengthening. Ollivierre was approached. He was twenty-four, presumably without ties at home, for he agreed to stay in England and qualify for Derbyshire for the 1902 season. Said the *Derbyshire Times*: "C.A. Ollivierre has promised to live in Derbyshire with the intention at the end of his two years necessary residence to play for the county as an amateur. Mr Ollivierre, who is a coloured gentleman, was employed in the Government office in Trinidad as a clerk and he has been promised a situation in Derby as an inducement to remain." St Vincent might have been a paradise island to some, with its beautiful thickly-wooded volcanic hills and picturesque valleys, its pleasant climate. But it was small, only eighteen miles long, no more than eleven miles wide, perhaps too stifling for a young man who would find the attractions of England over-

whelming. Perhaps he remembered, too, the hurricane which had swept through his homeland only two years earlier, destroying life and property.

For a season and a half Ollivierre played club cricket as he went through his two years of qualification which were completed in July 1902. He gave several spectacular batting displays including a magnificent innings of 167 against Warwickshire. He did not play long for Derbyshire, being forced to retire in 1907, when still only thirty-one, because of eye trouble. He scored three centuries in those six seasons, but one of them was a stupendous innings of 229 in a game still looked on as Derbyshire's finest moment. They won by nine wickets after facing an Essex first innings total of 597, and Ollivierre scored 321 runs in the match in 280 minutes for once out.

The game was played at Chesterfield, in the delightful Queens Park and from where the crooked spire of the parish church looks more crooked than ever. Ollivierre's first visit to the ground, according to the England player Fred Root who himself played for Derbyshire, came after the county had started the season with three successes on a southern tour. Ollivierre had done well and on the long return trip from Bournemouth he found time to celebrate. Having snatched an hour or two's sleep he arrived late on the ground where he went into the slips, not feeling at all well. He put down four slip catches, which was unlike him, kicked the ball back to the bowler, Arnold Warren, after the last one and then, hands on hips, surveyed the view. Suddenly he dashed off to the pavilion and was found dousing his head in a wash-bowl of ice-cold water. He returned to the field but clearly, all was not well. "After gazing at the spire with much the same 'peeking' action as a captured pigeon, he made a bee-line for the skipper and said," wrote Fred Root: "'It's no use, captain, you must find a substitute for a bit; I am ill, awfully ill. No wonder I drop catches. Why, even the church steeple seems to be falling on me!' He took a lot of convincing that the famous spire seemed to be falling on everyone else, too."

Olivierre soon learned to live with the spire and in July 1904, during a spell of particularly hot weather in the middle of a glorious summer, he unexpectedly stepped into history. The game, against Essex, started on a Monday, 18th July. The first day belonged to Percy Perrin, a man who never played for England despite 30,000 runs and 66 centuries, but who later helped to pick England Test teams. "Perrin is the hero of yesterday's cricket field," proclaimed the *Manchester Guardian* the following morning. "He has never played better than he did against the Derbyshire bowlers — men who are far from being contemptible. He hit often and he hit with force and sureness of aim and with unvarying decisiveness. Perrin is a terrible opponent for any bowlers when he gets well settled. His strength is enormous and he can go on for hours without tiring." Perrin had gone in to bat with Essex 12 for one after Herbert Carpenter had been bowled. He mastered the bowling from the first over and he and his captain, Fred Fane, put on 120 in 70 minutes for the second wicket. The hard-hitting Charlie McGahey dominated a stand of 47, the reverend gentleman, F.H. Gillingham, assisted in a stand of 126 in 70 minutes, and Perrin was missed when 152. Essex became 314 for six but Perrin, after his life, found another useful partner in Johnny Douglas. Together they put on 130 in 75 minutes and Perrin, who survived several chances in the outfield, ended the hot, tiring day with 295 not out in Essex's 524 for eight. He was still there with 343 — in 345 minutes — when the innings ended at 597 the following morning.

The daunting Essex total did not inhibit Ollivierre who, in typical West Indian style, launched an assault on the bowling that brought Derbyshire 50 runs in half an hour and 100 in 55 minutes. Ollivierre hit 11 boundaries in his own 50 which took 45 minutes and at lunch on the second day, Derbyshire were 144 for none. The morning session had produced 217 runs. "Olivierre's late cutting was beautiful to watch and the crowd cheered with delight at his huge drives," said the *Derbyshire Times*. A few minutes after lunch Ollivierre reached his hundred, in 95 minutes, and his opening stand was worth 191 in 100 minutes before forty-two year old Levi Wright, who had scored 68, was out. Another great partnership followed, this time with Billy Storer who scored 44 out of 128 in 75 minutes as Ollivierre, full of daring and unorthodox strokes, went on to play one of the finest innings in Derbyshire's history. He hit Bill Reeves for three fours in an over, twice over the spectators' heads, and when he reached his 200, in 190 minutes, his captain, Edward Ashcroft, took out a drink to what the *Derbyshire Times* described as "his dusky colleague". Perhaps it packed a punch for Ollivierre hit the next two balls over the scoreboard and the cinder track in the direction of the bottom lodge. His 229 took 225 minutes and by the close Derbyshire, who had started their innings just before one o'clock needing 448 to avoid the follow-on, were two runs away with six wickets in hand. In all, 1,043 runs had been scored in two days.

Derbyshire's innings closed the following morning for 548 and no game could have looked more certain to finish in a draw. But in 45 minutes to lunch Bill Bestwick, "making the ball bump a lot," and Arnold Warren bowled so well that six wickets went down for 27 runs. A large crowd gathered after lunch after the news had rapidly spread in the town. The Rev. Gillingham, who had been ordered to stay in bed in Nottingham by the doctor, received an urgent wire from his captain, requesting his return. Despite the pain the reverend amateur gamely responded and left his bed to return to Chesterfield. He missed his train by three minutes and when he arrived in Chesterfield by the next, the innings was over. He went to the ground but was evidently far from well. So, too, was the Essex innings, all over in 110 minutes, following their 597 of Tuesday with 97 on Wednesday. Derbyshire were left to score 147 to win in 125 minutes, and nothing was going to stop them now. The first ball of their second innings brought an appeal for a catch behind off Wright. The umpire turned it down but Wright admitted later that he "touched the leather". Not that it affected the result for Wright was out for one, leaving Ollivierre to reach his 50 in as many minutes as Derbyshire steamed towards victory. In an hour Derbyshire were 100, could Ollivierre complete the triumph with a century to add to his double of the first innings? His partner was the old Derbyshire pro, Billy Storer, thirty-six years old, who had first played in 1887 and was near the end of a career that had seen him play six times for England. There was bonus money of a guinea for a professional who reached 50 and that was more important to him that an amateur's century. So as one raced for 100 the other headed for 50 and one Essex player at least, Ted Sewell, was of the opinion that each tried to run the other out. In the end neither got there. Ollivierre, on his twenty-eighth birthday, finished 92 not out, Storer 48 not out, but Derbyshire had gained an astounding win, having scored 149 for one in 80 minutes. The £173 taken at the gate suggested, said one writer, that Chesterfield should at least have three championship matches instead of two and a friendly.

The luckless Ollivierre played only three more years for Derbyshire before being forced to retire after persistent eye trouble and scoring 377 runs for an average of 12.56 in 1907. He continued to play club cricket in Yorkshire and between the wars coached in Holland. He died in Pontefract, Yorkshire, in 1949 aged seventy-two.

It is worth recording that at the same time that Derbyshire were beating Essex, another remarkable game was being conducted at Trent Bridge. On the day when Perrin was getting his 295 not out, Gilbert Jessop was scoring 206 in less than two and a half hours for Gloucestershire against Nottinghamshire. In one little ten-minute dash after lunch he and Leigh Brownlee put on 48 runs. By the end of the day Gloucestershire were 591 for nine. Said the *Manchester Guardian*, with much circumspection, "It was quite one of Jessop's most brilliant efforts marked now and again by some restraint, but by perhaps safer hitting than usual." Nottinghamshire opening batsmen James Iremonger and Arthur Jones put on 100 together in the first innings and 303 in 265 minutes in the second . . . and lost. From that opening stand of 303 Nottinghamshire were all out for 393 and lost by an innings and a run.

16 EDDIE PAYNTER

I guess I had better come clean right at the start. Eddie Paynter is here because I was fond of him. He was a Lancastrian, from Oswaldtwistle, a courageous little player, a warm, generous man with a lovely wife who made delicious rock buns. And he did score 322 in five hours at Hove. I got to know Eddie in his last few years and whenever I was in Yorkshire I would call on him at his flat, conveniently situated between the Chapel and the Working Men's Club. But what such a loyal, lively Lancastrian was doing in a Yorkshire village called Idle was beyond me.

Only one Englishman, Jack Robertson of Middlesex, has scored more runs in a day than Eddie achieved at Hove on 28th July, 1937. Oddly enough, the third highest, 316 by Richard Moore of Hampshire, was scored on the same day, about 80 miles down the coast at Bournemouth. Paynter had been at Old Trafford for his previous game, playing for England in the second Test against New Zealand, and at midnight on the last day of the match he settled down in a sleeper on the train from Manchester to London, on his way to join the Lancashire team at Hove. It was eight o'clock when he entered the Pier Hotel at Brighton and he just had time for breakfast and a shower before walking to the Hove ground. Lionel Lister won the toss for Lancashire and Paynter and Cyril Washbrook opened the innings, with a stand of 268 in 155 minutes. "The sea air gave us both a tremendous appetite for the Sussex bowling," Paynter wrote later, "and by lunchtime I had scored a century. The Sussex bowlers were bewildered by the storm of runs that had seized the initiative from them."

Washbrook hit the day's first ball for four and Sussex managed to bowl only two maiden overs before lunch as seven bowlers tried to stop the flow of runs that washed over them. Paynter's century before lunch arrived with quarter of an hour to spare while Washbrook, although unable to keep up with the sprightly Paynter, completed his 1,000 runs for the summer. The storm of the morning turned into a whirlwind in the afternoon with 93 runs coming in 35 minutes after lunch. Washbrook still could not keep up yet he scored 40 runs in that time and left with 108 out of 268 for one, the third highest opening stand in Lancashire's history.

The waiting had done Jack Iddon, the next batsman, no good at all. He slipped on to the field almost unnoticed as the deck chairs applauded Washbrook back to the pavilion, then slunk off just as unobtrusively when he was run out seven runs later. Norman Oldfield, however, quickly matched Paynter's mood and in the next two and a quarter hours they put on 271 runs, a scoring rate of 120 an hour. Paynter, driving, hooking, cutting, pulling with the power of an oil drill, reached his 200 in 205 minutes — his second hundred had occupied exactly 100 minutes of his valuable time — and another century had been claimed between lunch and tea. He took 17 off one over from Charlie Oakes, including a splendid straight drive for six, and at tea Lancashire were 411 for two with Paynter past 250. His first mistake came at 260.

Sussex were too bemused by then to accept the slip catch and Paynter was allowed to reach 322 out of Lancashire's 546 before he was third out, lbw to Jim Parks who was probably as suprised as anybody at getting the little man out. It was that rotten midnight train that had done it. As Paynter said: "I had thoroughly enjoyed myself but I was feeling the effects of my overnight train-journey by the time I was lbw to a full toss from Jim Parks."

Cyril Washbrook later said of the Hove innings: "By five o'clock that afternoon, Eddie was relaxing in the bath after going on to score 322 out of a Lancashire total at close of play of 640. The slowest scoring rate of the day came in the last hour's play, by which time Eddie was enjoying a quiet drink at one of the bars around one of the bars around the ground."

Len Hopwood, who went in to bat when Paynter was out, said: "He was so unorthodox and when he was in that mood you couldn't set a field for him. It was a beautiful wicket and Sussex started with a deep mid-off and deep mid-on. Washbrook and Paynter started with quick singles to them and when the fielders were brought in they would hit the ball over them for fours. We always said of Eddie that he'd scored over 300, had a shower, dressed and had a drink by six o'clock! George Duckworth and I put on 50 in the last half hour and we were given the bird for slow scoring. There was nothing anybody could do with Eddie in that mood. I just wouldn't bowl at him in the nets. He never tried to play cricket properly, but would just sling his bat at it and hit it all over Old Trafford. He scored 291 at Southampton the following year, in 1938, and Hampshire had a little spinner, Stuart Boyes. 'You'll have to pitch 'em up, Stuart,' Eddie told him. 'I can't keep hitting it out of the ground if you don't pitch it up.' And Boyes pitched them up and Eddie hit them." Paynter hit seven sixes in that innings, six of them out of the ground.

Paynter's score was — and still is — second only to Archie MacLaren's prodigious 424 at Taunton for Lancashire. He had hit three sixes and 39 fours and had sprinted the other 148 runs in the bracing Brighton air. "I only wish I had got it at Manchester," he said later. Ah, but if he had, he would not have been at the Ice Palace in Brighton that night, the toast of the Lancastrian holiday-makers in the audience. The compere insisted that Eddie go onto the ice-rink to be spotlighted for further applause and he shuffled reluctantly on to the ice. Before he had reached the compere Eddie completed a pirouette in trying to stay on his feet and brought the house down for the second time in the day.

Paynter was born in 1901, on Guy Fawkes day, quite a little chap and never to rise above 5ft 5½in nor weigh more than 10½ stone. Sons of working-class men started work themselves at twelve years old in those days and Eddie's day was divided between school and the cotton mill, a natural stepping-stone for an Oswaldtwistle boy. He finished school totally at thirteen and went to the brickworks where his father worked. There he lost the ends of the first and second fingers of his right hand in a brick press. Twenty-three years later he was forced to pull out of a Test match when one of the fingers was so badly bruised and swollen that he could not hold a bat. In September, 1975, Eddie, then aged seventy-three, was at Lord's to see Lancashire beat Middlesex for the Gillette Cup. When the players trooped into the dressing room after holding Middlesex to 180 for eight, Eddie was there. Clive Lloyd flopped down on the bench feeling the strain of a long season. "Na then, Clive," said

Eddie. "'Owsta feelin'?" "Fine," said Clive. "Just a bit tired." "Tired!" exclaimed Eddie. "Tell thi what. Tha'd a bin tired if tha'd worked i' t' brickyard."

Paynter's early cricket experience was spent with Enfield in the Lancashire League, the same club that produced Jack Simmons. Although he had a trial with Lancashire at eighteen and played in the second team at nineteen, he did not get on to the staff and into the first team until he was twenty-four. Another five years passed before he got a regular place in the Lancashire team and in that same season, 1931, when he was twenty-nine years old, he scored his first century and made his Test debut.

In 1932 Paynter played the innings he always regarded as his best — 152 out of Lancashire's total of 263 against Yorkshire at Bradford when he twice hit the left-arm spin of Hedley Verity into the stand and twice over the stand and on to the pitch of Bradford Park Avenue football ground. Maurice Leyland came on to bowl. "If tha can 'it me for six I'll buy thee a pint after," he said to Paynter. A shortish ball gave Paynter the opportunity and he hit it over the deep square leg boundary and hit the wall dividing the ground from a park. Did Leyland buy the pint? "Course he did," said Eddie, who had hit five sixes and 17 fours in his 152, the last 50 of which took half an hour.

When the first fifteen names of players to go to Australia in 1932-33 were announced, George Duckworth was the only Lancastrian. Two more names were added later, one of them Eddie Paynter, who was to become a hero by rising almost Lazarus style from his sick bed in Brisbane to win a Test match for England. Paynter, a spare part batsman in the party, spent four days in hospital, suffering from tonsillitis, chiefly sustained, it is said, on a curious diet of cold chicken and iced champagne. Paynter had the satisfaction of hitting the winning runs with a six. The ball landed in the crowd but somehow, John Willy Pike, a friend of Paynter's, managed to get it for him. Eddie had the ball inscribed and mounted and in a place of honour at home. "When I'm dead, I want that ball to go to Lord's, into the museum," he once told me. I later wrote an article for *The Cricketer* and before sending it to the magazine I sent a copy to Eddie for approval. Back came a letter: "That's fine," he wrote. "But take out that bit about the ball going to Lord's. The wife says it's staying in the family."

Paynter played three Tests in Australia and two in New Zealand and although averaging 61.33 in Australia he did not play Test cricket again until 1937, the year of his great innings against Sussex at Hove. He was one of *Wisden*'s Cricketers of the Year but got into the first Test against Australia at Trent Bridge in 1938 only because Joe Hardstaff was injured. Eddie, in great style, scored 216 not out, a record in England against Australia. He averaged over 100 from six Test innings that summer and went to South Africa with Walter Hammond's team where one of his innings, against West Griqualand, included nine sixes. He averaged 81 in Test matches but still found himself dropped for the third and final Test against West Indies at the Oval in 1939. As luck would have it, one of the batsmen brought into the England team was Nottinghamshire's Walter Keeton — and Lancashire were playing at Trent Bridge when the team was announced. Paynter made up his mind to show the selectors. He did, with an innings of 154.

In 1977, two years before he died, Paynter got into an aircraft for the first time and went to Australia for the Centenary Test. He had at first decided to decline the invitation. Although flight and hotel were paid for he did not think he would have enough money for the extras. "I'm not standing in a corner unable to buy anybody a drink," he told me. Money was raised by a generous public, including a dinner in his honour by the Anglo-American Club, and Paynter went to Melbourne and had a wonderful time. The generous man gave me his dinner menu when he returned, signed by all sorts of people, chief among them being Eddie Paynter. I am not one for collecting cricket souvenirs, but that one I have kept. Bless you, Eddie.

17 WALTER READ

For a crack English batsman like Walter Read to be put in at number ten in a Test match on his home ground must have been like a slap across the face. If it had been a few years earlier he might well have whizzed his glove at the captain, Lord Harris, and settled the insult with pistols at dawn. But this was 1884. Mr Read, instead, took his annoyance out on the Australian bowlers, such worthies as Fred Spofforth, George Giffen, Henry Boyle and George Palmer, and in under two hours had hit a century that revived a flagging England. "From the very start Read hit with astounding rapidity and vigour," said one report. "Seldom has the Oval ring been treated to a display of more commanding batting. His leg hitting, it may be said without exaggeration, was the most brilliant both for timing and power that has been seen since the days of George Parr."

The match was only the fifth Test held in England and the third and last in the series of 1884. The first had been staged at Old Trafford — when the opening day had been totally washed out — England had won the second at Lord's after a magnificent century from A.G. Steel, and the decider, at the Oval, was played in brilliant, sunny weather. "The weather, being exceedingly hot, was all in our favour," wrote George Giffen. "The cold English days have often seriously incommoded Australians who have found their warm blood so chilled that they have been unable to enjoy fielding as it should be enjoyed and mistakes, otherwise unaccountable, have been made. On August 11, 1884, however, we were in our element. It was so warm that several of the spectators fainted."

Giffen reckoned that the English team of Lord Harris, the Hon. Alfred Lyttelton, Grace, Steel, Read, Barlow, Barnes, Shrewsbury, Peate, Ulyett and Scotton, was the strongest ever to represent the country. But the strength of England was buckling at the knee by the end of the first day when Australia were 363 for two with centuries from Billy Murdoch, Percy McDonnell and Henry Scott. Australia finished at 551 the following day with Murdoch scoring 211. "Every Englishman bowled and when all the cracks had failed Lyttleton went on and with underhand lobs took four wickets for nineteen runs," said Giffen. "With the wicket in such splendid order we entertained no real hope of getting England out twice; but so finely did Palmer bowl at a critical period of the first innings that for a short while we thought we might squeeze home as eight wickets had fallen for 181." Then Read went in.

Walter William Read was born at Reigate in Surrey in 1855 and was still only seventeen when he first played for Surrey against Yorkshire at the Oval in 1873. For eight years he could play just during the school holidays for he was assisting his father in his school at Reigate, and it was not until an official position was found for him at the Oval that he could play through the entire summer. He was first available for all matches in 1881, the year he scored 160 against Kent at Maidstone with three sixes and 29 fours, and went on the tour of Australia in 1882-83 when he played in

four Tests. He was in his sixth Test when he rescued a sagging England at the Oval in 1884.

The reasons given for Read batting so low in the order varied. Wrote C.F. Pardon: "So strong was the English batting side that W.W. Read was put in number ten." Sammy Woods, the Somerset captain who played for Australia and England, referred to Mr Read as "a sick man" but J.N. Pentelow, writing twenty years after the game, said Read "has confessed since that he did not at all like being number ten on the batting list. Perhaps the indignity of such a position (it was certainly not the place to which his skill rightly entitled him) made him all the more determined to do his best." *The Cricketer* magazine of 1905 said he was "considered to be somewhat out of form" while the same publication two years later suggested he "had begged to be sent in late". When Read went in to bat with England 181 for eight Billy Scotton, the dour Nottinghamshire professional, had already been batting for three and a half hours and was 53. Wrote Mr Pardon: "From the very start Read hit with astounding rapidity and vigour. Though his innings included 20 fours I don't think more than one of those fours was anything like a bad hit. He might have been caught by Spofforth when he was 23, the ball going back rather sharp and low to the bowler, a little to his left side. This, however, was the only mistake the Surrey amateur made and his brilliant cricket awoke the enthusiasm of the Oval crowd and worked them up to a tremendous pitch of excitement." Read hit fiercely and scored rapidly but his hitting did not degenerate into slogging. "A magnificent and masterly display," said Mr Pardon. "Read had never been seen to greater advantage."

The Australians tried all their bowlers. Palmer sent down his wily leg breaks and even off breaks; Spofforth tried every dodge he knew; Boyle's good length slowed the pace but could not break the stand; Midwinter and Giffen bowled, even Scott and Bonnor tried. But Read was in great form. He reached 50 in an hour with ten fours, at least two of which would have been sixes today as he hit Spofforth and Giffen into the crowd at square leg. After batting 105 minutes Read was level with Scotton on 84 and eight minutes later he had reached 100, scored out of 137 added while he was in. He went on to 117 — Scotton failed to reach his century — and for two hours the Australian bowling had been knocked all over the field. Read had gone in to bat at three o'clock, hitting hard and fast with Scotton playing steadily and safely, and it was not until ten past five that they were separated, having "saved the honour of England and accomplished a grand performance".

Nearly forty years later Sammy Woods recalled the match which he had seen as a seventeen-year-old, remembering that he had witnessed underhand bowling for the first time. "What impressed me most was the innings of W.W. Read who went in a sick man, at number ten, and got 117 while Scotton was pottering about at the other end for hours for 90. Still, it was the game to play and he, with the help of Read, saved the match."

Giffen, although impressed, did not waste too many words on the innings. "Then Walter Read came in — as *tenth* man mind — and knocked our bowling all over the field until he had made 117. Scotton, it will be remembered, played a grand defensive game and 151 runs were put on for the ninth wicket. I have a lively recollection of one incident of this match. The dense crowd had encroached upon the turf and once or twice I, who was in the long field, found them in the way. What happened but that Lord Harris, the English captain, most generous and genuine of sportsmen, told the people that if they did not keep back he would not go on with the match but would give us the game."

Read was near enough an England ever-present for a decade, playing in eighteen Tests, seventeen of them against Australia, and being captain in two, in Australia and South Africa, both of which were won. He never failed to punish a loose ball and was the first batsman to make full use of the pull shot. "It seemed to me," he said in 1905, "that with all the men on the offside it was a thousand pities to neglect any opportunity of getting the ball to the on. I found that by putting the left leg right across at an off ball and hitting almost exactly as you would to square leg, the desired effect was attained." His most famous shot, apart from the pull which he developed in his later years, was the stroke with horizontal bat which sent the ball between point and cover "like a shot from a gun".

He was an accomplished all-round sportsman. He played soccer, was a good skater, walker and billiard player, and was reported to be the life and soul of the gathering at smoking concerts. His years assisting his father at school probably also helped his Thespian leanings and Lord Hawke has recorded that on board ship to Australia he and Monty Bowden played with C. Aubrey Smith in Byron's farcical comedy, *Old Soldiers.*

He was a good all-round cricketer, too, for as well as being a distinguished batsman, he kept wicket and was a successful underhand bowler. It is said he spoke proudly of his lobs. If one story can be held to be typical he was a courageous fielder as well. During Ivo Bligh's tour of Australia in 1882-83 Yorkshire's Billy Bates was on a hat-trick after dismissing McDonnell and Giffen. George Bonnor, the big hitter, was next man and it was suggested that a silly mid-on be brought up for him. A.G. Steel reported the incident: "Bates faithfully promised to bowl a fast, shortish ball between the leg and the wicket and said he was quite certain that Bonnor would play slowly forward to it. Acting on the faith of this, W.W. Read volunteered to stand silly mid-on. In came the giant. Read crept nearer. A slow forward stroke to a fast, shortish leg-stump ball landed the ball in his hands not more than six feet from the bat. The crowd could not believe it and Bonnor was simply thunderstruck at mid-on's impertinence, but Bates had done the hat-trick for all that and what is more, he got a very smart silver hat for his pains."

Read played many other outstanding innings though none so distinguished as his 117 at the Oval. He scored 118 in 105 minutes at Oxford in 1887, 338 against Oxford University at the Oval in 1888, 161 against Yorkshire in 1894 — "a display of free and fearless hitting". His finest hour though, stayed with his only Test century, still the highest score by a number ten batsman, and a record partnership for the ninth wicket against Australia: "A magnificent and masterly display. The way in which he punished Spofforth, Palmer, Giffen and Boyle can never be forgotten by anyone who was so fortunate as to be present."

Read died at Addiscombe in Surrey in 1907 when he was fifty-one.

18 RAVI SHASTRI

One day early in January 1985 — it was a Saturday — somebody threw an orange at Ravi Shastri as he chased a ball near the boundary edge at Calcutta. Presumably the spectator had brought it along specially to show his feelings at Shastri's seven-and-a-half-hour century, scored earlier in the third Test against England. The following Thursday Shastri was back home in Bombay a thousand miles away, being showered with bouquets as he hit the fastest double century of all time which included six sixes in one over. He had beaten Gilbert Jessop and Clive Lloyd's double-hundred record and equalled Gary Sobers's six sixes; exalted company for a twenty-two-year-old who entered Test cricket as a left-arm spinner batting at number ten.

In February 1981, while the Indian team was on a tour of Australia and New Zealand, Shastri was at home, helping Bombay qualify for the final stages of the Ranji Trophy. He scored 58 and took four for 41 against Baroda and four for 17 against Gujarat. He did nothing in the quarter-final match against Uttar Pradesh at Kanpur but in the middle of it received a telegram from Sunil Gavaskar, India's captain, telling him he was needed in New Zealand. The eighteen-year-old Shastri, who had managed to get two "ducks" in Bombay's totals of 441 and 327 for six, and had not taken a wicket, packed his bags and was soon in Wellington where his next match was his Test debut.

Shastri had caught Gavaskar's eye in the pre-season nets in Bombay and had impressed enough to be thrust straight into the Wellington Test as a replacement for Dilip Doshi who was injured. Shastri arrived the evening before the Test match and two days later finished with three for 54 in the first innings including the last two wickets in two balls. He took the last three wickets in one over in the second innings to complete an impressive Test debut with six for 63. He batted at number ten in those days and while his bowling was impressive with 15 wickets in the three-match series his batting brought him only 48 runs.

Shastri still hovered between the middle and end of the batting order through the six-match Test series at home against England but the failure of two of the specialist openers in England in 1982, saw him elevated to opener. He scored 93 and 24 not out in his first match, against the Combined Oxford and Cambridge University team, 51 and 20 against Cambridgeshire, all of which was more than enough to take him into the second Test as Gavaskar's partner. Unhappily, there was no immediate fairy-tale ending. He got a "duck". In the final Test, however, he scored 66 at the Oval. His first century came against Pakistan in Karachi the following year, and the second three months later against the West Indies. It took him five and a quarter hours.

Shastri had shown himself a capable all-rounder, nothing explosive like Ian Botham or Kapil Dev, but still a valuable member of the side. Soon, he overtook Kapil Dev as the pin-up boy of the Indian team, popular, idolised, favoured, a young man with an acceptable background. Both his parents were professionals and Shastri

was educated at a top Jesuit school in Bombay. He was influenced a good deal in his early cricket by Gavaskar who was his captain both in the Calcutta Test in 1985, when he scored 111 in seven-and-a-half hours, and in the Ranji Trophy match a few days later when he created his unlikely record.

Shastri's bowling, which is how he came to get into the Test team in the first place, would not have been enough for him to have held his place in the side during England's visit in 1984-85. He took seven wickets in five matches as his batting took over to such an extent that he scored two centuries in the series and averaged above 50. He started with 142 in the Bombay Test which India won, but it was at Calcutta where he earned the wrath of his own countrymen as India carried their first innings into the fourth day before declaring. Shastri took six hours getting to 90, then spent another hour crawling along to his fourth Test hundred, an innings that was an offence against the sport.

The Calcutta Test thankfully came to an end on Saturday, 5th January, not long after the orange had shrivelled in the sun, and Shastri was probably happy to desert Calcutta and get back to Bombay and the prospect of a quiet Ranji Trophy match against Baroda. Shastri had not played in Bombay's previous Trophy game after arriving late, but he was well on time for this game, played at the Wankhede Stadium, scene of England's Test defeat. Bombay were into their second innings and Gavaskar must have been weighing up his declaration when Shastri went to the crease, a heavier than usual bat swinging from his hand, the prospect of some happy-go-lucky runs facing him. He was dropped four times on the way to his first century, reached in 71 minutes, but it was his second century which saw him timing the ball to perfection, hitting cleanly and taking 42 minutes more to get to 200.

Shastri had reached 147 when he faced left-arm spinner Tilak Raj, a faster-than-normal spinner, more a Derek Underwood than a Ravi Shastri, I suppose. The first ball, however, was more a genuine spinner's tempter, so inviting that Shastri hit it straight for six. The second and third were hit over long-on and when the fourth was pitched down the legside Shastri hit it over square leg. Four balls ... four sixes. The fifth ball became the third to clear long-on and now there was only one ball to go, and Gary Sobers's record in sight. In the old days the bowler might have entered the spirit of the occasion and tossed it up. But who wants to go in the record books these days on the receiving end? Shastri gave himself room, Raj bowled wide of the off stump, but nothing was going to stop Shastri now. He was quickly in position and the sixth six flew at the sightscreen.

He had gone from 147 to 183 in an over and the double century arrived in 113 minutes, seven minutes faster than Jessop at Hove in 1903 and Lloyd at Swansea in 1976. Shastri had to hit further than Sobers for his sixes — Sobers, like Lloyd, was at Swansea — and he finished with 13 sixes and 13 fours. What would they think in Calcutta. How would the man with the orange have reacted? "They'll think it's the Eighth Wonder of the World," said Shastri. Gavaskar had been so enthralled by the record innings that his declaration, when it came, allowed Baroda an hour to score 498. They must have been as bewitched as Gavaskar — they finished at 81 for seven.

19 HERBERT SUTCLIFFE

Herbert Sutcliffe has come down through the years — at least, to me he has — as a quite immaculate, imperturbable man. Everybody talked about his clothes, his near elegance; there was never a hair out of place, his shirt had been ironed just so and if he got a "duck" you could bet it was the best-dressed "duck" of the day. I have always imagined him buckling on his pads or pulling on his gloves or fastening his shirt in front of a full-length mirror, flattening a loose eye-brow here, replacing a wayward hair there. Pelham Warner once referred to his "beautifully brushed" hair which never seemed to become ruffled during even the longest innings. His pride in his appearance, it seemed, bordered on paranoia. His batting was just as immaculate and I recall a description once which seemed to fit him perfectly. It referred to his innings of 232 against Surrey at the Oval in 1922, his fourth season in the game. He did not give a chance. "Indeed, he seldom, if ever, lifted the ball in the air," said the report, loftily. That, I suppose, is how he will be remembered, near perfection. Heavens, he even made every score from nought to 127, a curious, boring sort of statistic I agree, but it does again show the nicely rounded-off character of the man. Not a score out of place. Truly, a Herbert — not a Bert. So the occasional break from the everyday Sutcliffe is worth recording; like finding a Bishop on the front row at Raymond's Revuebar. He hit ten sixes at Kettering, a few of them over the stand, 94 in 40 minutes at Scarborough, and, the point of this exercise, an innings of 132 in under two hours against Gloucestershire at Bradford to record his hundredth hundred in 1932.

Sutcliffe started the 1932 season — his fourteenth in the first-class game — with 93 centuries. May was wet. Games at Chesterfield and Sheffield were totally washed out; games at Lord's, against M.C.C., at Cambridge and Edgbaston did not get past the first innings. Yorkshire lost to Lancashire by an innings and Sutcliffe perhaps did well just to squeeze out one century that month, in the game against Warwickshire at Edgbaston. June was much drier and kinder and much more productive for the thirty-seven-year-old Sutcliffe. Inside three weeks he hit five centuries — one of them a double, another a treble — three of them coming in a week. It was great stuff, starting with 104 not out in three hours against Hampshire, and 153 not out in five hours against Warwickshire. Pedestrian stuff really, especially for our purposes, but hundreds accumulated with grace and command. No histrionics, no hairs out of place. The famous innings of 313 and the stand of 555 with Percy Holmes arrived on 16th June against Essex at Leyton, followed in the next match with 96 and an unbeaten 110 for the North v. the South in a Test trial at Old Trafford. He had spent four and a half hours over his 110. In his next innings, Sutcliffe hit his ninety-ninth century, a chanceless 270 in over six hours against Sussex at Headingley.

Sutcliffe went into the Test match against All India at Lord's with the incredible aggregate of 789 runs from four consecutive innings. He scored three and 19 in the

Test match — the first ever against India in this country — and returned to join Yorkshire for their match at Northampton, the ground where Sutcliffe had scored his first century in 1919. Sutcliffe thought he had an excellent chance of getting his hundredth there but was lbw to Vallance Jupp for 28 just when he thought he was settled. He failed to get into double figures in either innings in the next match and went to Bradford to face Gloucestershire and Walter Hammond, still searching for his hundredth. It was Wednesday, 6th July 1932. "My first innings score was 83 when Wally Hammond caught me in the slips off Rogers," wrote Sutcliffe, "and it was left to that fine batsman, Arthur Mitchell, to make the first century of what was to prove a most extraordinary match. Sinfield and Hammond had centuries in Gloucestershire's innings of 404 — we had declared at 472 for seven — and Hammond's was one of his best. He found the call of the football stand irresistible. When our second innings started it looked as though the game was doomed to be drawn, but we felt we had a chance of victory if we could get quick runs, and I know that when I started that second innings I never gave a thought to the likelihood of it producing my hundredth hundred. I went for the bowling, found I could get runs, and simply went on scoring. It was a question of getting quick runs so that we could put Gloucestershire in again on a wicket that was beginning to show signs of wear. The runs came, but still I never thought of a century innings until I found myself there. Really, no one was more surprised than I was. I had expected to get out almost every over, but I had not cared about that because we were fighting to force a win."

Yorkshire won with the first ball of the game's final over when Bill Bowes knocked back Tom Goddard's off stump. Sutcliffe had played a significant part in the win with 132 in 115 minutes as Yorkshire scored 240 for six declared at the rate of 125 runs an over. Sutcliffe left with eight sixes and eight fours, a dramatic way to reach his hundredth hundred.

During the Australia-England Test at Headingley in 1985 I asked Bill Bowes, then aged seventy-six, about Sutcliffe. "He was immaculate in every way and developed an attitude from his pride in Yorkshire cricket," he said. "He hadn't as many shots as Jack Hobbs but we used to say if you wanted somebody to play for your life, it would be Sutcliffe. Their running was perfect, you know, he and Hobbs knew every left-handed fielder. He hit a lot of sixes when he was in the mood and once hit three in the opening over of a match against Lancashire. During the innings which brought him his hundredth hundred he, like Hammond, put a lot of balls on to the corrugated roof of the football stand. Arthur Wood, our wicketkeeper said: 'It's like the boy scout band passing by." Frank Dennis was twelfth man for that game and was fielding substitute at mid-off. "The ball was being hit over my head into or onto the football stand at what seemed almost every other ball at one time," he said.

The *Manchester Guardian* even mentioned Sutcliffe in its leading article the following morning: "He has never been a spectacular batsman and it is not often that he scores rapidly. Other players and particularly those who learned the game before the war may have a more brilliant repertory of strokes, but none has excelled Sutcliffe in the art of adjusting each stroke with an infinity of subtle modification to each ball's new problem."

Yorkshire steamed on towards the championship with Sutcliffe hitting more centuries against Lancashire and Derbyshire before heavily punishing Essex for the second time in the season. This time the game was at Scarborough and played in blazing sunshine with temperatures in the nineties. Essex, after their defeat by an innings and 313 runs at Leyton, scored 325 on the opening day with opening bowler Bill Bowes taking nine of their wickets for 121 runs in 44.1 overs. Yorkshire batted for 25 minutes on the opening day so Sutcliffe did not go in this time until the fall of the second wicket. Arthur Mitchell hit 80 but his dismissal brought Sutcliffe and Maurice Leyland together in one of the most remarkable partnerships Yorkshire have ever experienced. In 55 minutes they put on 149 runs. At one period 75 runs were taken off four overs from fast bowler Ken Farnes and six successive overs from Farnes, Nichols and O'Connor brought 102 runs. "Oh dear," wrote Bowes. "I've never seen such batting. The faster they bowled the further they were hit." Sutcliffe spent an hour and a quarter reaching 50, got to his hundred in 125 minutes, and then spent 40 minutes getting another 94 runs. There were three sixes and 20 fours in an innings of 194 in 165 minutes, which included five chances. Yorkshire declared at 476 for nine and by lunchtime on the final day they had again walloped Essex by an innings. Bowes, who took 13 wickets in the match, recalled seeing Farnes soon after the Sutcliffe onslaught. He burst into tears. "I'll never make a fast bowler," he said. Bowes told him to try to get to know the batsmen. "You don't bowl bouncers at Sutcliffe and Leyland in that mood," he said.

Frank Dennis wrote of that match. "Bowes had to bear the full burden of the attack on a very hot day. He bowled over 40 overs for nine wickets and was utterly exhausted. But he still managed to bowl a few bumpers and as one Essex batsman was going off the field he remarked: 'We've got some buggers who can bounce 'em,' meaning Farnes, Nichols and Brown. So bounce they did. As it was late on the first day Sutcliffe was held back until number four next day and carted those fast bowlers all over Scarborough, with sixes behind square leg, over long-on, behind point."

Sutcliffe finished top of the English averages that summer with 3,336 runs (74.13) and 14 centuries, the last of which was also at Scarborough for Leveson Gower's XI against the Indians. Eight of his hundreds were scored in his own county where he averaged over 90. He scored six centuries in August to help him reach 1,006 runs that month from thirteen innings and his total for the season is the highest ever by a Northern batsman.

Another fine hitting innings was played at Kettering the following year, after Northamptonshire had been bowled out for 27 and Yorkshire had lost Holmes and Mitchell for four. Sutcliffe then hit 113 in two hours with ten sixes to the short legside boundary, an easy prey for his favourite shot, the hook. Sutcliffe, who had been up until four o'clock that morning, attending a ball at Cambridge with Mrs Sutcliffe, dancing away the night and tucking into bacon and eggs in the early hours, had decided to have a bang on the rain-affected pitch. "The stand on the low side of the ground was conveniently near," he recalled. "and somehow it seemed that I just had to lift the ball over it. Most of the sixes were taken off the man who at one time was one of my bogey men — V.W.C. Jupp."

Sutcliffe has all sorts of records, especially with Percy Holmes and Jack Hobbs, but the most impressive fact, I think, is his 7,687 runs in the twenty-four months from May 1931. He died in 1978 aged eighty-three and left behind a century of records including more than 50,000 runs.

20 BRUCE TAYLOR

In a seventeen-year career Bruce Taylor only ever scored four centuries. Yet two of them were stunning contributions to New Zealand Test cricket with 105 in 158 minutes against India in his first match and a staggering century in 86 minutes against West Indies at Auckland, both of them in the 1960s. Taylor had played just three first-class games when he was chosen to go with New Zealand on the 1965 tour of India, Pakistan and England. His fourth, after being overlooked for the first Test in Madras, was the second Test in Calcutta where he came into the team as an opening right-arm medium pace bowler and a left-handed number eight batsman to replace Barry Sinclair who became ill on the morning of the match. After winning the toss John Reid hit four sixes and ten fours in a spectacular 82 and New Zealand were 233 for six when the twenty-one-year-old Taylor walked out for his first Test innings and to join the vastly experienced Bert Sutcliffe. He reached 50 in 71 minutes and hit Nadkarni for six to take New Zealand to 300. In 158 minutes Sutcliffe and Taylor added 163 runs, of which Taylor had hit 105 with three sixes — the other two were off Venkat — and 14 fours. Then, when India batted, he took five wickets for 86 runs to complete an impressive debut.

That Calcutta innings was still Taylor's only first-class century when he faced West Indies four years and, for him, twelve Tests later. The West Indies, under Gary Sobers, had just lost the Test series in Australia 3-1 and started the New Zealand part of their tour with a three-day drawn game against South Island at Dunedin. They started that game on 22nd February, 1969, only hours after arriving from Australia, and on 27th February the first Test started at Auckland.

Sobers won the toss, put New Zealand in to bat, and although Bev Congdon scored a valuable 85 in two and a half hours, New Zealand were 152 for six when Taylor started his innings. His claim to fame was still his century and five wickets on his debut, but on this day he was to surpass it with the fastest century ever for New Zealand and the fifth fastest of all Test hundreds. He reached 50 in half an hour which equalled the third fastest in Test cricket, and powerful driving and pulling took him to tea with 93 runs in 74 minutes. He reached his century, in 86 minutes, with his fifth six, a towering hit into the stand off Richard Edwards. It was the fastest Test century for fourteen years and Taylor finished with 124 in 111 minutes, including five sixes and 14 fours. He also had the satisfaction of recording the first century for New Zealand against West Indies, in the tenth Test between the teams. More good batting followed when West Indies, given 315 minutes in which to score 345 to win, galloped to a five-wicket victory with Seymour Nurse scoring 168 and Basil Butcher 78 not out.

Taylor, born at Timaru in 1943, impressed with his bowling at schoolboy and youth level and by the 1963-64 season, when he was still just twenty, he forced his way into the Canterbury 'B' and under-23 teams and the New Zealand under-23s.

His first-class debut came that year, for the under-23s against Auckland when he scored 23 and 34, took four for 65 and one for 54, and was described as "a most interesting prospect". A sign of his hitting ability came in an innings of 61 not out in 36 minutes against Ashburton County. The 1964-65 season proved the turning point for Taylor who put together a string of outstanding performances that earned him a place on Canterbury's northern tour when Dick Motz pulled out injured. He scored 49 and took three for 57 against Auckland, hit 31 and took five for 49 and two for 38 against Northern Districts and bingo, within a week and after G.A. Bartlett had been rejected on medical grounds, he was named in the New Zealand touring party for India, Pakistan and England, over five months away from home with ten Test matches.

After his remarkable debut, Taylor stayed in the New Zealand team for the remaining five Tests against India and Pakistan, finishing with 15 wickets against India, but only six against Pakistan and playing just one more innings of consequence, 76 in 96 minutes against Pakistan at Rawalpindi. Taylor celebrated his twenty-second birthday in England — in Leeds to be more precise — and played in two of the three Tests with the only distinguished feature coming in his first Test innings when he scored 51.

Dick Brittenden said of Taylor in his book, *Red Leather Silver Fern*: "His road to the top was strewn with the sick and the maimed but surely New Zealand cricket will long be grateful to the pulled muscles and dysentery which lifted Taylor from obscurity to enduring fame."

In all, Taylor toured England three times, played in 30 Tests, took 111 wickets, and was probably seen at his best in the 1971-72 tour of West Indies when he took 27 wickets in four Tests to equal the record for a visiting bowler. All the Tests were drawn and Taylor's best return came in the third Test at Bridgetown where he took seven for 74. It was in the second innings of that match that Gary Sobers edged a ball from Taylor into the slips where Terry Jarvis let the chance go. Sobers, 88 at the time and with West Indies in grave danger of defeat, went on to score 142 and share in a stand of 254 with Charlie Davis that saved the game.

Taylor carried on playing cricket until 1980 but hit only two more first-class centuries to go with his Test hundreds, both of them when he moved to Wellington. His highest was 173 against Otago at Dunedin in 1973, going in at 42 for four and sharing in a run-a-minute stand of 255 with twenty-year-old Jeremy Coney. Taylor, who had a runner for most of his innings after injuring his knee, hit three sixes.

Taylor the cricketer was something of a complex character. As one writer said: "With Bruce Taylor, nobody knew what to expect — unless it was the unexpected. Taylor more than any other top-class cricketer was a captive of his own emotions; when he felt good he played well, even if he didn't look good doing it."

INDEX

BIBLIOGRAPHY

The outstanding book with reference to "the Great Blows of Cricket and of Those who Struck Them" is Gerald Brodribb's *Hit for Six*, published by Heinemann in 1960. I tried hard to ignore it all the time I was researching and writing, afraid that in the end I would rely too heavily and too easily on it. But when I did get in a corner I turned to it for the way out. It is a reliable book. *Wisden*, of course, for any year from 1881 to 1985, was always in use and I referred frequently to the magazines, *The Cricketer* and *Wisden Cricket Monthly*. *The Times*, *Daily Telegraph* and *Guardian* were frequently turned to along with many evening and local newspapers throughout the country. Several libraries were of great help, particularly the one at Old Trafford, and many of the books to which I referred are mentioned in the text. My other main sources were:

Talking of Cricket, by Ian Peebles.
Viv Richards, by Trevor McDonald.
Cricket Between Two Wars, by Sir Pelham Warner.
With Bat and Ball, by George Giffen.
The Book of Cricket, by Sir Pelham Warner.
A Cricket Pro's Lot, by Fred Root.
For England and Yorkshire, by Herbert Sutcliffe.
Living for Cricket, by Clive Lloyd.
Clive Lloyd, by Trevor McDonald.
A Cricketer's Log, by Gilbert Jessop.
Cricket, by W.G. Grace.
Woolley, by Ian Peebles.
Alletson's Innings, by John Arlott.
My Life Story, by Jack Hobbs.
West Indies Cricket, by Christopher Nicole.
A History of Leicestershire, by E.E. Snow.
Nottinghamshire Cricket and Cricketers, by F.S. Ashley-Cooper.
Sussex Cricket, by A.E.R. Gilligan.
Great Cricketers, edited by Denzil Batchelor.
Northamptonshire Cricket, by J.D. Coldham.
Sussex Cricket, by John Marshall.
The Incredible Tests 1981, by Ian Botham.
Phoenix from the Ashes, by Mike Brearley.
The Hand that Bowled Bradman, by Bill Andrews.
Harold Gimblett, by David Foot.
An Illustrated History of Australian Cricket, by R.S. Whitington.
Cricket All The Way, by Eddie Paynter.
Forty Seasons of First-Class Cricket, by R.G. Barlow.
Fifty Years Cricket Reminiscences of a Non-Player, by W.E. Howard.
Cricket Triumphs and Troubles, by Cecil Parkin.
The Fast Men, by David Frith.
Crusoe on Cricket, by R.C. Robertson-Glasgow.
The Slow Men, by David Frith.
Kings of Cricket, by Richard Daft.
Old English Cricketers, by 'Old Ebor'.